I0799864

Postcard History Series

Sebastian and Crawford Counties

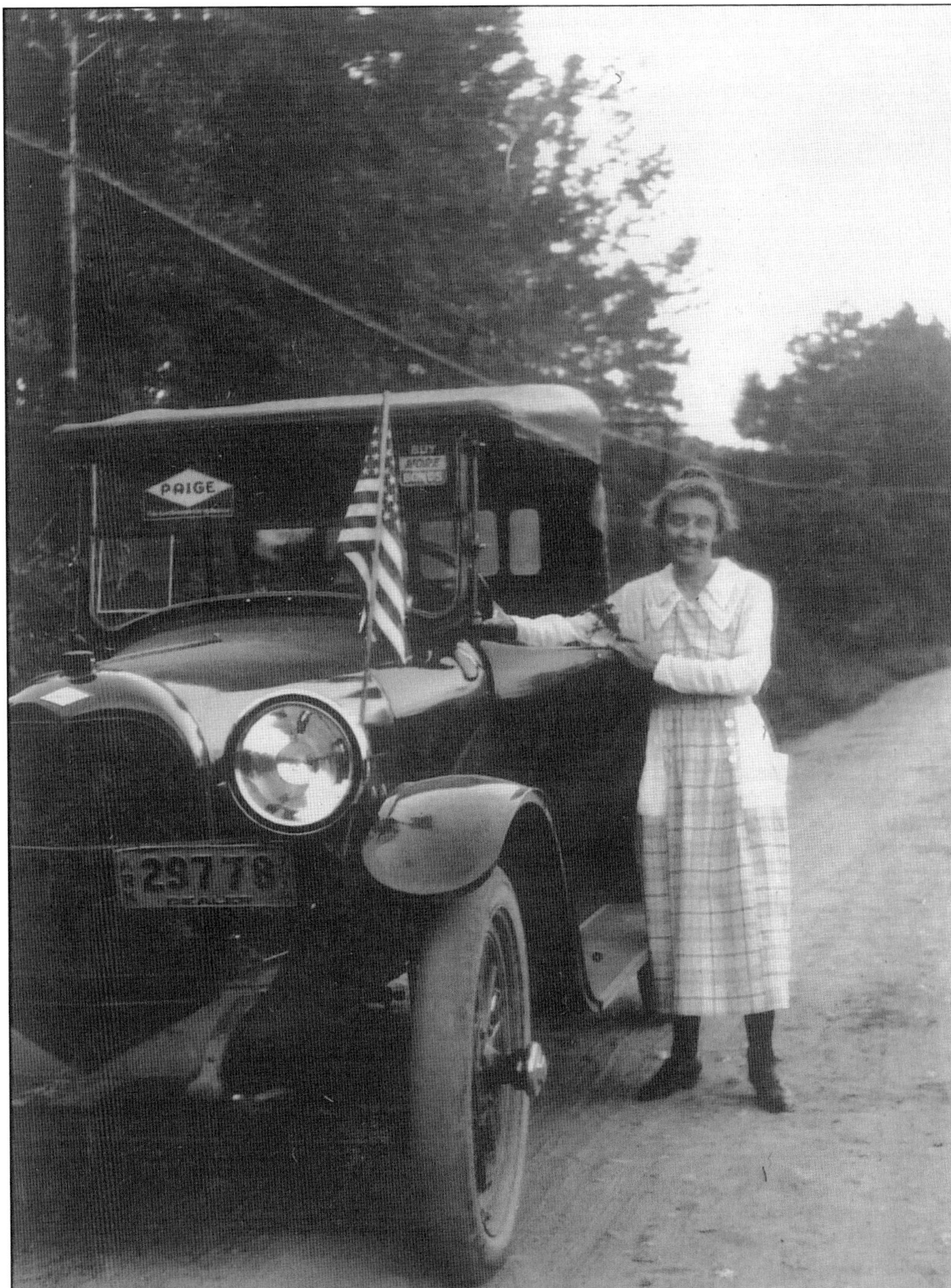

In 1918, America was fighting the "War to make the world safe for democracy," and this unidentified woman was doing her part in Sebastian County as World War I raged in Europe. Her car has a "dealer" license plate, and the sticker on the visor urges "Buy More Bonds," an effort to promote the sale of war bonds funding the American commitment to defeat the German Kaiser's forces in Europe.

POSTCARD HISTORY SERIES

Sebastian and Crawford Counties

Steven Hanley and Ray Hanley

ARCADIA
PUBLISHING

ISBN 978-0-7385-0051-5

Published by Arcadia Publishing
Charleston, South Carolina

Printed in the United States of America

Library of Congress Catalog Card Number: 99-65128

For all general information contact Arcadia Publishing at:
Telephone 843-853-2070
Fax 843-853-0044
E-mail sales@arcadiapublishing.com
For customer service and orders:
Toll-Free 1-888-313-2665

Visit us on the Internet at www.arcadiapublishing.com

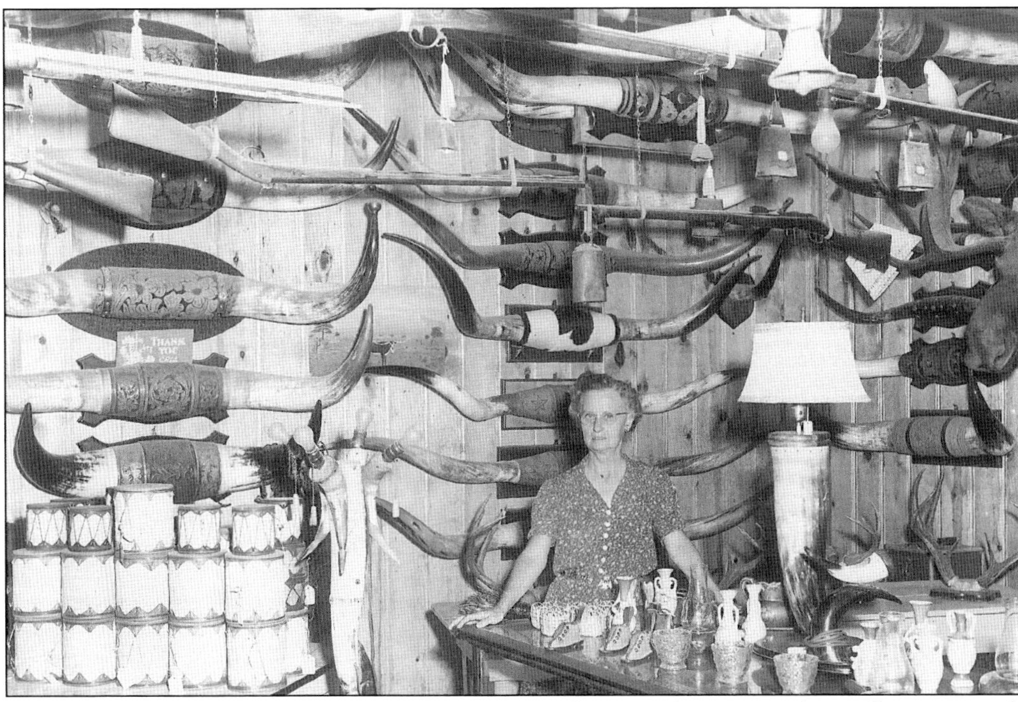

Tourists leaving Van Buren and heading to Fayetteville were often tempted to pull over, outside of Van Buren, to browse in the Long Horn Museum, an establishment that might have earned the "tourist trap" label. Owned by Floyd Hall, the business on Van Buren's Route 1 sold a variety of souvenirs, including the large supply of toy "Indian" drums stacked to the left of the unidentified woman. The museum aspect of the attraction was in the form of the many steer horns and muskets on display. The business, shown in this c. 1954 postcard, closed a number of years ago.

Contents

Acknowledgments 6

Introduction 7

1. Fort Smith 11

2. Rural Settlements and Sights in Sebastian County 69

3. Van Buren 81

4. Crossroad Villages and "Tourist Traps" 109

Acknowledgments

While the postcards found in this work came from the author's personal collection, without the "story behind the pictures," this book would not be the unique and readable history that we hope it is. We hope this book will be enjoyed for many years. We are grateful for the help of a number of people, led especially by Mrs. Amelia Martin of Fort Smith, who provided invaluable details and advice about her city. Across the Arkansas River, Mr. and Mrs. Louis Peer were kind enough to do some very helpful research for us in Van Buren and Crawford County, and Mrs. Doris West helped out with additional Crawford County details.

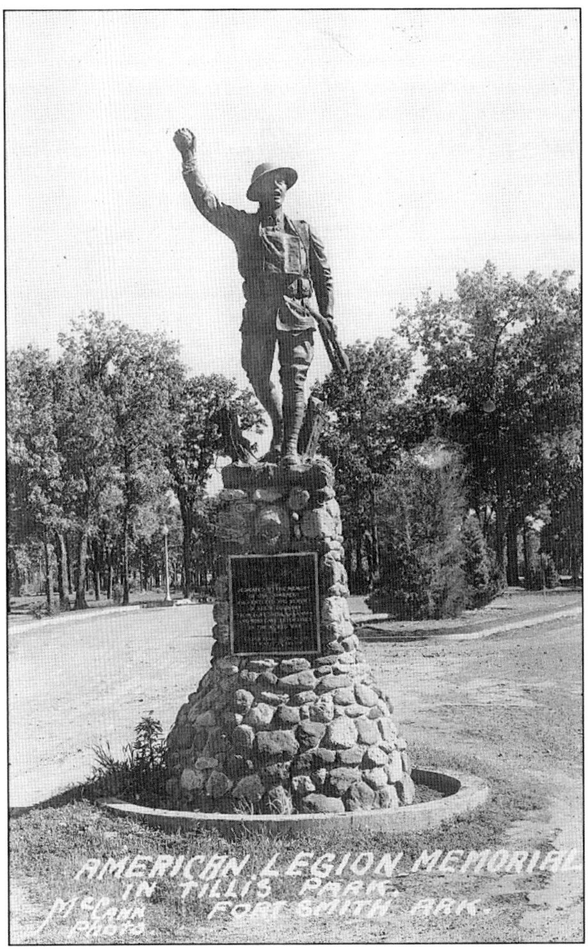

On July 4, 1930, some 2,000 people gathered at Tillis Park, in Fort Smith, to unveil and dedicate the *Spirit of the American Doughboy* statue. Honoring those who died in WW I, the statue was the work of noted sculptor E.M. Viquesney. The day's festivities included a band concert and the first nighttime tennis match ever held in the city. For half a century, the statue stood in the park, but in 1980, it was removed by the city because of vandalism. Restored in 1990, the statue was placed in front of the local American Legion headquarters, where it stands today.

Introduction

As the American frontier moved rapidly west in the latter years of the 19th century, it seemingly paused and bypassed (in ways both obvious and subtle) western Arkansas in Sebastian and Crawford Counties. The area's proximity to the "Indian Territory," as wild and rugged Oklahoma was labeled on many maps until its 1907 statehood, contributed greatly to the mixture of imagery and fact in the lore of the region. The area, so rich in history, has grown into the state's second-largest metropolitan area. Fortunately, much of the area's historical legacy (i.e. events that are fading memories and buildings that are greatly altered or now gone) was captured on picture postcards, which can still be revisited by those who live in a much-changed world.

The postcards that illustrate this work followed the birth of the picture postcards, which were first produced in the United States for the World's Colombian Exhibition held in Chicago in 1893. The postcard craze had developed first in Europe and began to spread across the United States after that great fair, accelerating to a huge phenomenon around 1905. This phenomenon was considered to be the golden age of postcards, from 1905 to around 1915. One commentary on the passion of the new hobby was found in *American Magazine* in 1906: "It often happens that collectors . . . have not enough friends to increase their hoards (of postcards) in a normal manner. Hundreds of them haunt establishments where the causes of their besetting sin are exposed for sale, select such as strike their fancy, stamp them and mail them to their own addresses. . . ." This article was written with tongue in cheek, and sarcastically told how the nation had gone postcard mad: "From small beginnings the pasteboard souvenir industry has fattened upon epistolary sloth and collecting manias. . . Bookstores which formerly did a thriving trade in literature are now devoted almost entirely to their sale. There were in Atlantic City last season ten establishments where nothing else was sold, and Chicago, Boston, Pittsburgh, and New York have emporiums where postals constitute the entire stock. Ten large factories are working overtime in this country to supply the demand and many smaller ones are selling their output as fast as it is produced."

The postcard fad eventually reached the south, arriving in force in such places as western Arkansas two or three years after interest in the hobby first washed over the East Coast. Local merchants and photographers foresaw the potential, from reading the accounts in popular publications reporting on the postcard fad. However, with the transition of the fad to rural and small-town America, the subjects of the postcards began to reflect more the everyday lives of common families. Today we can see life in a period that is separated from ours by two world wars and mind-boggling leaps in technology. A 1910 issue of *American Magazine* offered further commentary on this evolution: "When mother decides that she will stay overnight with her daughter in the next town, she sends word home to the family on a souvenir postcard of the library. When father's dry goods store burns down, he photographs the catastrophe, prints a souvenir postcard from it and requests the insurance adjuster to drop into town immediately. . . Baby's arrival, his first tooth, his first trousers, his first bicycle, his first girl and his first baby, all go to the family circle by souvenir postal, for anyone with a camera can make his own postcards these days. . . ."

The postcards from Sebastian and Crawford Counties that went into the nation's postal system shortly after the turn of the century captured views of towns only a decade or so removed from the "Wild West" with its dirt streets, hordes of outlaws, and hanging judges. The images in this book include such frontier scenes, as well as other postcards that trace the history of both counties through the first six decades of the 20th century.

Sebastian County, Arkansas, was created in 1851, carved from parts of Crawford, Scott, and Polk counties. It was named for Arkansas's U.S. Senator William K. Sebastian. Initially the town of Greenwood was selected to be the county seat, but after a decade of feuding and controversy, Fort Smith was given dual status so that Sebastian County found itself with two county seats and two courthouses. Fort Smith, among the most historical communities in Arkansas, quickly came to be the dominant city in the western part of the state.

While the city of Fort Smith has grown today to be the state's second largest (after Little Rock), it had its beginnings well before the creation of Sebastian County. Fort Smith began not as a town but literally as a fort, an army post on the remote, wild frontier of the Arkansas Territory. Established in 1817, Fort Smith was one of a cordon of many military posts along the eastern edge of the Indian Territory (present-day Oklahoma). The original fort, a small log and stone stockade, was located on Belle Point, a promontory on the bank of the Poteau River near where it joined the much larger Arkansas River. Named to honor General Thomas A. Smith, commander of the Ninth Military District, the fort's mission was to interpose federal troops between the Osage Indians upstream, who had been there for generations, and the recently arrived Cherokees downstream. The Cherokees were not there of their own accord, but rather had been forced to emigrate from their homelands in the eastern United States. The fort also gave protection to white trappers and traders, while encouraging settlement in the sparsely populated area.

The first Fort Smith was occupied for only seven years before its garrison was ordered westward to establish Fort Coffee, Indian Territory. However, in 1838, in response to settlers' fears of Indian raids, the army began constructing a second fort near the ruins of the first one at Belle Point. From 1841 to 1844, Colonel Zachary Taylor served as the commander of the Second Military Department, which included Fort Smith. The future president of the United States chose to live in the town that was growing up in the shadow of his military post. However, Taylor felt the new fort was not needed, asserting that "a more useless expenditure of money and labor was never made by this or any other people. . . The sooner it is arrested the better." Colonel Taylor's view eventually prevailed, and the would-be fort was converted into an army supply depot in 1845.

By the time of this conversion, the town of Fort Smith had over 500 residents. In 1848, when gold was discovered in California, the community became a thriving supply center for wagon trains bound for the gold fields. The boon was short-lived, and with the outbreak of the Civil War in 1861, Fort Smith was seized by Confederate forces. The post would change hands several times during the conflict, although no major battles were fought in the area. The post commissary building was alternately used as a prison and as a refuge for women and children during the war.

At the war's end, the U.S. Army again activated Fort Smith. In September of 1865, the fort hosted a Grand Council at which Native American tribes agreed to cede almost half of all land that had been claimed by them before the Civil War. Thus, by 1871, the "Indian frontier" had moved so far west that the fort could no longer even serve as a supply depot, and it was abandoned by the army. In the following year, the Federal Court for the Western District of Arkansas moved into one of the vacant barracks buildings.

The new court had criminal jurisdiction over western Arkansas, as well as the vast and lawless Indian Territory just across the Arkansas River. This broad commission served to open up another remarkable chapter in the history of Fort Smith. Judge Isaac C. Parker presided over the court from 1875 until 1896, and during his 21 years on the bench he heard more than 13,000 cases. Over 9,000 of the defendants were convicted or pleaded guilty. Among these defendants, 344 were tried for capital offenses and 160 were sentenced to hang (79 actually met their end on the gallows near Judge Parker's courthouse). For its first 14 years, Parker's court was unique in that sentences could not be appealed except to the president of the United States or the Federal Circuit Court. "It was not I who hung them, I never hung a man," reflected the "Hanging Judge" in later years, "It was the law." Indeed, in many cases he had no choice, as during Parker's era the Revised Statutes of the United States commanded that anyone convicted of murder or rape "shall suffer death."

More than 200 U.S. deputy marshals rode for Parker's Fort Smith court, bringing lawbreakers to justice. One such marshal was depicted in the Charles Portis novel, *True Grit*, and was portrayed in the movie version by none other than John Wayne. Parker's marshals were indeed formidable, and so was the judge himself. It is said that one outlaw, upon being captured by one of Judge Parker's deputy marshals, pleaded "Don't take me before the judge. You might just as well kill me now." Sixty-five of these U.S. marshals were killed in the line of duty.

Gradually, Congress established new courts in the adjacent Indian Territory, and each of these courts whittled away at Judge Parker's jurisdiction. Finally, in September of 1896, Congress removed his court's territorial authority completely, and less than three months later, at the age of 58, the ailing judge died of Bright's disease. Judge Parker's death marked the passing of the frontier era for western Arkansas and signaled a new future for the city of Fort Smith.

The 20th century dawned upon Fort Smith, bright with promise. According to the 1900 census, the city had a population of more than 11,000, some three times its population only 12 years earlier. Fort Smith boasted electric lights, streetcars, and sidewalks. The discovery of natural gas and coal deposits soon transformed the city into a major manufacturing center. Within a decade of the census, the city would again double its population, establishing itself firmly as the state's second-largest community.

Crawford County, located across the river from Fort Smith and Sebastian County, is eighth oldest among Arkansas's counties. It was created in 1820, some 16 years before statehood. Initially the county encompassed a vast sprawling wilderness, taking in much of the Arkansas Territory south of the Arkansas River and also much of present-day Oklahoma. Boundary changes and American Indian treaties eventually pulled the borders of Crawford County into an area north of the river. The county was named for William Harris Crawford, who was the U.S. secretary of the treasury when the county was formed. The Georgia native was an unsuccessful candidate for president in 1824.

The original county seat of Crawford County was located on a point of the Arkansas River some 18 miles below present-day Van Buren, a site that proved out of the path of developing commerce. Before the close of the 1830s, a town was beginning to grow up across from the military fort, though the first white settler on the Arkansas River site is said to have been a squatter, Thomas Martin, who arrived around 1820. The first settler to claim land ownership in the area was James Phillips, whose family operated a wood yard on the banks of the river, supplying the steamboats that plied the waterway. Phillips in turn sold the town site to John Drennen and David Thompson in 1836, the year Arkansas became a state. When the first post office was designated in 1831, the name of the town had already been chosen to honor U.S. President Martin Van Buren.

Drennen and Thompson proceeded to try to turn a quick profit on their investment, by selling off pieces of the town they had bought. Ads ran in major newspapers across the South in 1837: "A public sale of lots in Van Buren, a flourishing town will commence on Monday, the 16th day of October next, and will be continued from day to day until all are sold. . . . The situation of the place is picturesque, and pleasing to the eye; a portion of the town site is high and with a commanding eminence. There is an abundant and never failing supply of palatable and pure water. . . . The site is easily approachable." Settlers were soon drawn to Van Buren, and the city rapidly prospered across the Arkansas River from Fort Smith.

Today, the city of Van Buren proudly lays claim to having what is likely Arkansas's most intact, restored main street from the era of the late 1800s. The most photographed part of the city for postcards in that era was also along Main Street. These postcards would prove vital to those who took on the challenge of restoring the downtown area in the 1970s, making possible a historic district that stretches for several blocks. This lovely town draws visitors off nearby Interstate 40 and has even attracted Hollywood movie makers. The television mini-series *North & South* was shot, in part, on Van Buren's Main Street, with few changes needed other than covering the pavement with dirt.

Elsewhere in Crawford County, small villages grew up around farms and railroad stops. Postcard views of these areas offer a glimpse of communities once very remote and isolated that later either became much-visited tourist stops or faded from memory, depending on the chosen routes of railroads and highways as the 20th century advanced.

It is hoped that the reader will enjoy this depiction of some of the most historic counties in Arkansas, brought to life through the postcards of tourists and residents from decades past. Their record of life in Sebastian and Crawford Counties may perhaps provide inspiration to seek out, in person, some of the sights found within the pages of this book.

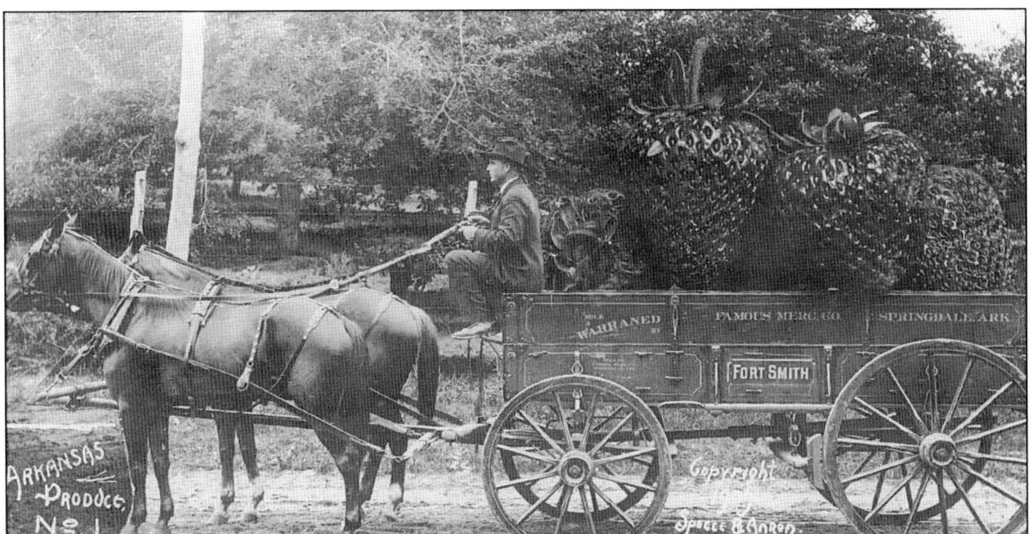

One of Fort Smith's best-known manufactured products at the turn of the century was Fort Smith Wagons, which were crafted from the abundant hardwood forests of Sebastian County. This particular wagon had been sold to Warraned Famous Mercantile Company of Springdale, Arkansas. The photograph was doctored to add giant strawberries to the wagon's load. The Fort Smith wagon nameplate shows on the side of the vehicle.

One

Fort Smith

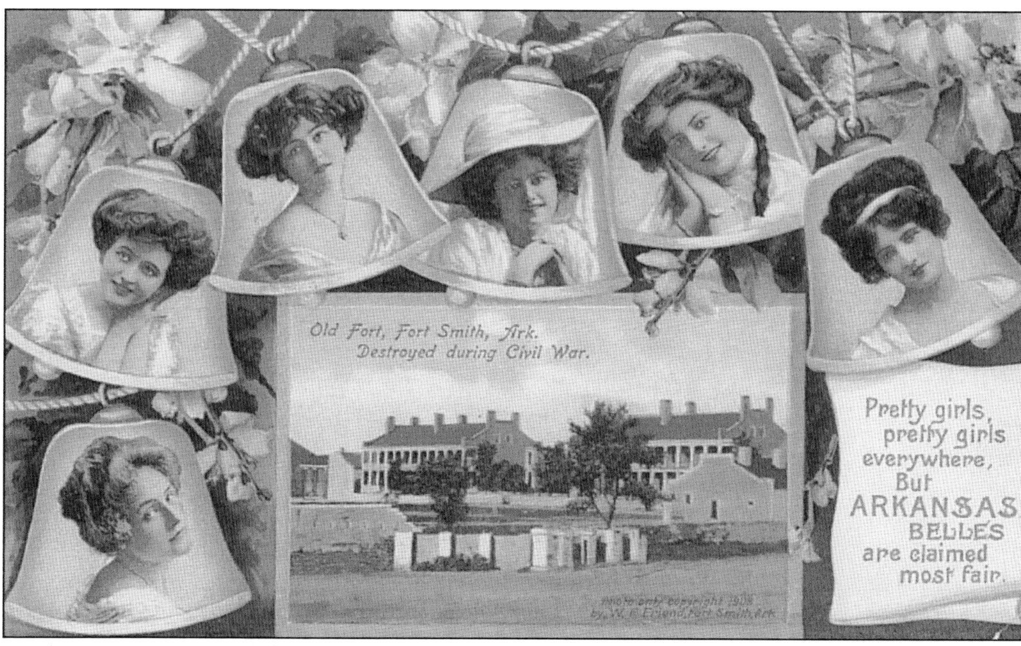

In this c. 1910 postcard, six Arkansas "Belles" frame an artist's conception of the second Fort Smith, with the post buildings surrounded by stone walls. The compound is incorrectly described on the face of the postcard as having been destroyed during the Civil War, for no fighting took place there. Most of the buildings were torn down, and the stones and lumber were recycled during construction around the growing town of Fort Smith before the end of the 19th century. Today, only two of the historic military post buildings survive, operating under the administration of the National Park Service.

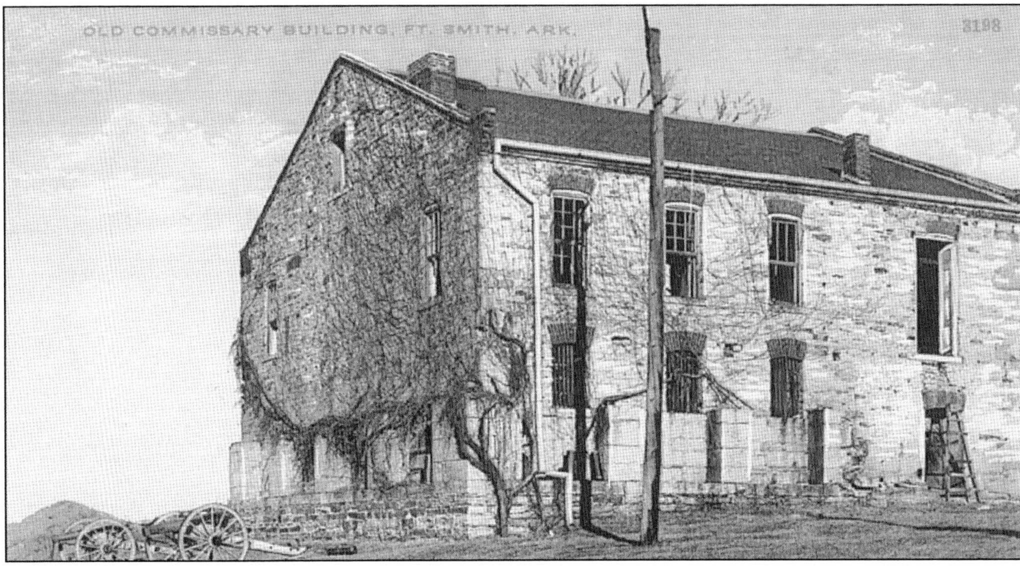

The Commissary Building, seen here around 1900, is the sole remaining unit of five original corner structures, or blockhouses, of the second Fort Smith constructed in 1838. Originally used as a storehouse, the building served as a prison during the Civil War, and famed Judge Isaac Parker had an office in the building for much of his 21 years on the bench. It was only about a half-mile walk to the courthouse where Judge Parker admonished juries, "Permit no innocent man to be punished, let no guilty man escape."

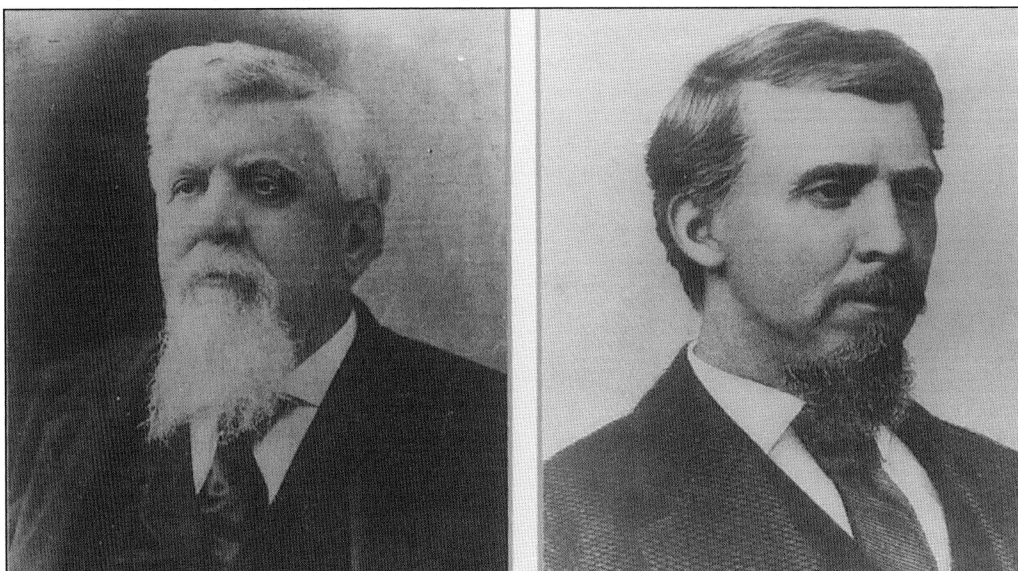

Appointed by President U.S. Grant, Isaac C. Parker was only 35 years old when he came to Fort Smith in 1875, the youngest judge on the federal bench at the time. His court was often in session 12 hours a day, 6 days a week. Upon adjourning for the day, Judge Parker usually retreated to his chambers, where he studied late into the night in preparation for the next day's cases. The photograph on the left was taken not long before Parker's death in 1896, contrasting sharply with the earlier image on the right. The years of hard work had left their mark on the man known as the "hanging judge."

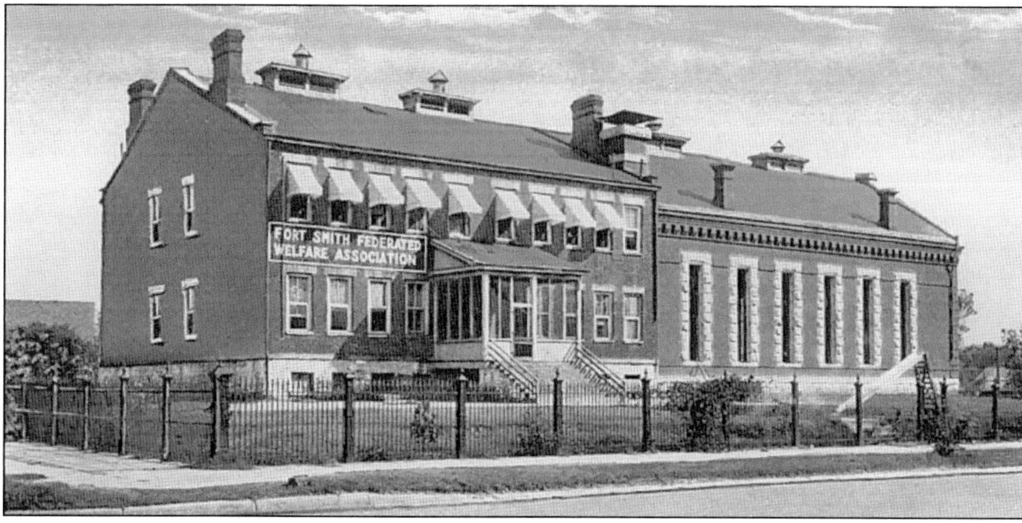

Rebuilt after being destroyed by the 1849 fire, this building served as the enlisted men's barracks until the army left the fort in 1871. The following year, the Federal Court for the Western District of Arkansas moved into the building, and Judge Parker presided over cases here from 1875 until 1889, when the court proceedings moved to a new location a few blocks away. When this photograph was taken in the 1930s, the building housed the offices of the Fort Smith Federated Welfare Association, complete with a slide on the front lawn for children. Today, the restored building is the heart of the National Park Service's Fort Smith National Historic Site.

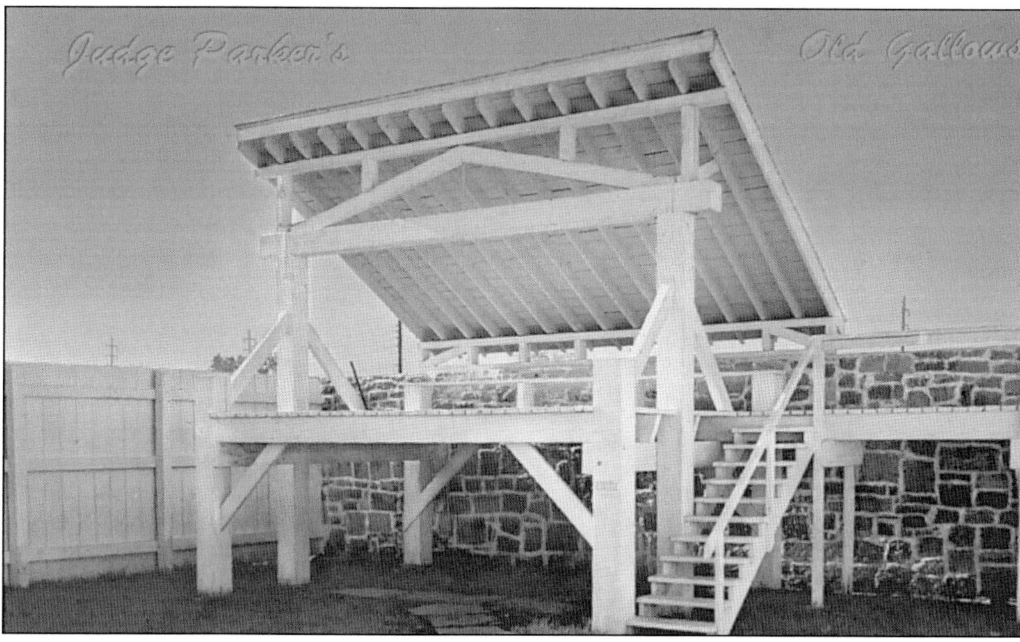

"May God whose laws you have broken have mercy on your soul." Thus intoned Judge Parker to at least one of the 160 convicted men he sentenced to hang during his 21-year tenure. Of these men, 79 actually were put to death on the gallows; the others died in prison, were killed attempting to escape, or were pardoned. The gallows seen in this c. 1955 postcard is a replica of the one built in 1886, which stood behind Judge Parker's court. It was designed to hang as many as twelve criminals at a time, but the greatest number ever dispatched at once was six.

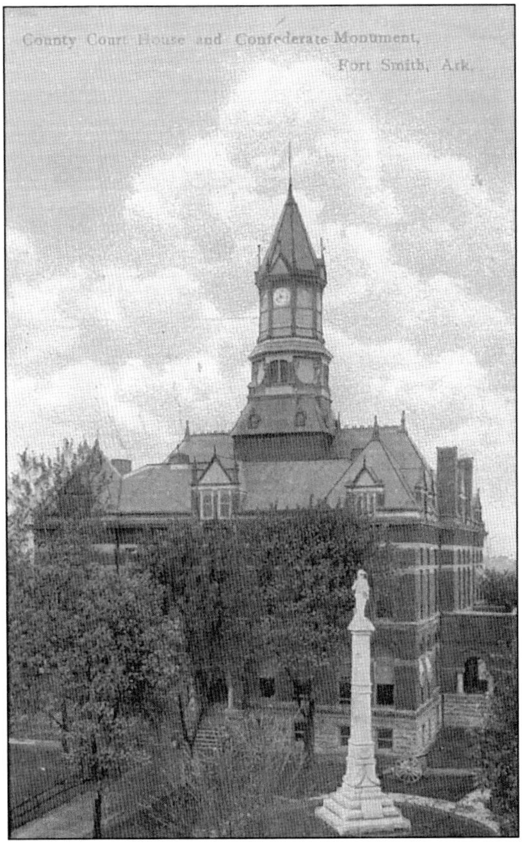

The Sebastian County Courthouse seen here was built in 1889, during the time Judge Parker was presiding in the nearby Federal Courthouse. The impressive, rounded tower seen in the view to the left was struck by lightning in 1910. The tower was rebuilt in a square shape, but the vibrations of the restored clock proved hazardous as they caused plaster to fall within the building. The ill-fated tower was finally removed, as can be seen in the c. 1915 postcard below. The building would serve until the erection of the new courthouse in the late 1930s, which is still in use. Today, the old building is but a faded memory, preserved only on postcards.

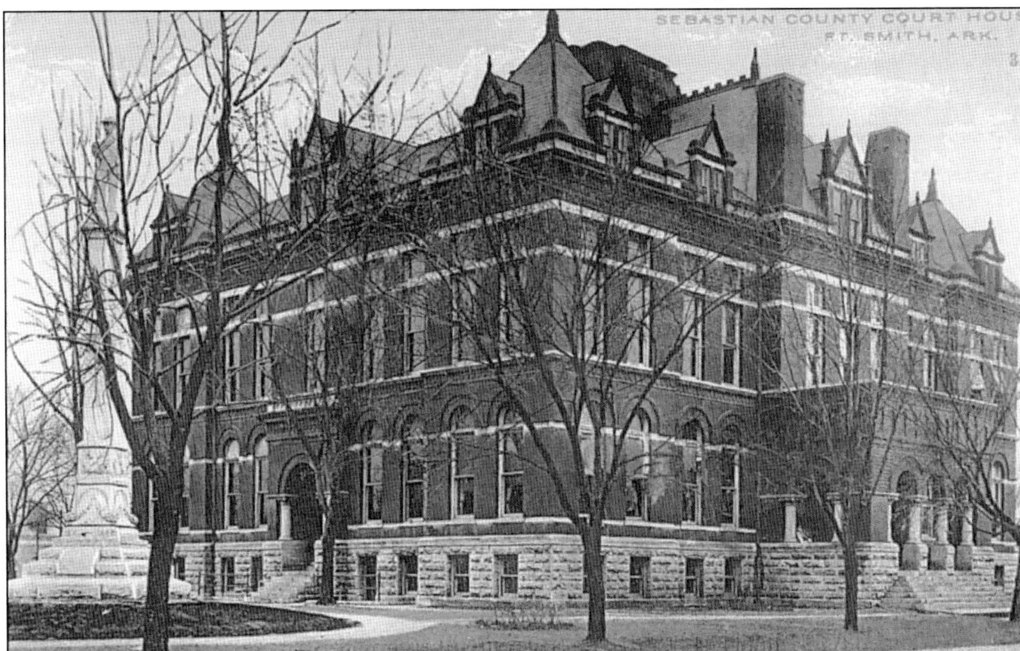

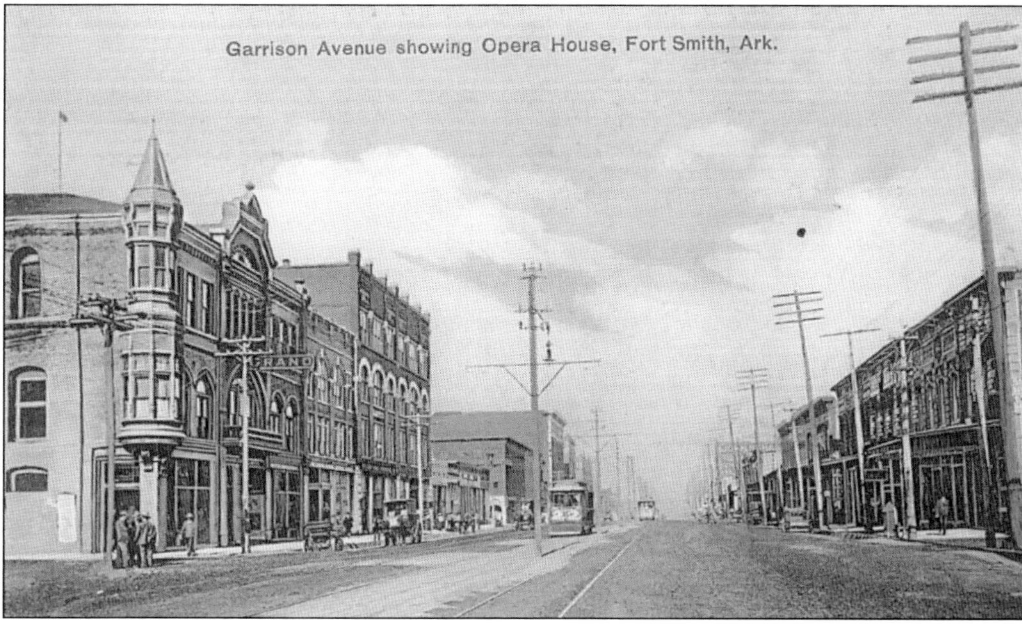

Garrison Avenue, originally leading from the military post located at one end, has always been Fort Smith's "main street." The wide boulevard became the premier avenue of western Arkansas. Early in the century, the street was often referred to as the "Great White Way," apparently because of the extensive use of electrical lights turned on each night. Among the attractions on Garrison Avenue was the Opera House (seen to the left, at 420 Garrison, in this postcard from around 1908). Built in 1887 at a cost of $50,000, some of the best-known stage names in the Southwest, including Jenny Lind, performed there before the business ceased operation in 1911. Used later as a grocery warehouse, the building burned to the ground in 1941. In the c. 1905 view of Garrison Avenue below, a parade of some kind is moving along either side of the streetcar tracks.

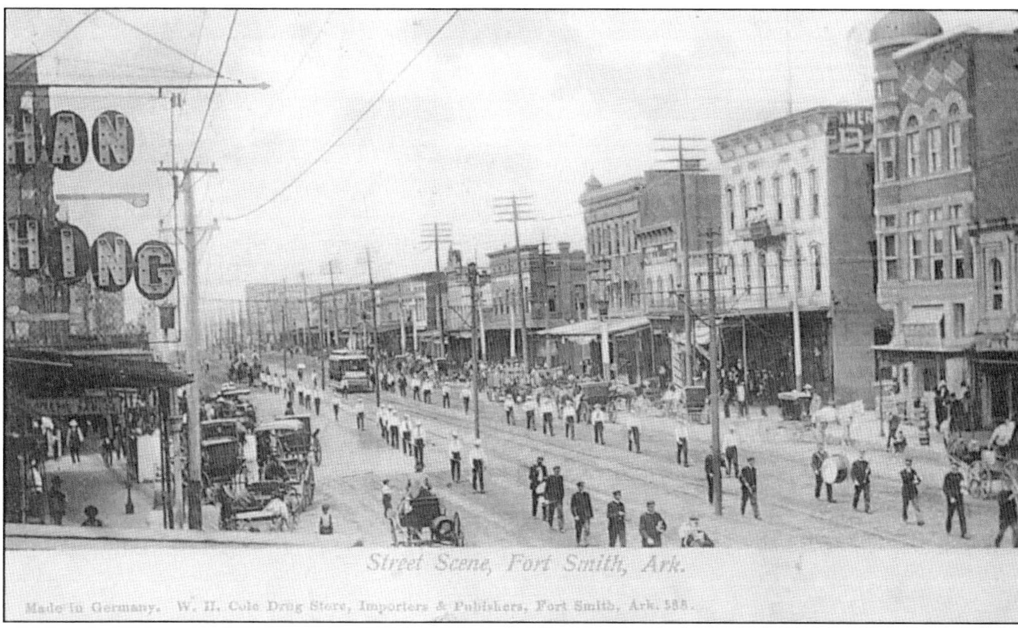

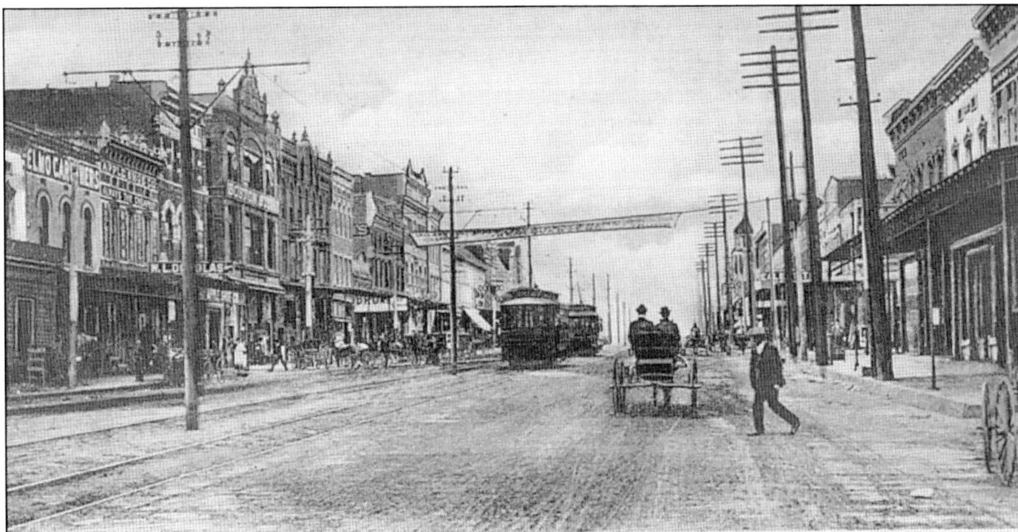

Gar Ave., Fort Smith, Ark., in 1907.

In this 1907 postcard view, streetcar tracks can be seen running both ways on Garrison Avenue, sharing the dirt street with wagons and pedestrians. Seen above, the Anheuser-Busch building, (left, with a peaked front), was home to the Boston Store, one of Fort Smith's early successful retailers. Begun in 1879, by Julius and Sigmund Baer at 315 Garrison, the store was initially housed in a 12-foot by 20-foot building and was stocked with an initial capital investment of only $350. In the c. 1910 postcard below can be seen the carpet department of the Boston Store, whose rugs went into the town's finest homes. The postcard was mailed by the store to a customer in Chismville, Arkansas. It reads as follows: "Beg to say you failed to enclose the sample of Lace Banding and we are unable to fill order." The Anheuser-Busch building was demolished years ago, but the Boston Store would prosper in Ft. Smith (in one location or another) for more than 100 years, before closing in the 1980s.

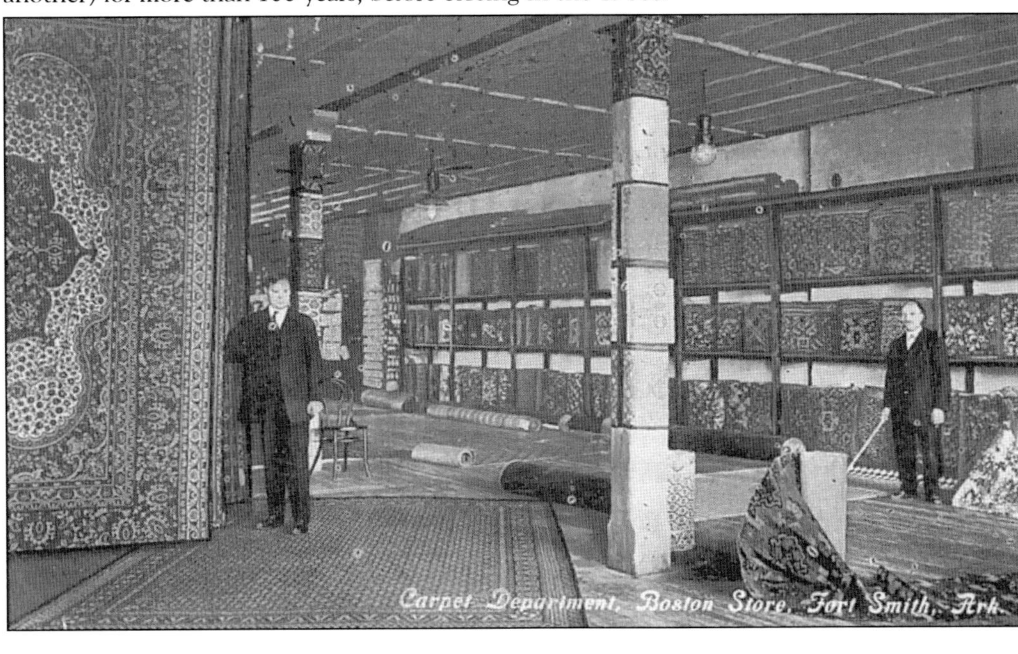

Carpet Department, Boston Store, Fort Smith, Ark.

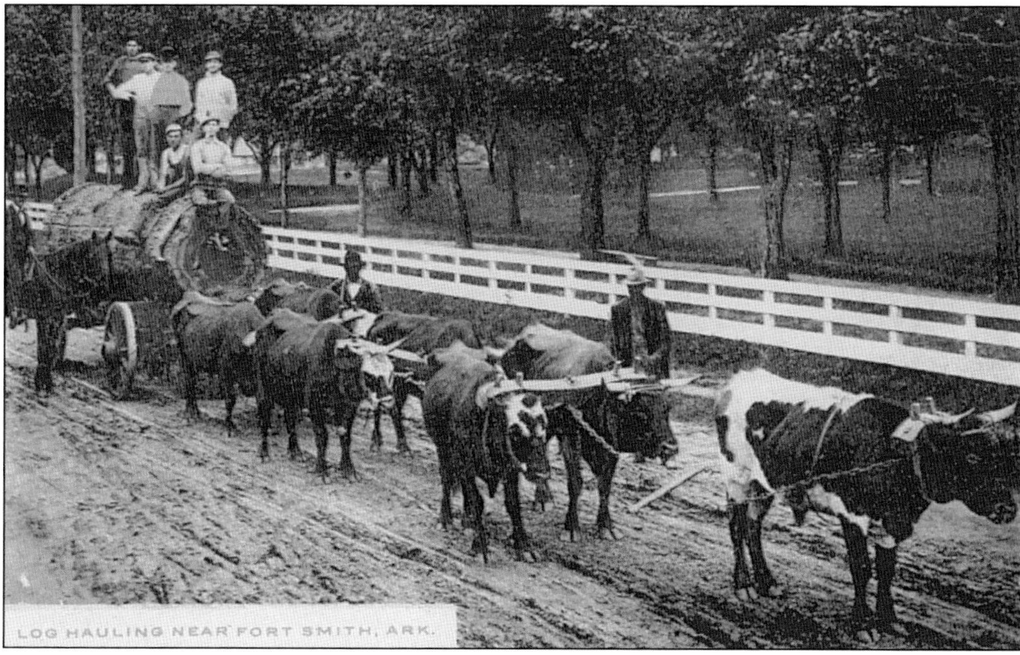

The river bottoms of Sebastian County were once home to ancient oak trees that had stood before the signing of the Declaration of Independence. The labor of man and beast alike turned almost all of these great trees into lumber and furniture. The immensity of such trees is evident in this 1910 postcard; it took seven oxen to haul but one log, upon which are seated six men.

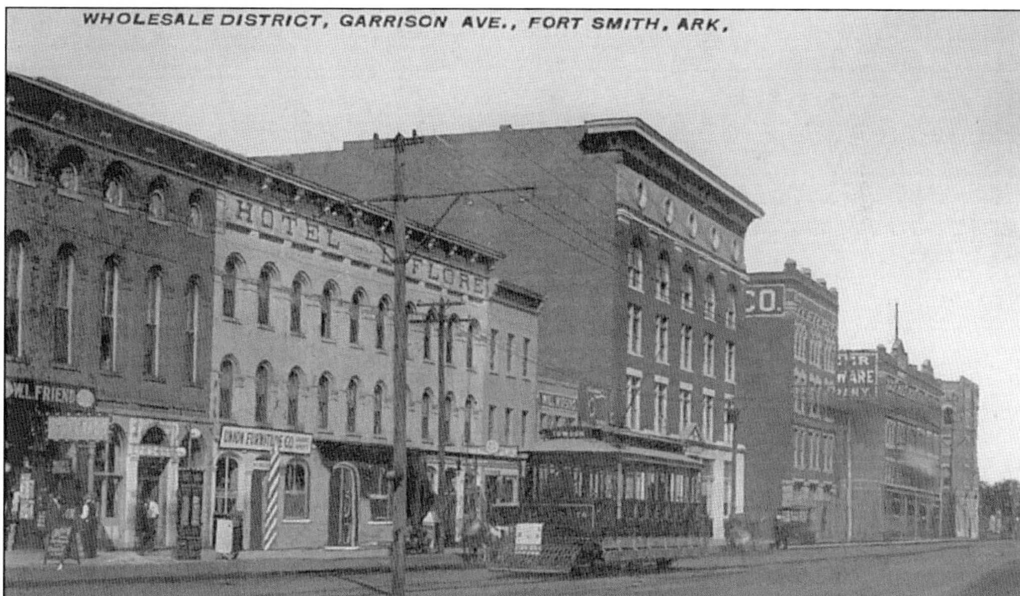

The nearby hardwood forests had made Fort Smith one of the South's leading furniture manufacturing centers by the turn of the century. One of the outlets for these furniture products was the Union Furniture Company at 318 Garrison. It can be seen here in the center of the photograph, below the Hotel Leflore, located on the lower end of Garrison Avenue in what is labeled as the town's wholesale district. This entire block of buildings is gone today.

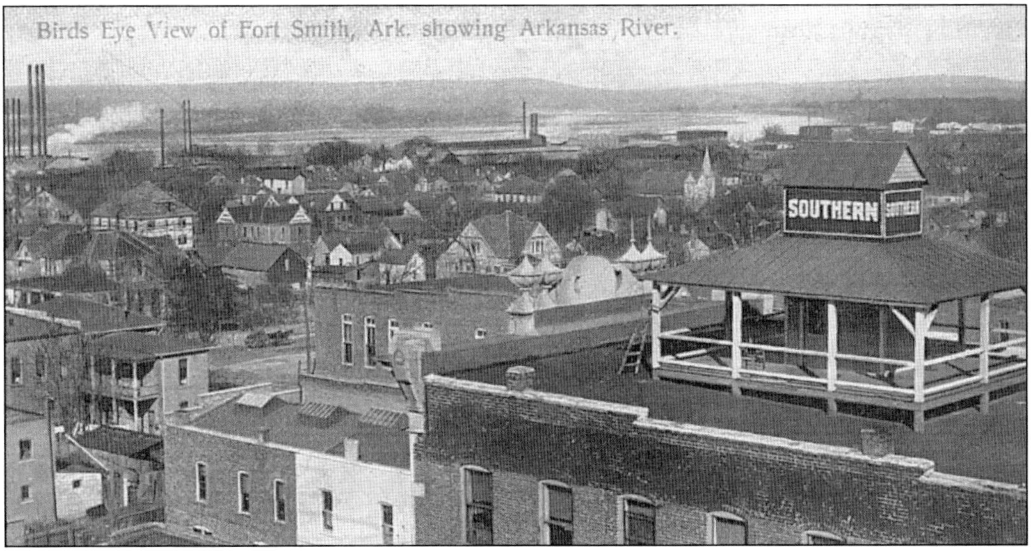

While most postcards were taken from the ground level, some were produced as "bird's-eye views," a popular technique early in the century. In Fort Smith, photographers occasionally climbed atop buildings along Garrison Avenue. This *c.* 1910 view looks over the city to the northwest, with the Arkansas River in the distance. Large homes and churches are visible between downtown and the river, along with the roof of the Hotel Southern at 609 Garrison. The hotel has since been demolished.

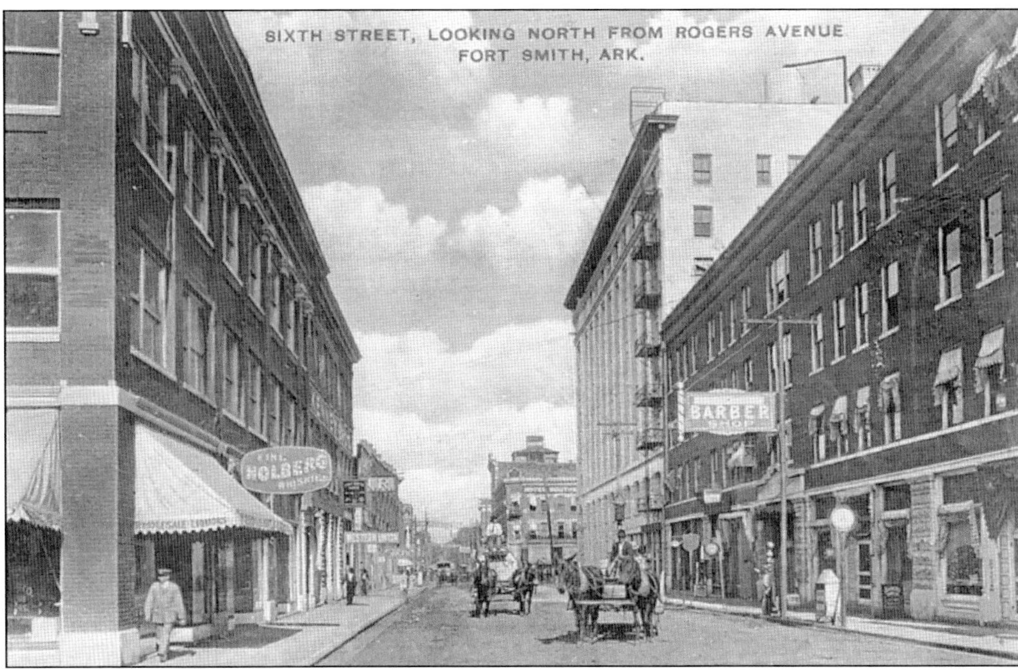

Sixth Street is shown here around 1910, in a view looking toward Garrison from Rogers Avenue, as wagons and pedestrians go about their business. On the left are the Holberg Whiskies store, the Western Union station, and the Eagles Club; on the right is a barbershop. The building in the distance is the Hotel Southern, the roof of which is seen in the bird's-eye view at the top of this page.

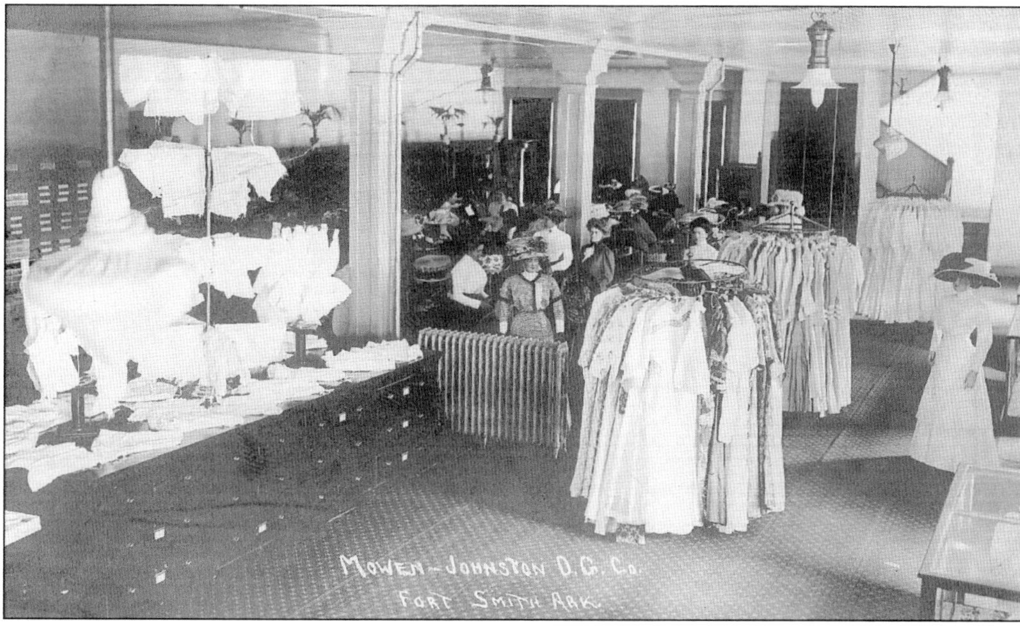

Many postcards were made of the business buildings along the wide streets of Fort Smith, most of which showed only the outside of the structures. Some of the rarest of postcards are the few that survive showing interior scenes; two such examples are found here. In the 1911 view above, the interior of the Mowen & Johnston Dry Goods store at 821-823 Garrison is seen, showing women's fine clothing department. The women in the center appear to be dressing a mannequin behind the radiator that would have helped heat the store on cold days. To the right, another mannequin is already sporting a fine dress and hat of the era. In the *c.* 1910 postcard below, two young Fort Smith barbers pose with a reclining customer in what may be a three-chair shop somewhere in Fort Smith, likely on Garrison Avenue.

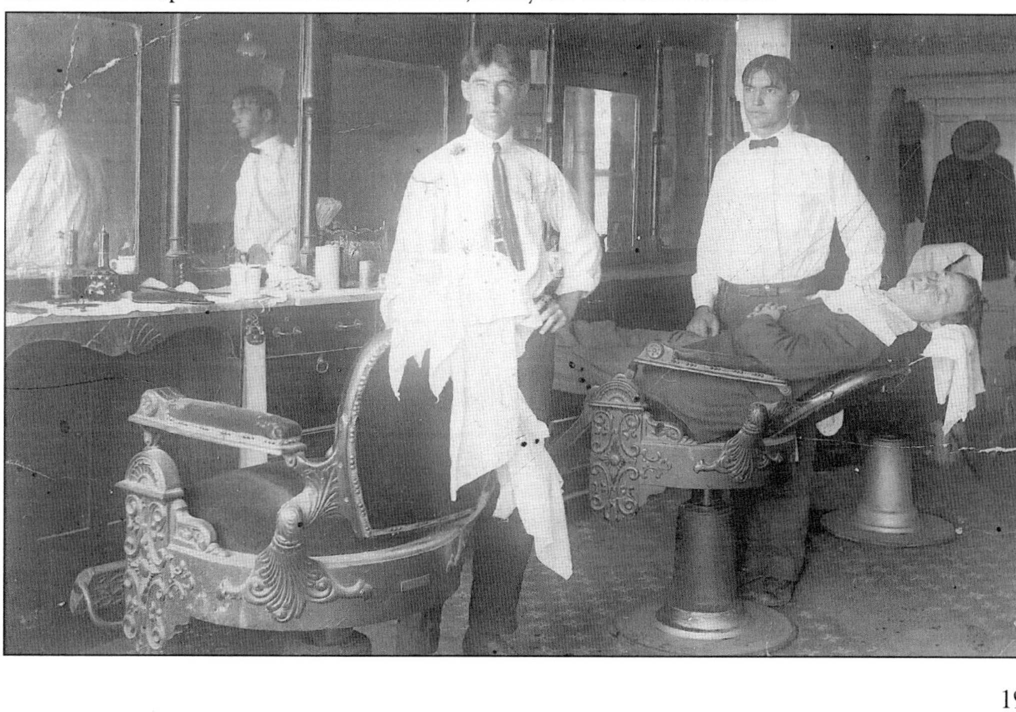

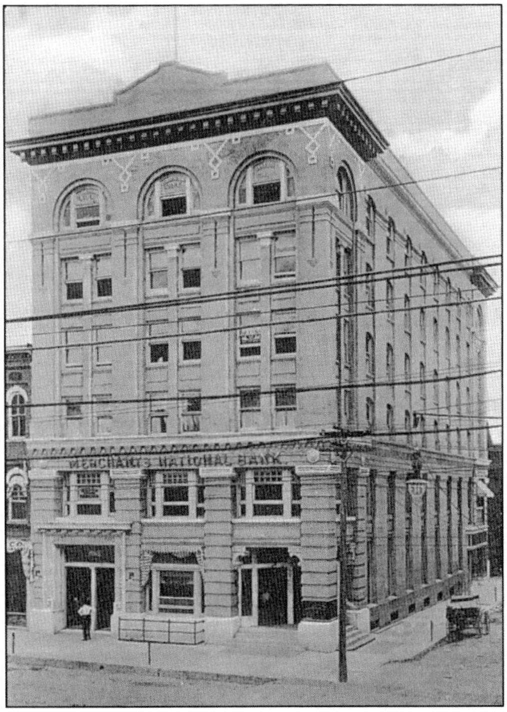

The prosperity of Fort Smith was reflected in the grandeur and number of banks that arose in the city as it benefited from expanding railroads and industry. Merchant's National Bank erected this six-story building at 623 Garrison Avenue in 1907 in a key corner location, as banks often sought. William Echols, a grocer who initially used his store safe for the valuables of neighbors, founded the bank in 1882, and his family controlled it until it was sold 100 years later, in 1982. In the c. 1910 postcard below, the interior of the bank is shown, with teller's cages set above polished wood and marble. Benches to the right furnished a spot for tired customers to sit and perhaps to wait their turn on a busy day. The bank later relocated, and its historic building is today occupied by the City of Fort Smith offices.

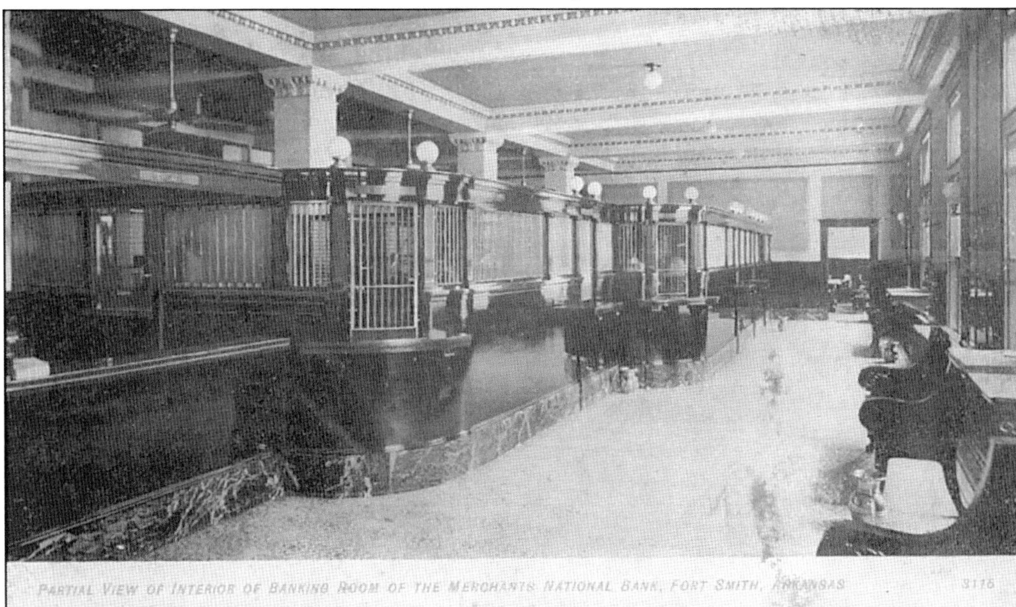

First National Bank was organized in 1872 with $100,000 in assets, and its success led to the erection of this white brick building towering over the corner of Sixth Street and Garrison Avenue in 1910. The new bank cast a shadow over its neighbor, the Hotel Main, in front of which is parked a delivery wagon from the J.W. Williams's Creamery. The c. 1910 postcard below reveals the elaborate interior of the bank, with spittoons on the floor in front of the tellers' cages for use by the tobacco-chewing depositors. The curved door to the right, behind the potted plant, bears a "Ladies Room" sign above the door. The building still serves the bank today.

HOTEL MAIN AND FIRST NATIONAL BANK BUILDING. FORT SMITH, ARK.

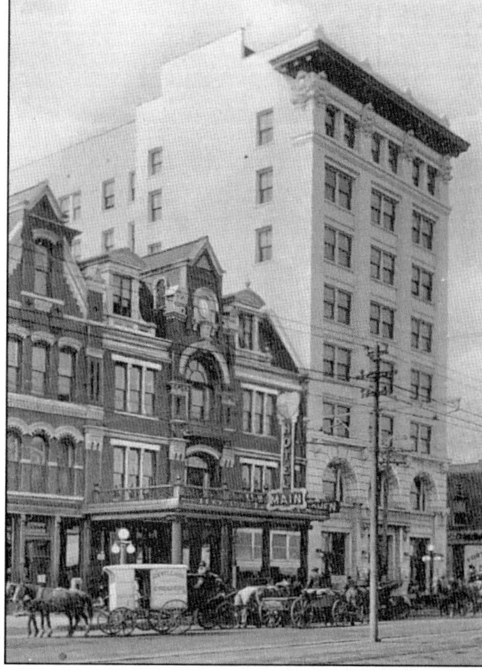

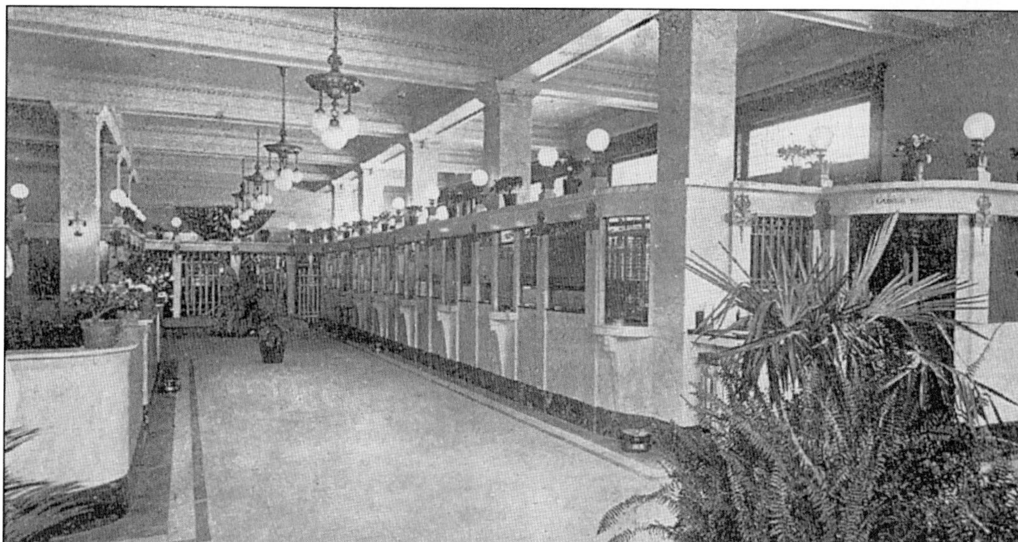

BANKING ROOM, FIRST NATIONAL BANK, FORT SMITH, ARKANSAS

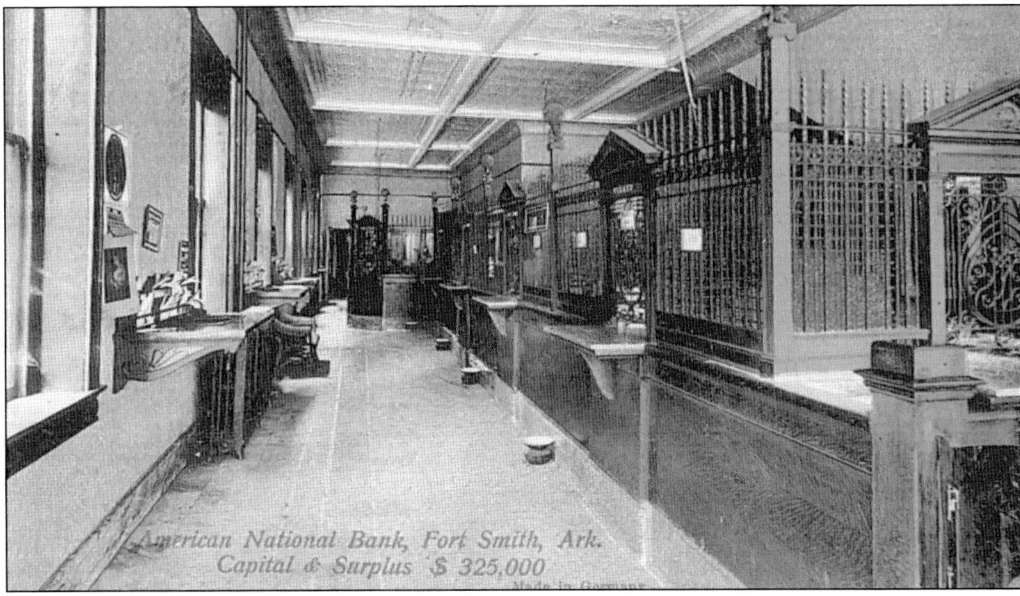

The American National Bank, seen on this 1908 postcard of its lobby, boasted that it had "Capital & Surplus of $325,000." The ornate tellers' cages, with a spittoon for each, served customers who likely had stopped at the writing desks to the left to prepare their deposits. Each shelf seems to have a supply of deposit tickets and a calendar on the wall to aid the customer. "Send me a postcard sometime" is the message on the back of this postcard, which was printed in Germany, and was probably used to advertise the bank. The postcard below was mailed by the Arkansas Valley Trust Company and illustrates how banks often turned to postcards as a way to solicit new customers. The fictitious "Prosperity Bank of Prosperityville" had opened an account for "A. Wiseman." "Saving money is your duty—paying interest is ours," was part of the 1910 message from the bank.

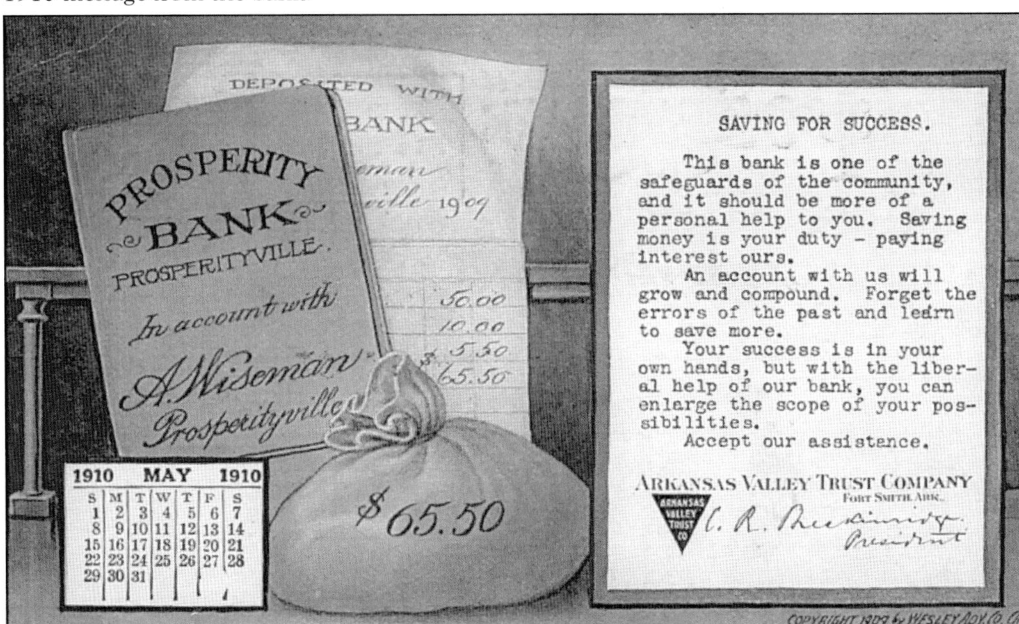

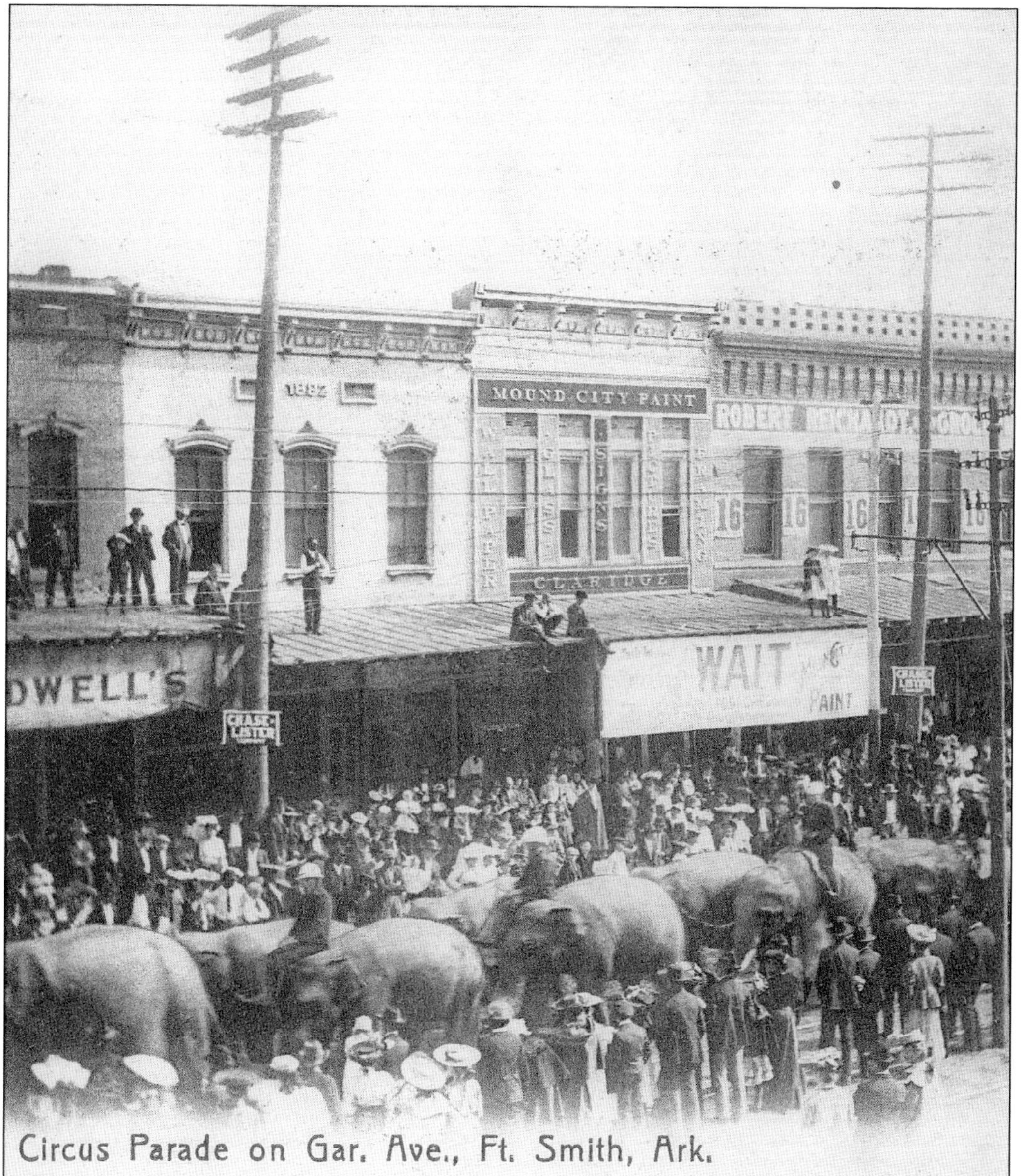

Garrison Avenue was not all business, and certainly even the buttoned-up bankers must have been tempted outside to watch the passage of a circus parade in 1906. The elephants and other attractions were off-loaded from railcars and were marched down the street on their way to the show grounds, in part to spur ticket sales for the promoters of the circus. Some spectators had claimed a vantage spot atop the awnings over businesses like Mound City Paint.

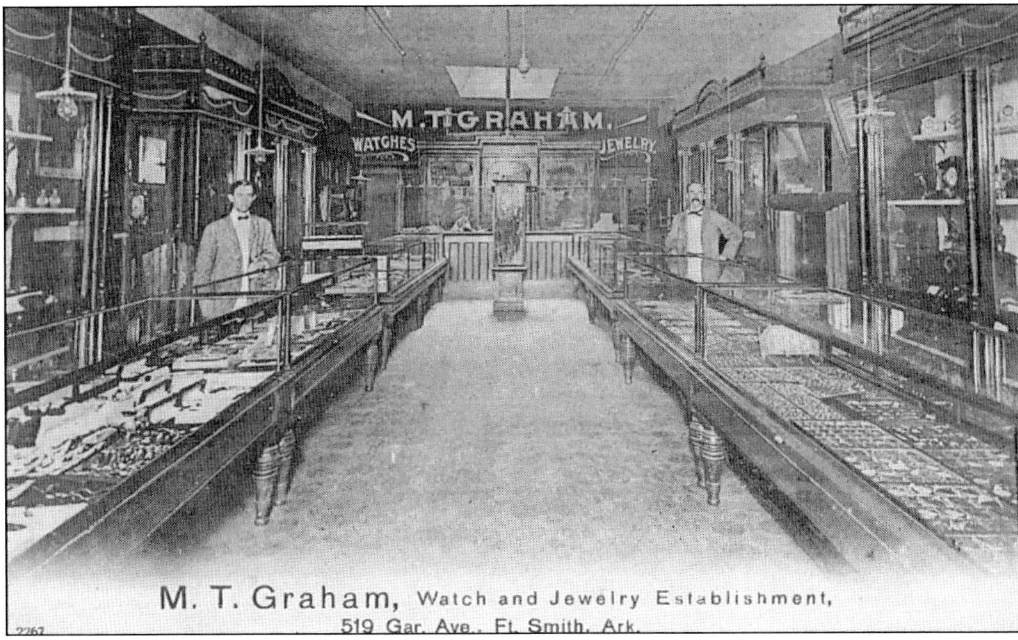

Among the businesses supported by Fort Smith's growing economy was M.T. Graham's watch and jewelry store located at 519 Garrison Avenue, seen here in a c. 1907 interior view. The glass case to the right contains a wide selection of men's pocket watches, an emblem of a bygone era. Above this case, on wall shelves, is an array of mantle clocks. A variety of rings and bracelets are displayed in the case to the left.

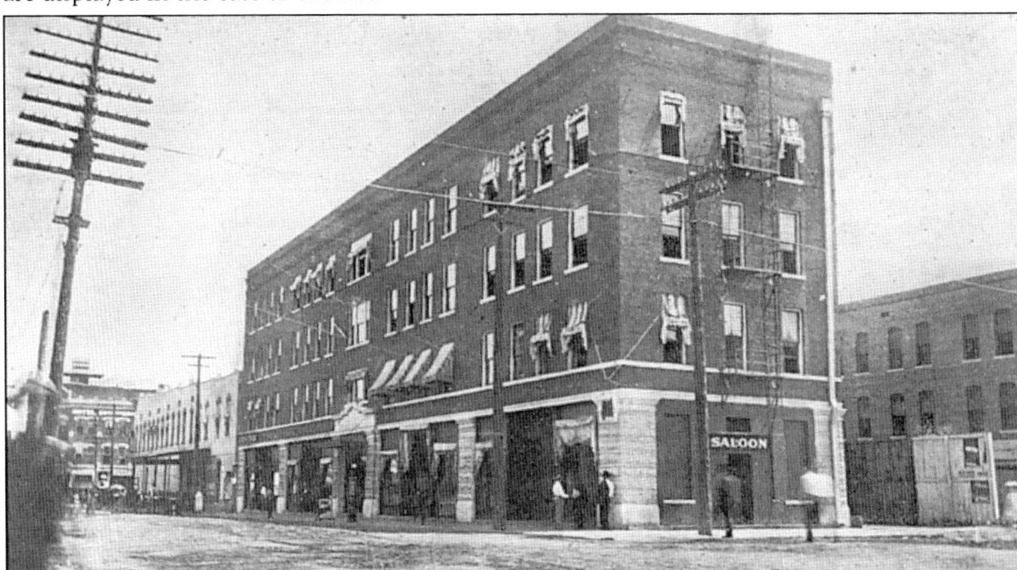

Located a block over from Garrison Avenue, at Sixth Street and Rogers Avenue, was the Kennedy Block, seen here around 1905. Taken from a similar angle as the postcard on the bottom of page 18, this postcard was made before the erection of First National Bank in 1910, notably absent beyond the building in this view. The long, narrow structure seen here housed, among other businesses, a saloon that fronted Rogers Avenue. The building was later demolished; today the site is a parking lot.

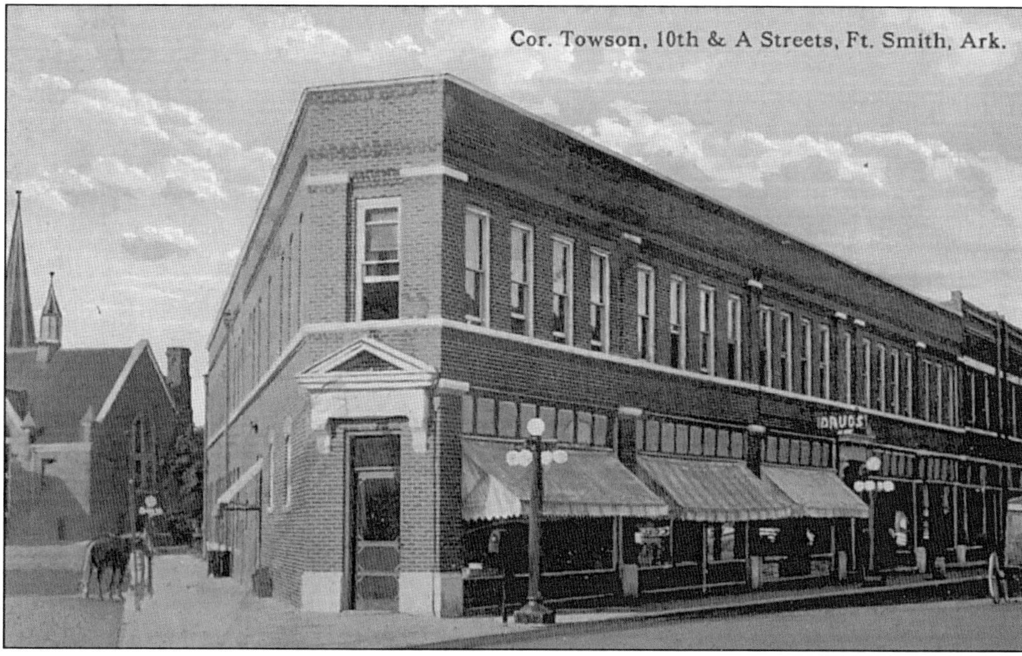

The commerce that fueled Fort Smith's growth gave birth to a number of attractive and unusual buildings. Fortunately, several of these buildings survive, but few have been so carefully restored as has this one at the intersection of Towson, Tenth, and A Streets. Dating from the turn of the century, it served as both a dance hall and a union hall in the 1920s, and today it is owned by the Union Hall Investment Co., so named for one of its historical tenants. The c. 1915 message on the above postcard reads as follows: "Am at Mother's now, left the boss (her husband) to batch, don't imagine what a house will find on my return home." As evidenced by the 1999 photograph below, the restoration of both the Union Hall building and the former Cumberland Presbyterian Church, in the background, are both remarkable. The restored church building today houses Architecture Plus, Inc. (Photograph by Ray Hanley.)

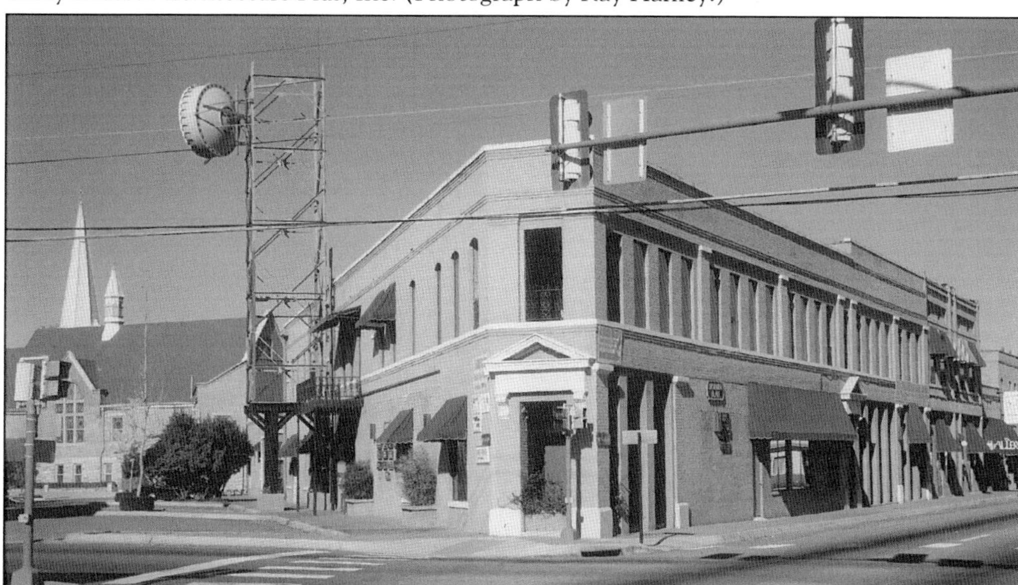

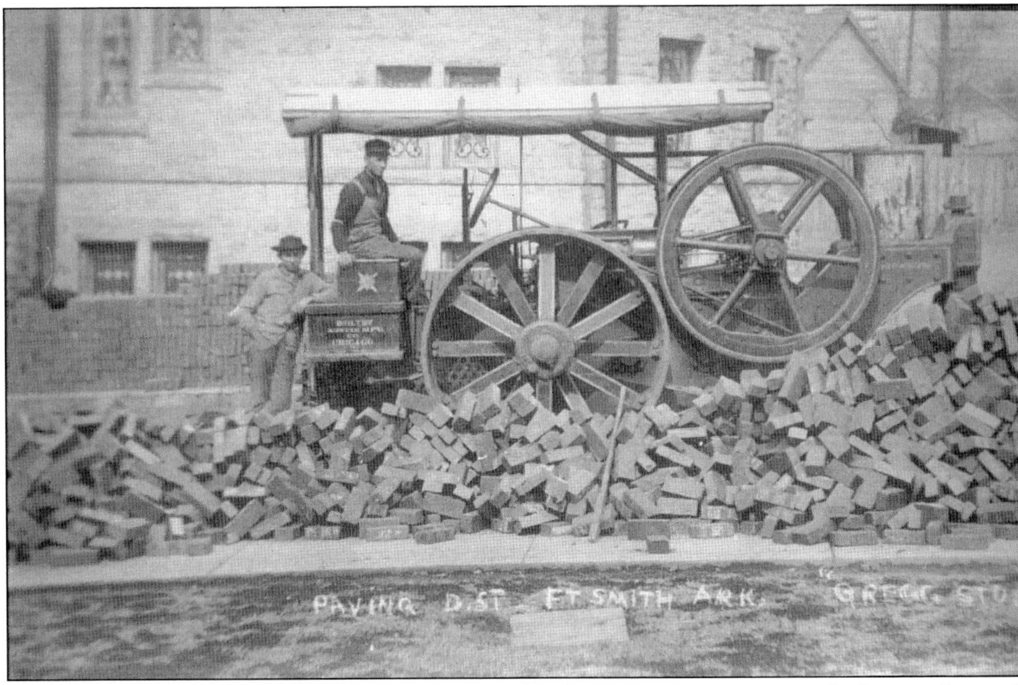

Fort Smith was striving to keep its city services developing at a pace to match the rapid growth of the Garrison Avenue business district in the early years of the century. A part of this effort brought this steam-powered paving machine into service around 1915. The machine was built by the Austin Mfg. Co. of Chicago, and it drew crowds of onlookers to watch it lay the brick pavement. (Postcard courtesy of Tom Mertens of Little Rock.)

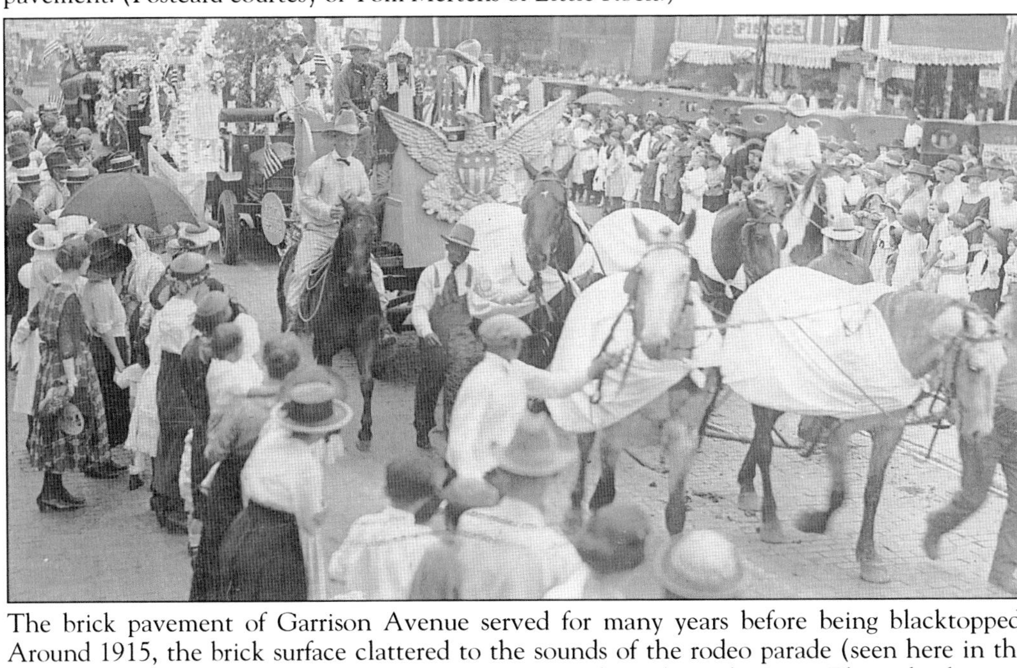

The brick pavement of Garrison Avenue served for many years before being blacktopped. Around 1915, the brick surface clattered to the sounds of the rodeo parade (seen here in the 800 block), which packed the sidewalks with viewers along the wide street. The rodeo became an annual fixture for Fort Smith and western Arkansas.

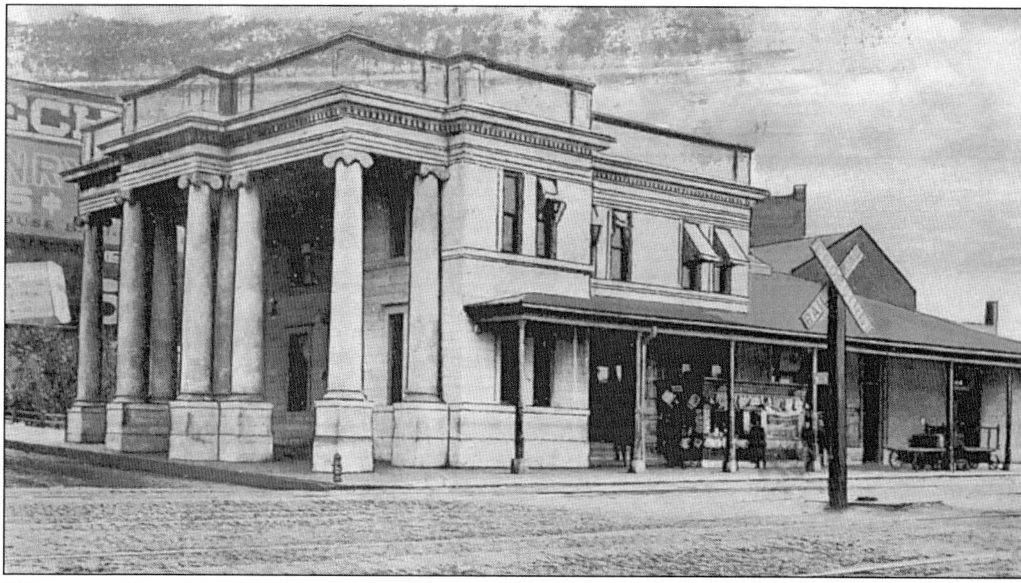

"How are the rabbits and the plain cooking?" read the 1911 message to Oklahoma on the back of a postcard of the Frisco railroad depot. The Frisco depot, with service reaching from southern Missouri through Fayetteville to Fort Smith, proved a vital link in the growth of Sebastian County's economy in the early years of the century. This depot was built just after the turn of the century near the Arkansas River, at 100 Garrison Avenue. The depot no longer welcomes trains but still stands today, having served as a restaurant and an office building in later incarnations.

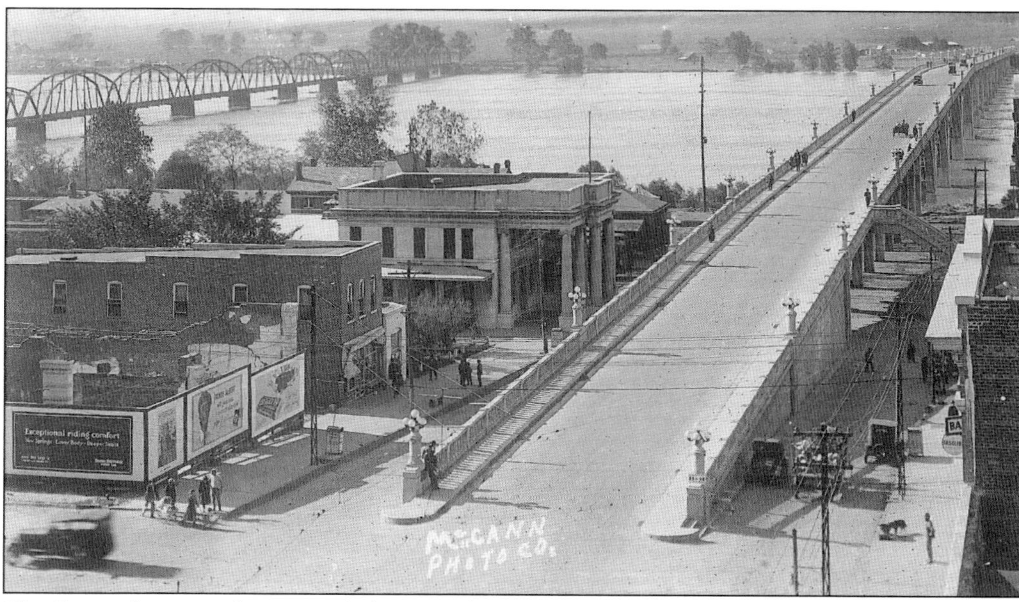

The Frisco depot, in this *c.* 1925 photograph, seems rather forlorn as it sits in the shadow of the new highway bridge that linked Fort Smith and Oklahoma upon its 1922 opening. Of note are the billboards to the lower left of the image, surrounding the ruins of a building. One billboard advertises Prince Albert tobacco. The bridge had more pedestrians than automobiles on the day the photograph was made. The bridge was in use until it was torn down and replaced in 1971.

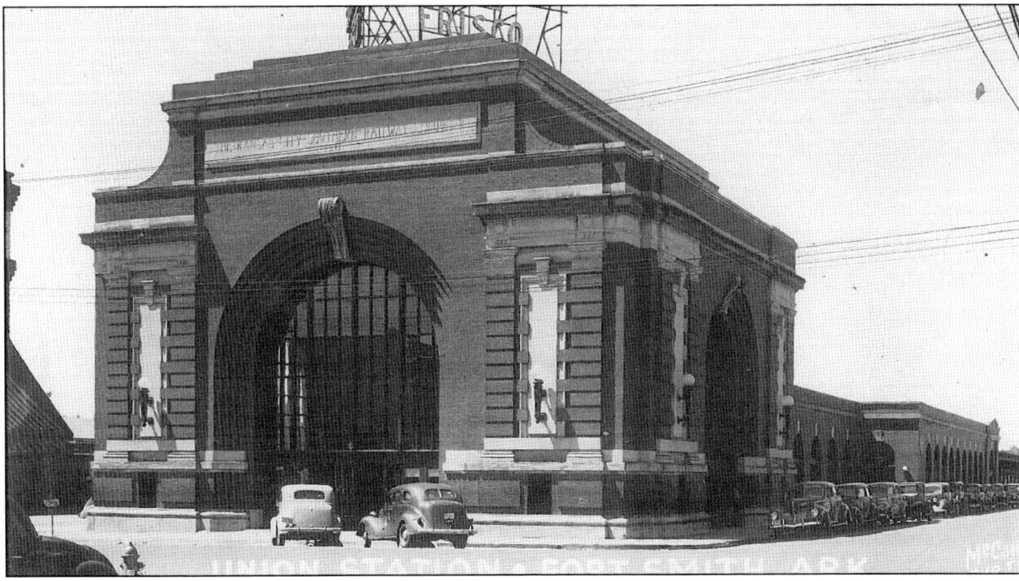

One of the most imposing train stations in Arkansas was completed in 1913 at Rogers Avenue and Seventh Street. The soaring, multi-storied, glass-paneled building (seen here around 1940) served two railroads, the Frisco and the Kansas City Southern, for many years. Sadly, this magnificent piece of the state's history fell victim to the wrecking ball in 1960 (after passenger service had ended) to make way for yet another parking lot. Later, a Holiday Inn was erected on the site.

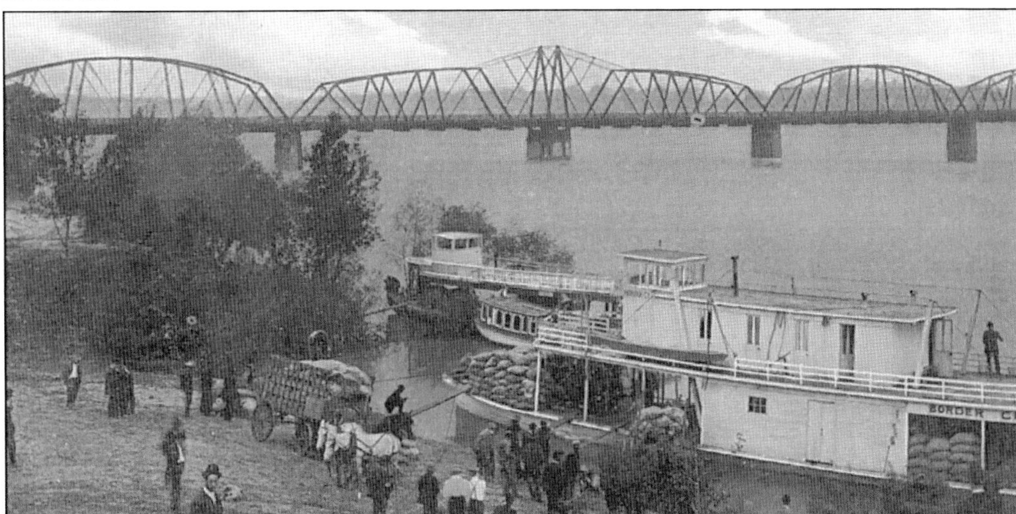

Fort Smith was served not only by the network of iron rails entering the city from all directions, but also by the powerful Arkansas River that flowed at its feet. In this c. 1910 postcard, a shipment of potatoes is being loaded from wagons onto the steam-powered vessel, the *Border City*, for shipment to downstream markets. The *Border City* was built at Fort Smith in 1908, and was used for a number of years to carry cargoes of grain and potatoes. The treacherous river was both a blessing and a hazard to commercial shipping for decades, before being tamed by a series of locks and dams in the 1960s. Today, many tons of products pass Fort Smith by barge, bound for points around the globe.

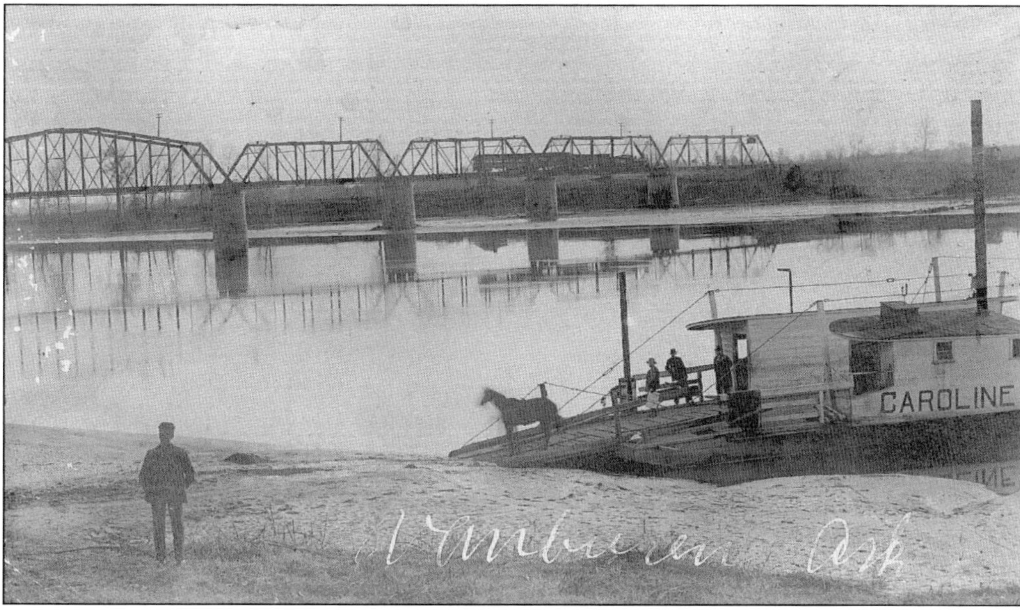

The boats that docked at the edge of Fort Smith on their journey up or down the Arkansas River were not the mighty steamboats of Mississippi River fame, but were instead much smaller. Shapes and styles varied with the purpose of the craft and the financial resources of the owner. The 1908 postcard above shows the ferryboat *Caroline* unloading a horse on the Van Buren side of the river, perhaps having just ferried it over from Fort Smith. The owner of the *Caroline*, Phillip Scott, named the vessel for his young daughter. The charge for the ferry was 75¢ for a two-horse wagon, 50¢ for a one-horse wagon, 25¢ for a mounted rider, and 10¢ for a foot passenger. In the background, a train is seen speeding across the Frisco Railroad Bridge toward the station in Fort Smith. In the photograph below, the *Driftwood* is seen around 1920 with its larger paddlewheel for a heavier craft and an almost totally enclosed deck, with many windows for light and air. The metal frame at the top would have supported a canvas cover to allow additional protected space during bad weather.

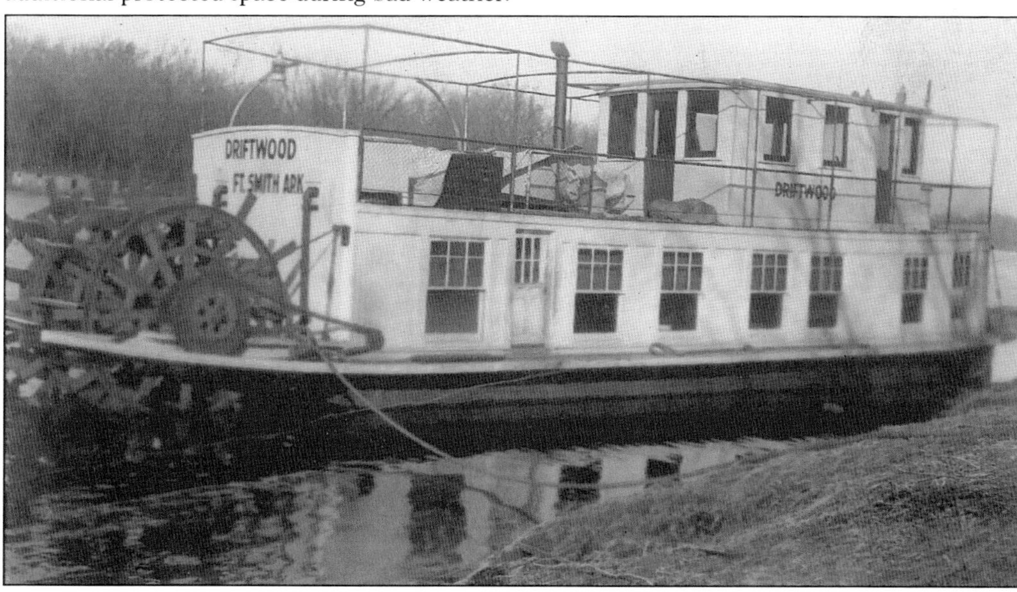

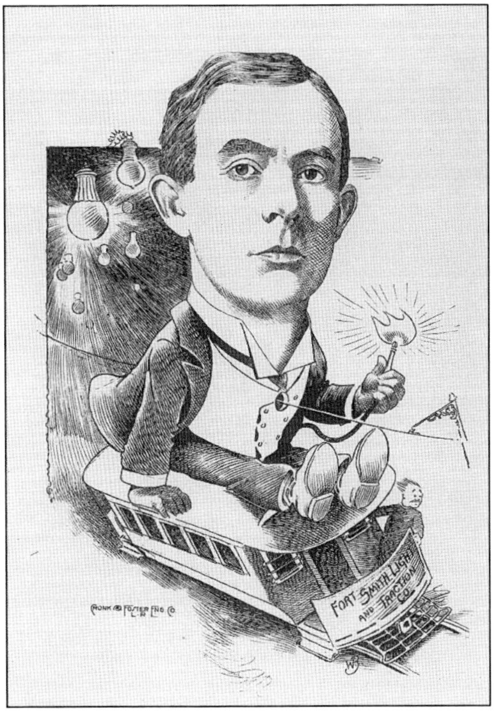

Visitors and residents of Fort Smith had a new option for traveling around town beginning in 1893, when electric trolley service took over from the horse-drawn system that had begun a decade earlier. What became the Fort Smith Light and Traction Company in 1903 made even greater strides under the leadership of general manager J. Walter Gillette, who is depicted here. Faced with an Arkansas law banning Sunday baseball games, which gave fare-paying customers a reason to stay home, Gillette was soon taking his electric cars across the Arkansas River on Sundays, to where baseball games packed the stands in Arkhoma, Oklahoma. Newspaper reports of Gillette's Sunday effort said his electric cars transported 10,000 people the first Sunday they ran across the railroad bridge to Oklahoma. (Postcard c. 1905, courtesy of Arkansas History Commission.)

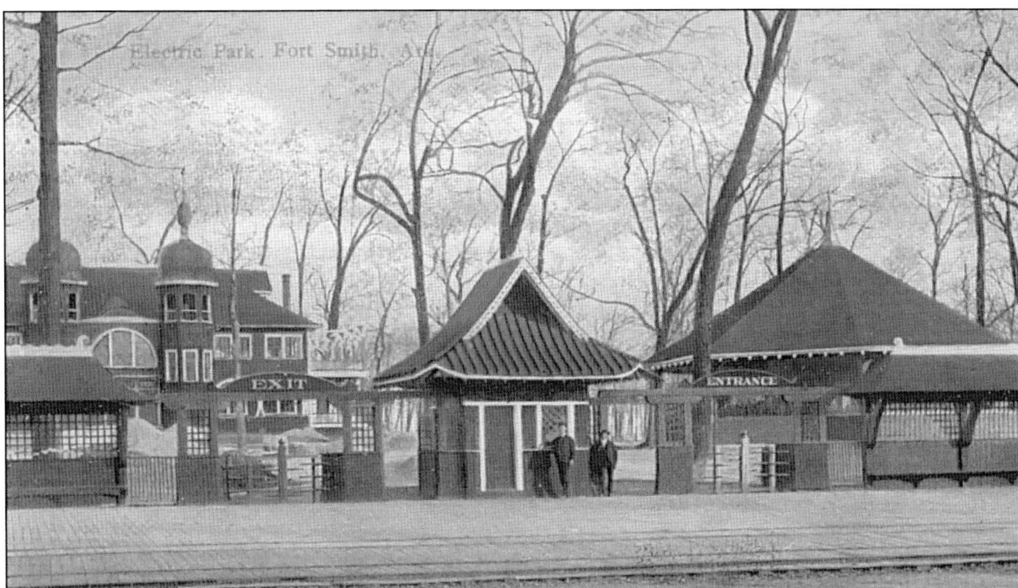

The most prominent contribution to Fort Smith's history by J. Walter Gillette came when the streetcar tracks were extended out North Eleventh Street, to an area known as McCloud Park, to which Gillette made major improvements and renamed "Electric Park." He gambled that the park, at that time quite a way from the heart of the city, would increase streetcar business if the attractions were enough of a draw. A success it was, and in 1908, Gillette added a roller coaster, among other features. This c. 1910 postcard shows the entrance to the park, where visitors would have alighted from the streetcars to purchase a ticket and proceed through the gates.

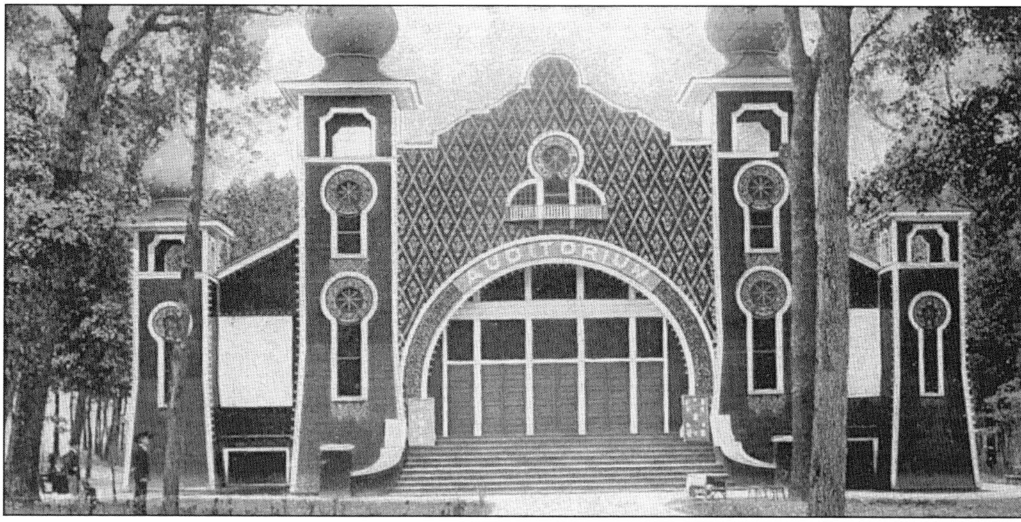

Among the features of Electric Park was this Moorish-style auditorium, which measured 240 feet by 110 feet. The building seated 2,200 patrons in front of a fully-equipped stage that included 15 different sets of scenery and 16 dressing rooms. Seats could be reserved at the streetcar company's downtown Fort Smith office before passengers boarded to come to the park to view vaudeville acts and various traveling stock company productions. Streetcars traveled through Fort Smith, adorned with removable billboards advertising the latest attractions appearing at the auditorium or elsewhere in the park.

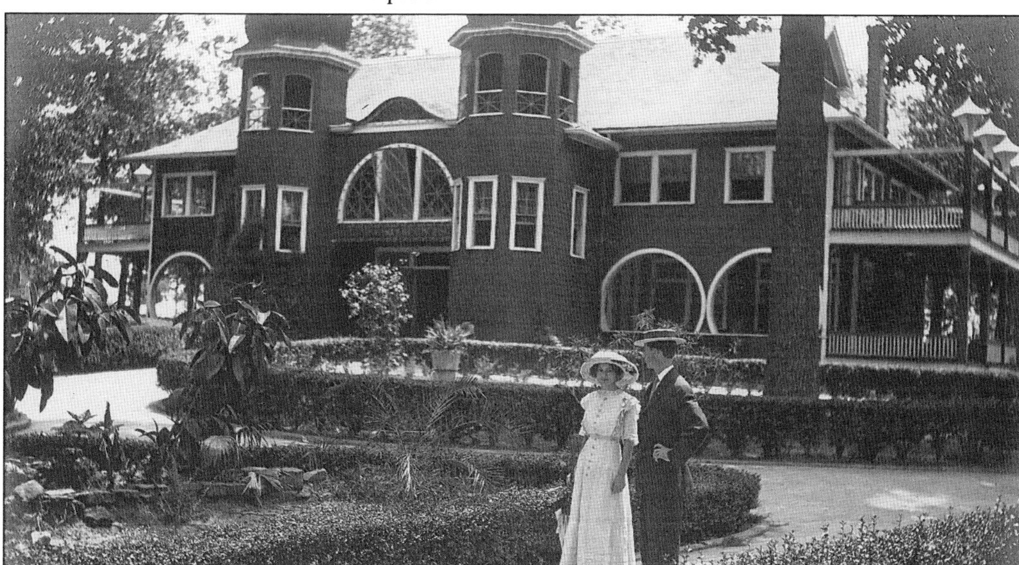

The other large building at Electric Park was called the Casino, and while some card games likely took place in its smoking rooms adjacent to the dining hall, the building's most-used area was the 60-foot by 90-foot dance hall. Its archways opened onto broad balconies overlooking gardens that often found young couples strolling among landscaped paths. The Casino building, which is seen in the background in this 1910 view, was adorned with 5,600 electric lights that blazed at night. Under the rules of the park's owners, Fort Smith Light and Traction Company, no intoxicating beverages were sold on the grounds, but certainly some found their way, on occasion, into the park.

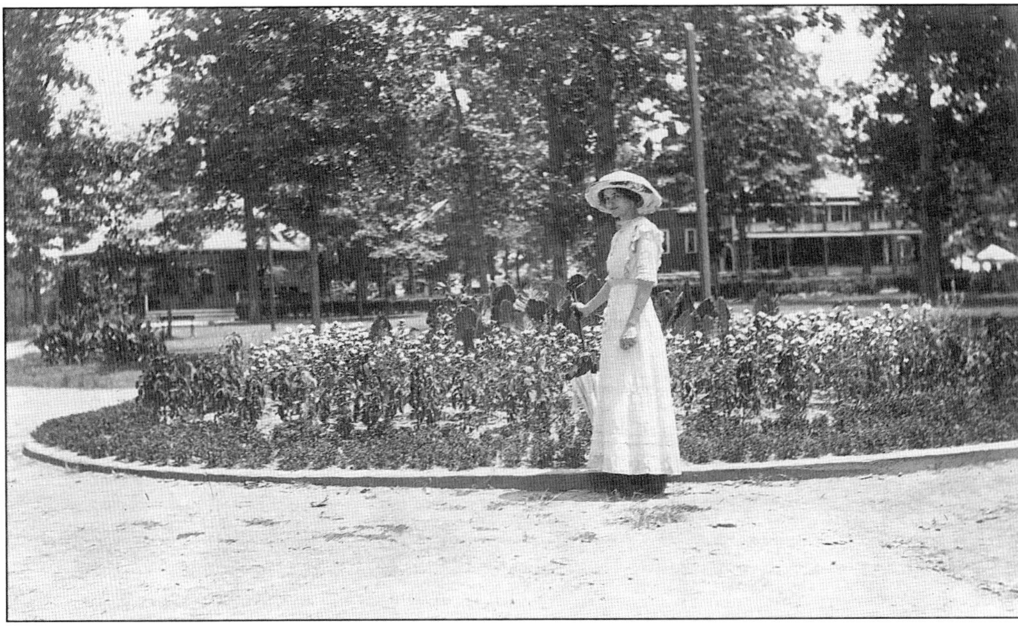

The landscaped grounds of Electric Park, enhanced by the park's own greenhouse, was a major recreational draw for Fort Smith citizens of all ages, as evidenced by these photos of ladies and children. The park had its own water and sewer system, a penny arcade, and even a baseball park that hosted local leagues. The team sponsored by the Light & Traction Company was called the Trolley Dodgers. Shifting priorities of the company and the growing numbers of automobiles led to the closing and eventual demolition of the park buildings around 1915. The site is presently occupied by Kay Rodgers Park, though without the elaborate features of Electric Park. The streetcars were replaced by buses in the 1930s, but today, one restored car runs a short route from the Trolley Museum in Fort Smith to give visitors a memory of how things used to be.

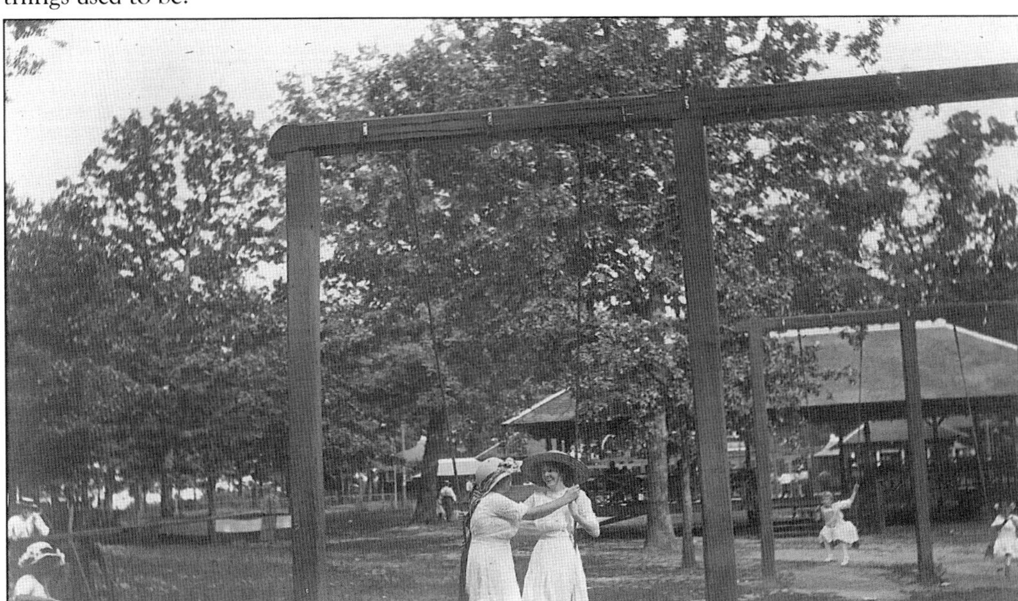

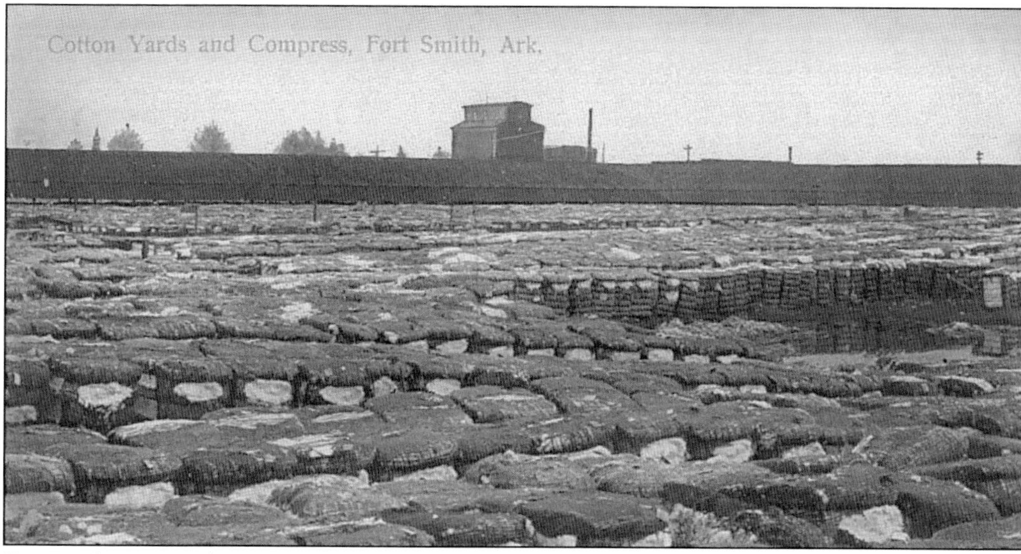

Despite the postcard attention given to carefree places like Electric Park, there was much hard work done in Sebastian County to put food on the table for many people. Some of the hardest work involved bringing the cotton to the point seen here, at the local compress in Fort Smith. Each of the bales in this view weighed some 500 pounds. In 1908, when this postcard was mailed, cotton was grown in 73 of Arkansas's 75 counties, making it truly the king of crops at the time. From the compress, the huge bales of cotton could be shipped to distant factories by river or rail.

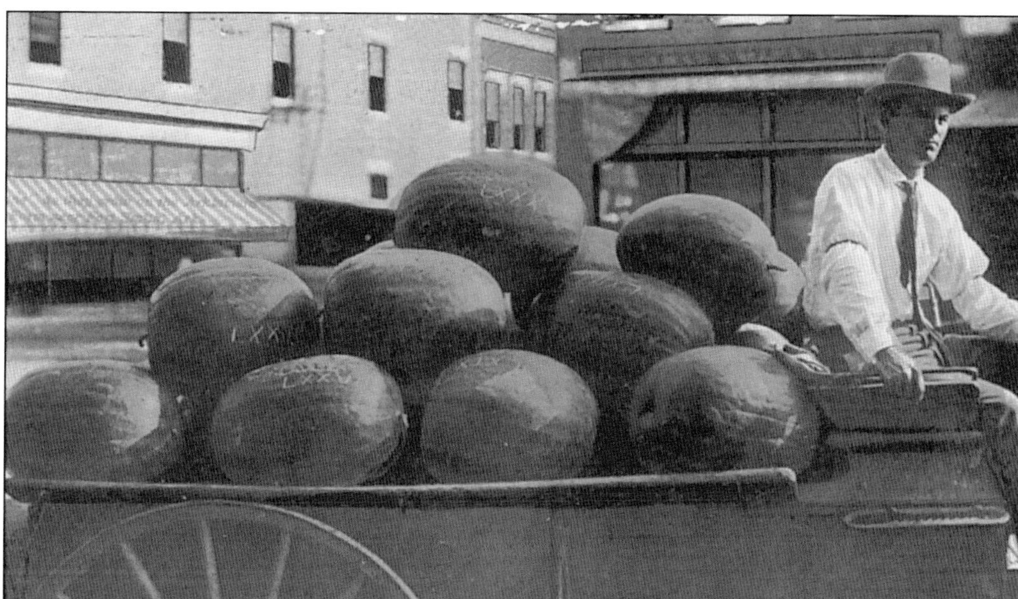

The slowly improving roads of Sebastian County were important to the owners of the Arklavista Farm, who depended on wagons like this one to transport their watermelons into Fort Smith for sale and rail shipment. In this 1910 postcard, the wagon driver was sitting atop a load of melons, nattily attired in a shirt, tie, and bowler hat. Each melon had its weight carved into its surface in Roman numerals, and the one just over the rear wheel is marked as weighing 75 pounds (LXXV).

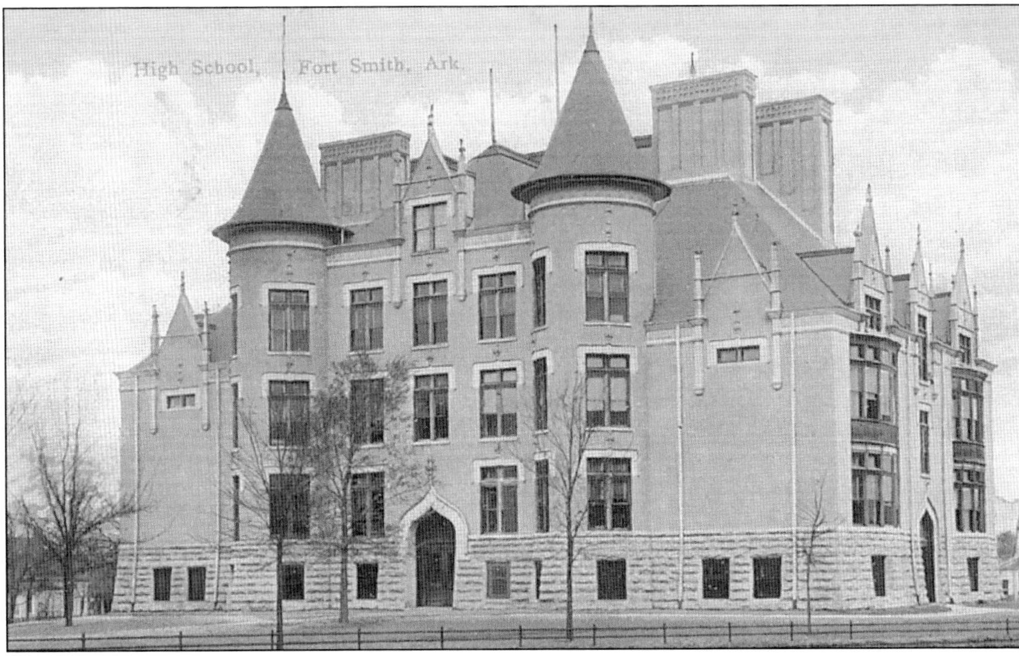

Fort Smith erected this magnificent high school building with great pride in 1897, only to see it suffer major damage just three months later in a deadly tornado that raked the area. The school was restored and back in business by 1900, a year that found the average Arkansas teacher's annual salary at $166. The school was gutted by a 1912 fire but was later restored to serve the community once again.

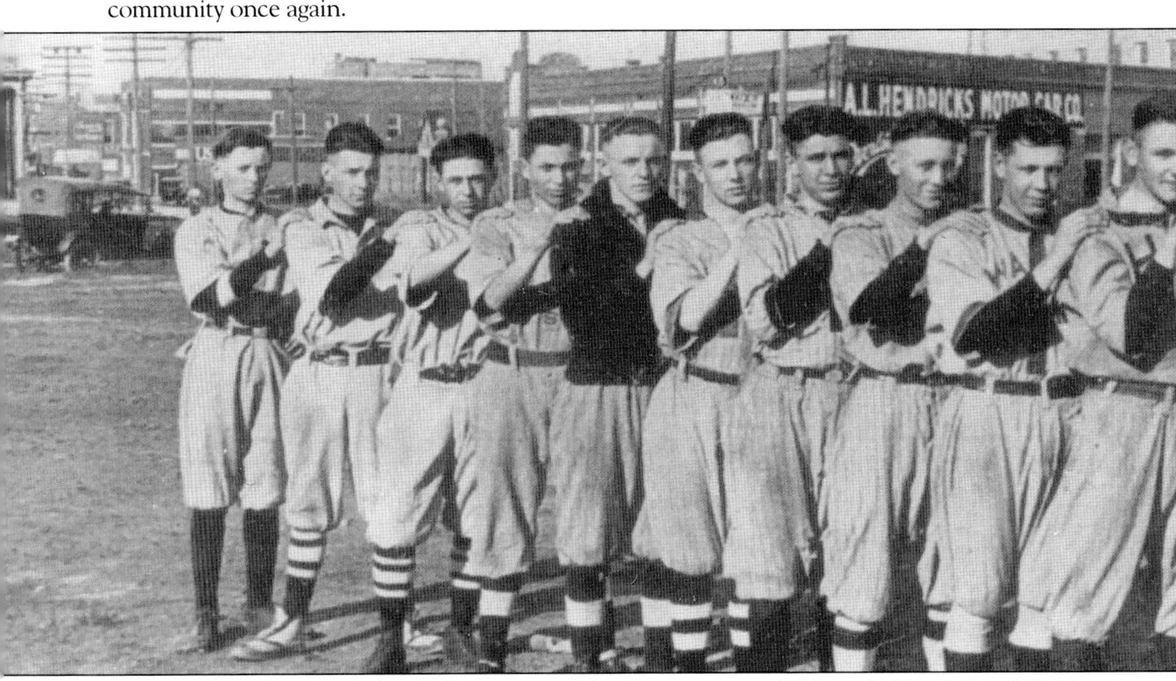

Fort Smith High School's baseball team posed for this picture in 1920, with Coach Frank Bridges in the front of their line and the city as a backdrop. At the time the photograph was made, the team was preparing to play Little Rock for the state championship. Listed among the players on the roster

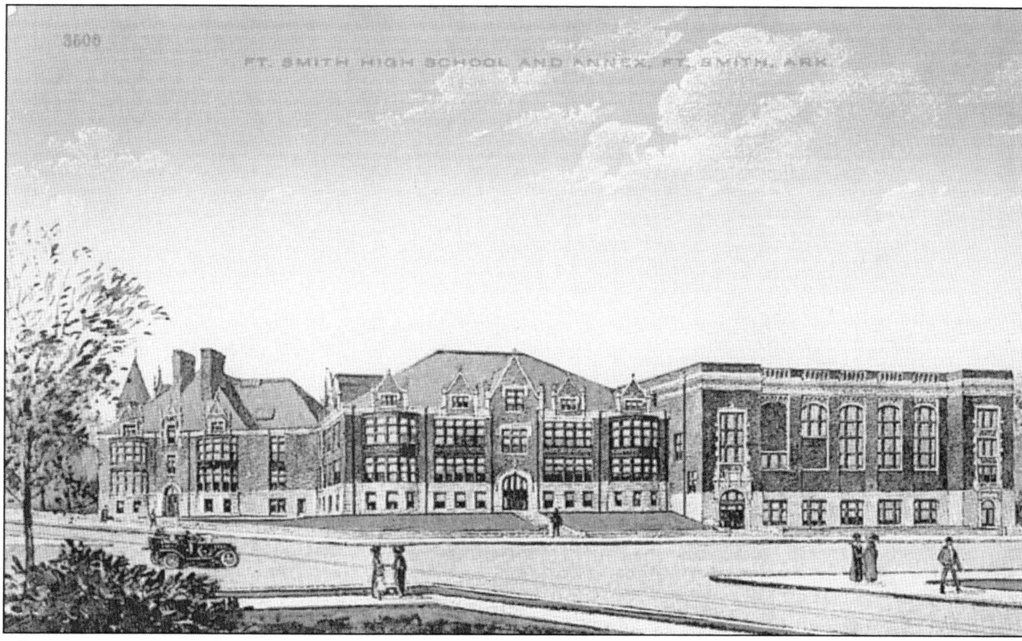

The Fort Smith High School was given annexes on at least two occasions, seen here around 1915, expanding from the original 1897 structure to the left. Over the years it would serve as Fort Smith High School, Fort Smith Junior High, and Darby Junior High before being demolished in 1968 to make way for a new school building.

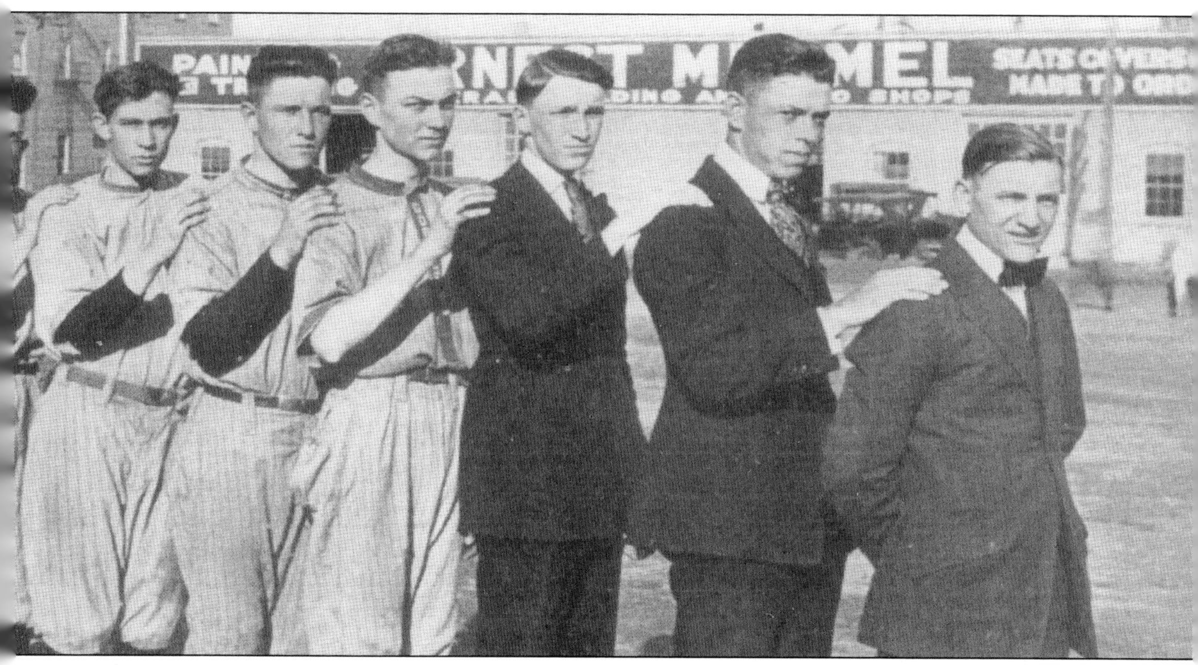

were lettered players Degen Boyd, Armando Porta, and Farley Klewein, to cite some unusual names of the era. Following the very successful 1920 season, Coach Bridges left to become the baseball coach at Baylor College in Waco, Texas.

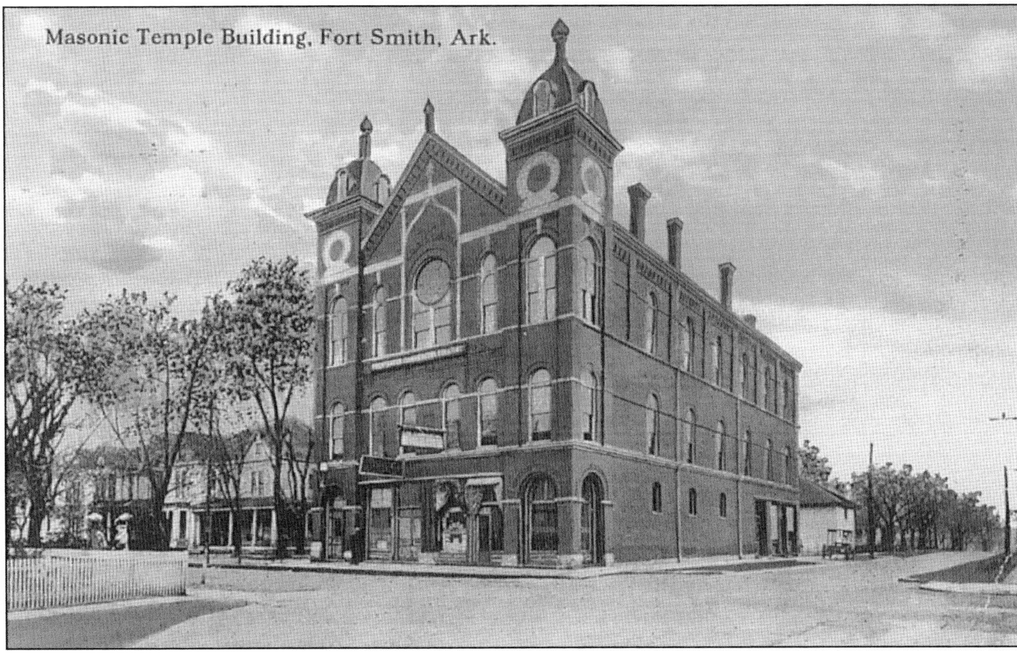

Among the first successful post-secondary educational enterprises in Sebastian County was the Fort Smith Commercial College that opened in the Masonic Temple (called the Baer Memorial Temple) in 1888. The college, located on North Sixth Street across from St. John's Episcopal Church, graduated 15 students its first year, from classes housed on the first floor of the temple. The view below offers a look at the mixed residential and commercial neighborhoods located within a few blocks of busy Garrison Avenue. The temple building was severely damaged by a fire in 1919, losing in the process many of the historic Masonic documents. The building was restored but was left with only two floors. Today the building still stands, housing mostly offices.

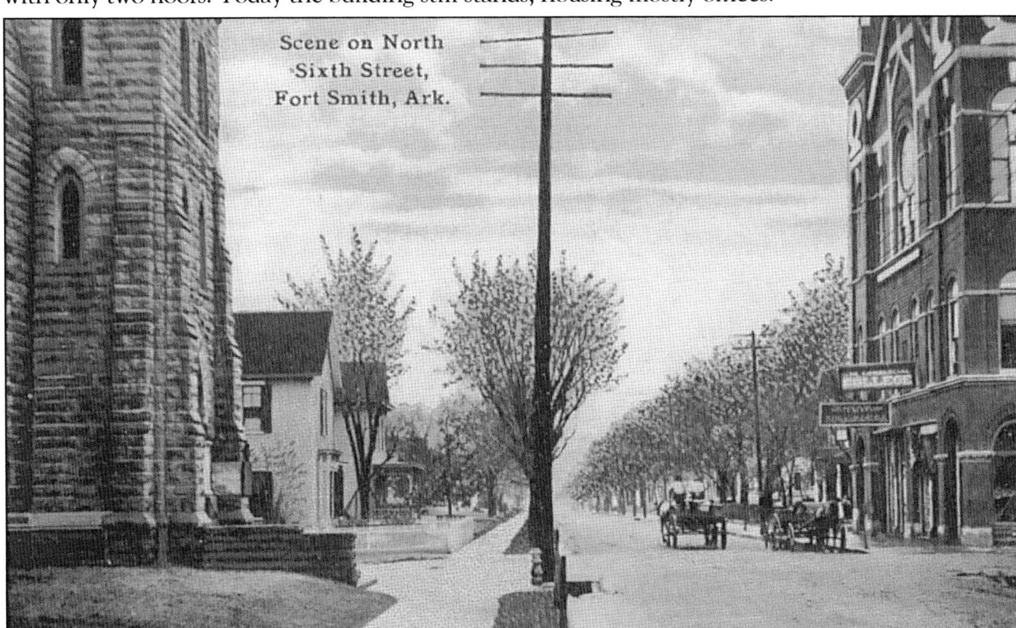

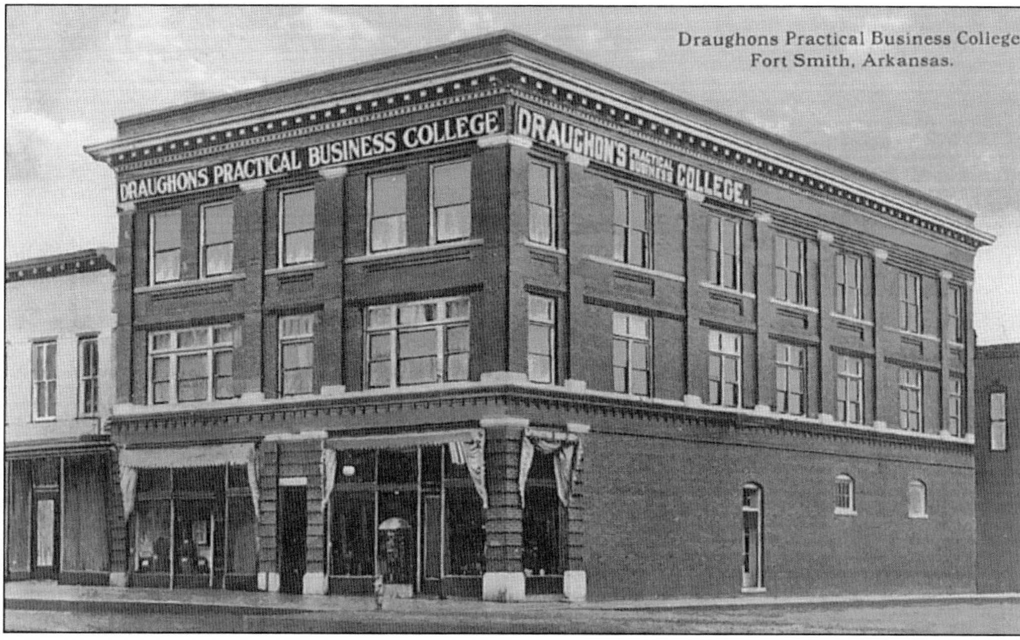

Draughon's Practical Business College was a fixture at Eighth Street and Garrison Avenue from 1912 until its demolition in 1942. The Fort Smith location of Draughon's was a part of an affiliated network of business schools operating in several states, with one in Little Rock for more than 50 years. Today, apparently all are gone, but at the time of this c. 1915 postcard, Draughon's afforded young people the chance to acquire business and office skills in an era when most people didn't finish high school, much less attend college.

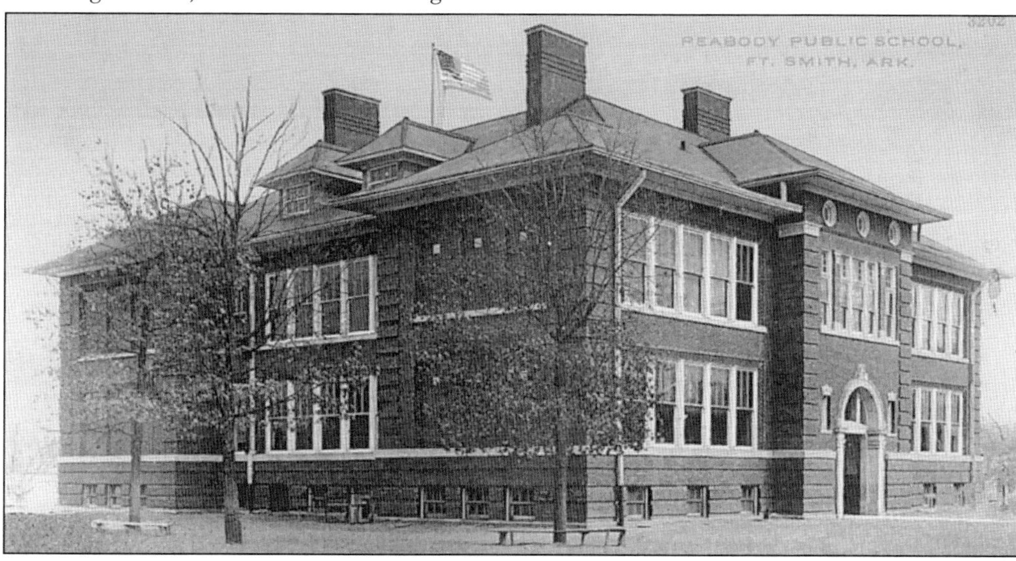

Peabody School was built in 1905, between South Twentieth and Twenty-first Streets, just off Rogers Avenue. The school seen in this c. 1910 postcard took its name from its benefactor, George Peabody of Massachusetts, who devoted much of his family's great wealth to funding the construction of schools. The Fort Smith school was one of those fortunate to be gifted by the philanthropist. Still standing, the old school has in recent years served as an adult education school operated by the Fort Smith School System.

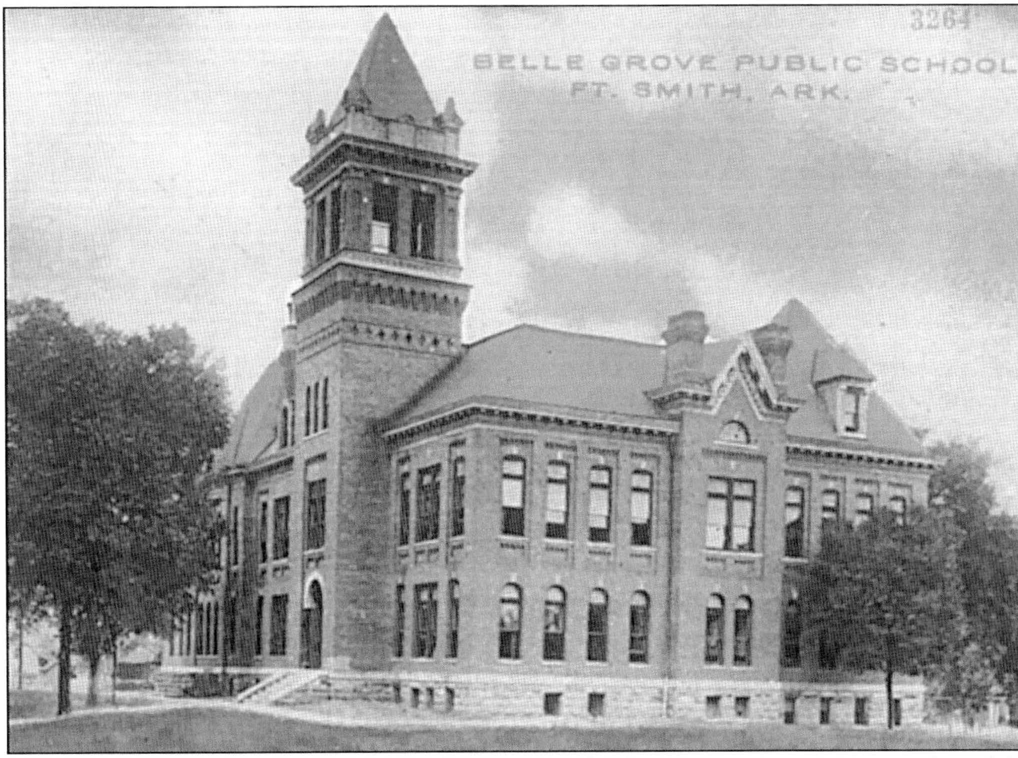

Belle Point, located at the confluence of the Poteau and Arkansas Rivers, was the site selected for the original Fort Smith in 1817. The area became home to impressive public school buildings after President Chester Arthur signed the land over to the city of Fort Smith for a school site in 1884. Seen on the 1910 postcard below is the Belle Point Public School, which occupied a city block at South Ninth Streets and Wheeler Avenue. The first class, in 1887, graduated two students. The building was torn down in 1918. The impressive, towered building in the upper photo, the Belle Grove School, was erected in 1886 and replaced an earlier building that had housed an Episcopal academy for young ladies. The building was converted to apartments and still stands today.

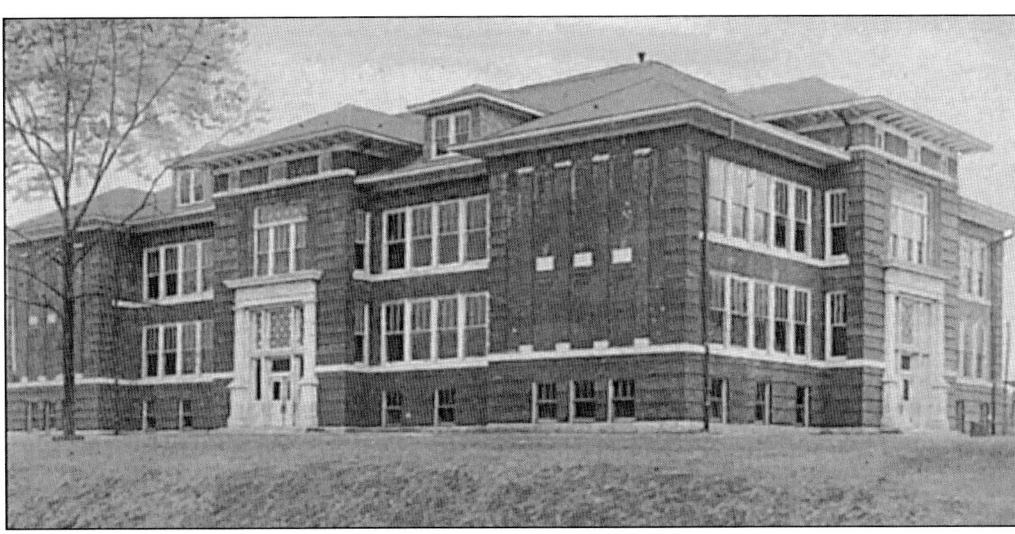

First Presbyterian Church was formed in Fort Smith in 1846, the same year the Methodist Church was formed, and they apparently represent the first two churches planted in the city. To the strains of the hymn "The Precious Firmament on High," the Presbyterian congregation ceremoniously laid the cornerstone for this new Gothic-styled church in 1898, at North Twelfth and B Streets. Completed in 1900 at a cost of $18,000, the imposing church featured a stained-glass rose window dedicated to the Travelers Protective Association and was intended to welcome lonely traveling salesmen to a house of worship. One newspaper article at the time speculated the following: "The broad beautiful aisles will prove a great temptation to many young ladies who have, up to this time, been heroically resisting the entreaties of sighing swains that would name the day, to walk down the long dream aisle, under the light of 125 electric bulbs all 'done up in silk and satin and flowing veils.'" The message on the 1910 postcard below reads, "This is the street on which I live, you can see part of our house." The church still serves today.

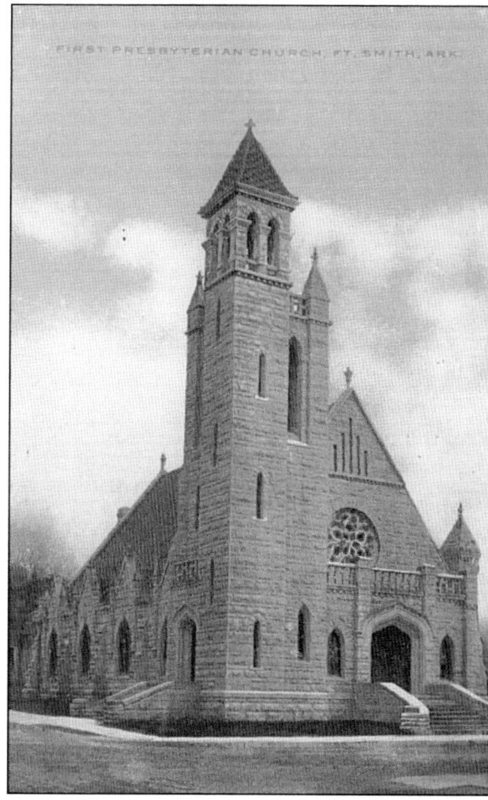

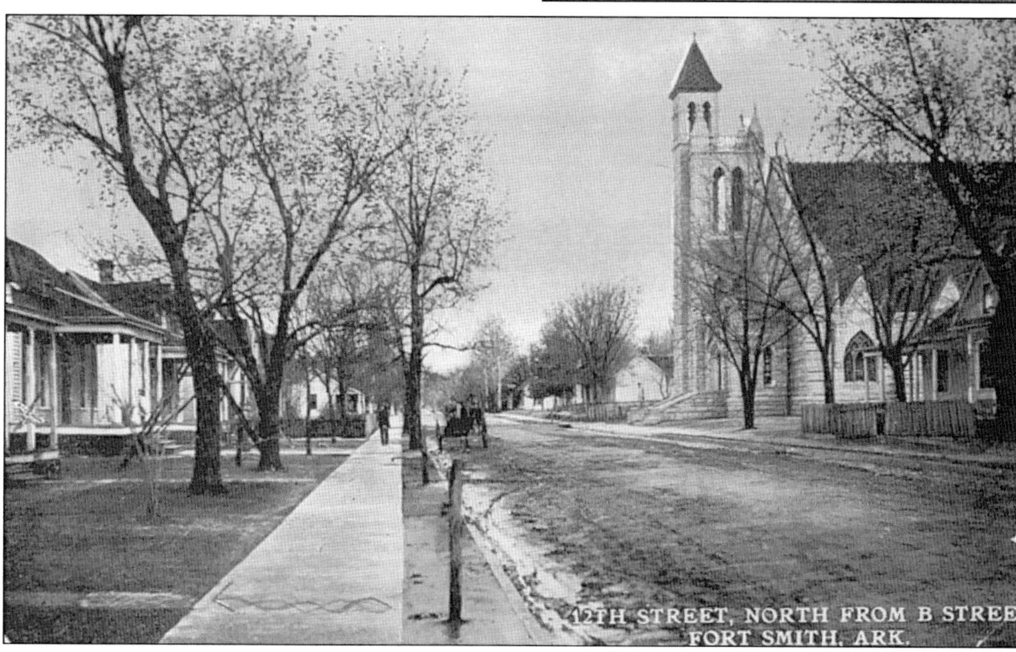

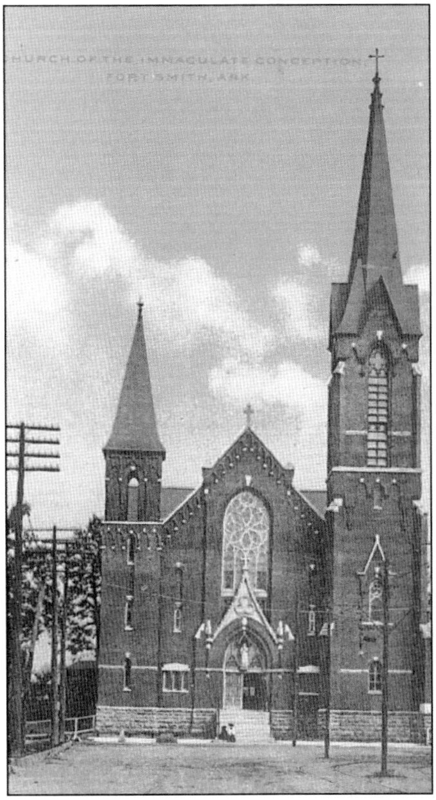

The Irish potato famine of 1845 reportedly caused the deaths of 500,000 people and the emigration of 6 million Irish people, most to the United States. Some of the Irish Catholic families who paid $5 each for crowded passage on what some called "coffin ships" would eventually find a home in Fort Smith. The first Immaculate Conception Church had formed in Fort Smith in 1849 to serve the handful of Catholics in the area. It would, however, be the arrival of ten Irish families in 1851 that gave the church its spark. During the 1880s, Bishop Edward Fitzgerald added to the Catholic numbers in Arkansas by helping a larger number of immigrants find their way to Arkansas and Fort Smith. The faith of these new residents, combined with the first wave from 1851, helped raise this impressive new Immaculate Conception Church in 1898 at the head of Garrison Avenue, giving the city perhaps its most striking landmark. The towering church, its tallest spire soaring to 110 feet, replaced a frame building damaged in an 1898 tornado. The church, one of three Catholic parishes in modern Fort Smith, still stands today. The interior (seen below) lost much of its ornate adornment during the Depression, in order to remove all signs of opulence. The Church celebrated its 150th birthday in May of 1999.

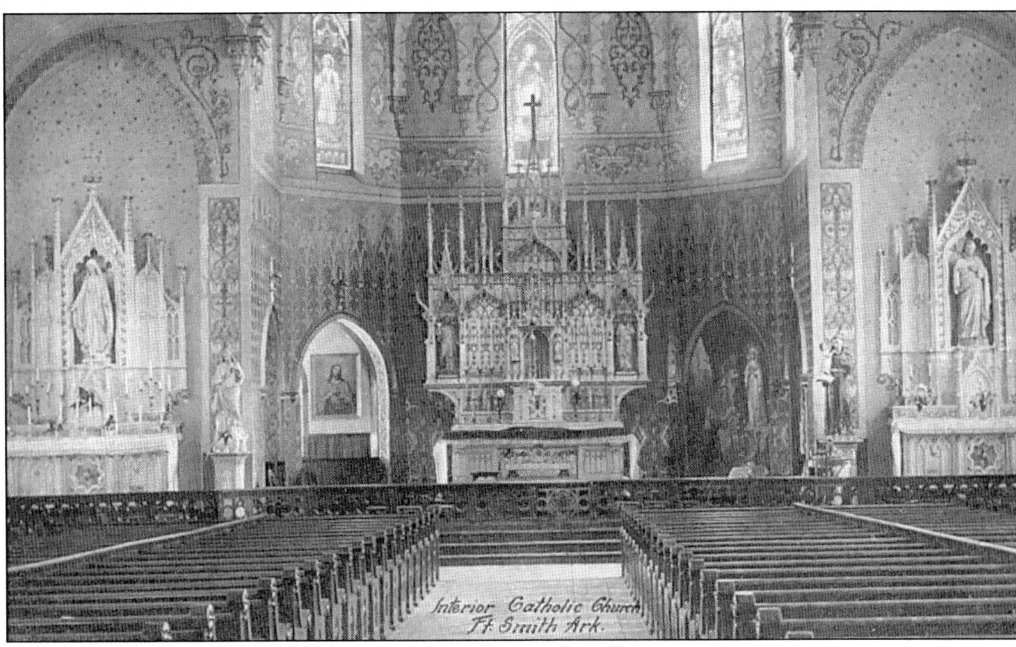

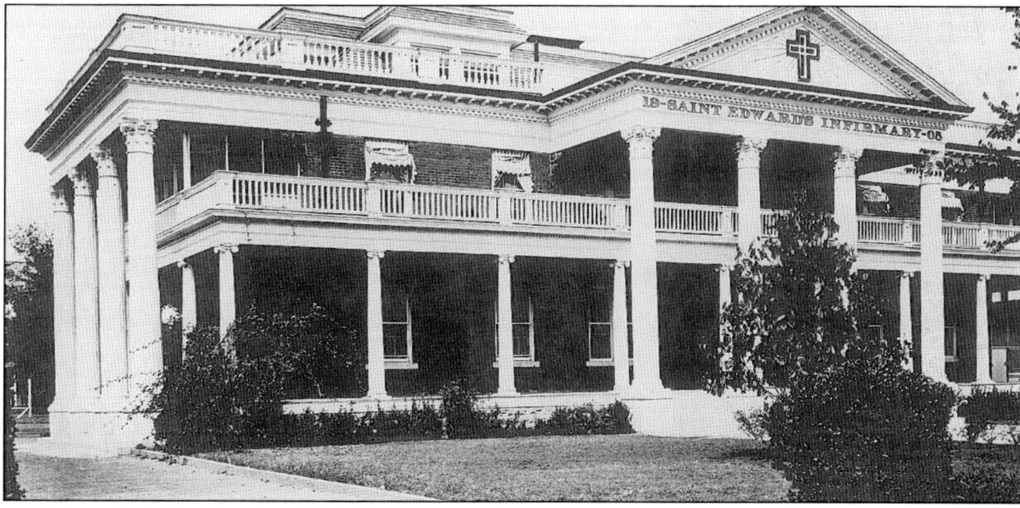

While the Catholic population of Arkansas has always been small, the church has given back to the state far in excess of what might be expected. Much of that contribution has come in the area of health care. The Sisters of Mercy tended the wounded during the Civil War in Fort Smith, and in 1869, they converted their convent, enlarging it to add columns and porches. The Fifteenth Street facility shown in this *c.* 1915 postcard became St. Edward's Infirmary in 1905, named to honor Edward Fitzgerald, Bishop of the Diocese of Little Rock. At the time, he was ill and partially paralyzed.

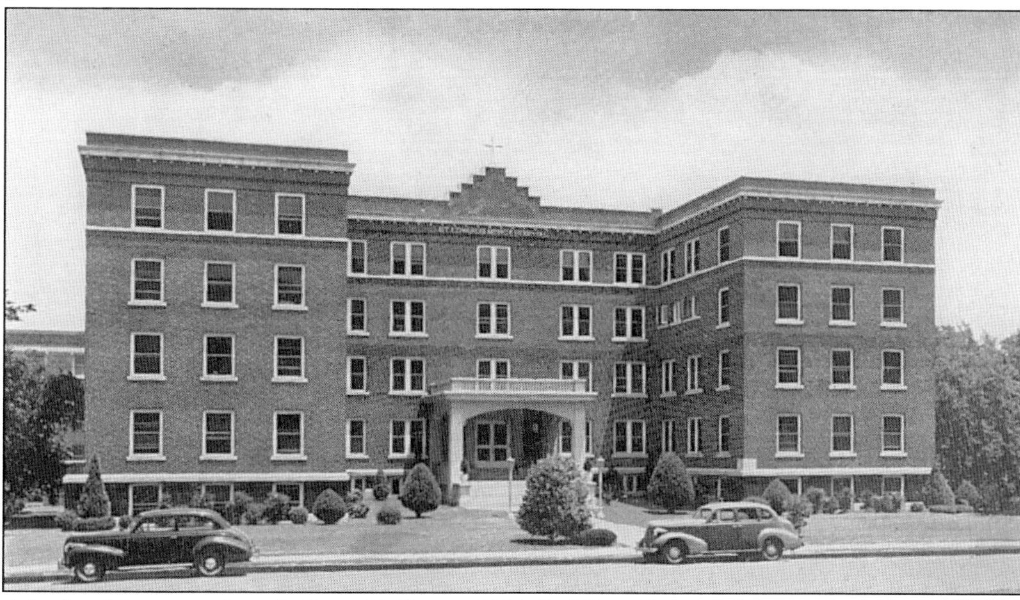

After breaking ground on St. Patrick's Day in 1921, St. Edward's moved in 1922 to its second home, just behind the Immaculate Conception Church. The move represented a continuing effort to expand the church's service, expressing the Christian mission through the delivery of health care for area residents. The building served until 1975, when the hospital moved to a new state-of-the-art medical center campus on Rogers Avenue. President Gerald Ford spoke at the ribbon-cutting ceremony, taking note of the work of the Sisters of Mercy in a state so far removed from the larger concentrations of American Catholicism found elsewhere in the nation. The hospital has since expanded its services to staff rural area hospitals and clinics.

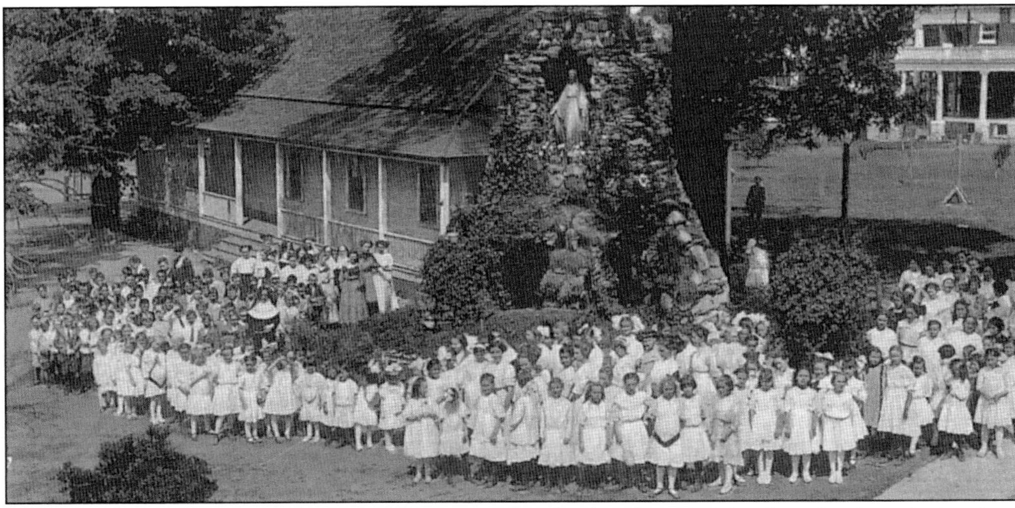

Fort Smith's Catholic migration gave rise to another landmark in 1906, when St. Anne's Academy was erected east of Immaculate Conception Church on Garrison Avenue. It operated as a girls' boarding and day school. Seen in this 1912 postcard is a large group of girls dressed in white on the day of their first communion. The large building to the right was razed in 1974, but the school, with more modern buildings, served for a number of years after that.

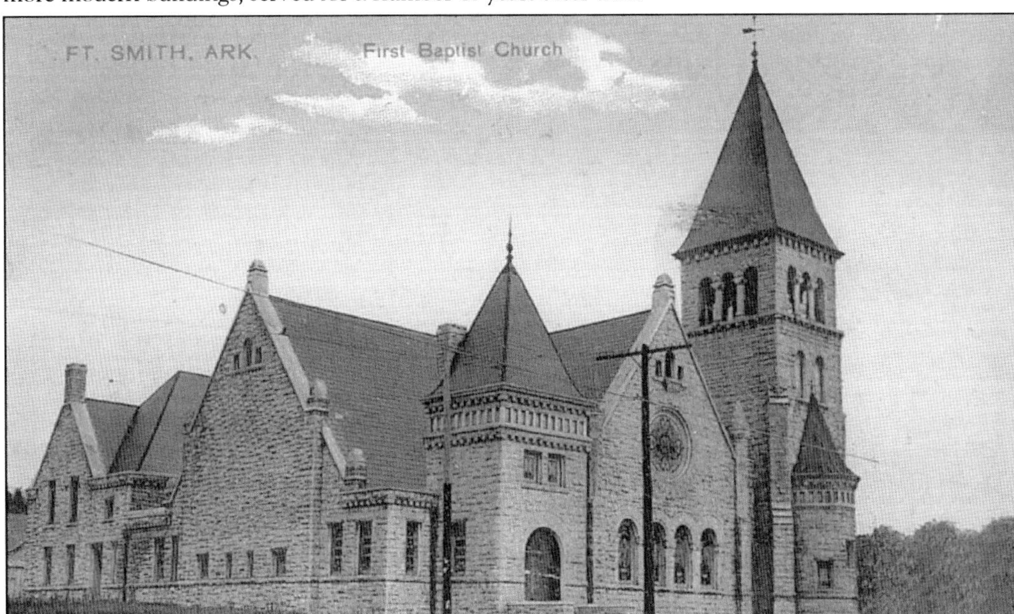

First Baptist Church of Fort Smith, organized in 1857, was initially in the home of William H. Byers, an elder who was elected the church's first pastor upon a promise that he would preach a monthly sermon. The church's first building was on North Fourth and B Streets, and it was sold for $50 to the city's "colored Baptists" after the Civil War. The next First Baptist Church, located on what is now Grand Avenue, was one of four churches and 100 homes to be lost in the tornado of 1898. The congregation quickly recovered and built the impressive, white limestone house of worship shown in this c. 1908 postcard in 1899, at Fourteenth Street and Grand Avenue. The church no longer stands, but the newest First Baptist Church stands adjacent to the site.

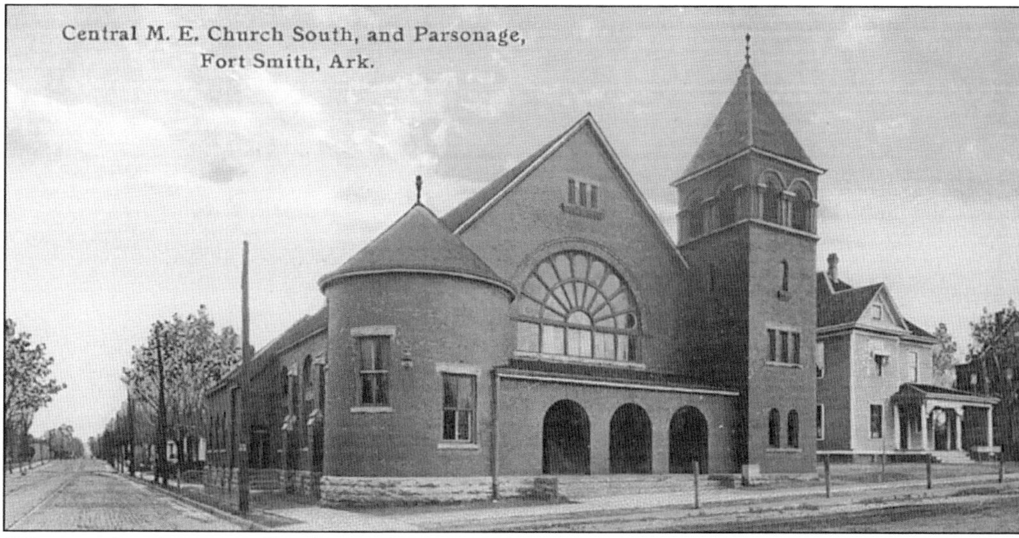

"This is a lovely city, will only stay here for a short time, am here at Southern Hotel," were the words written on a 1911 postcard of the Central Methodist Episcopal Church South and Parsonage, located at Thirteenth and B Streets. The church building, dating from the turn of the century, was bought by the Knights of Columbus, a Catholic men's organization, in 1919. It was later sold to become a restaurant called The Hall, operated by the proprietors of the Taliano restaurant, which was located in the former parsonage house to the right. A fire later destroyed the upper portion of the building, and the remaining part was repaired and painted white. It still stands today.

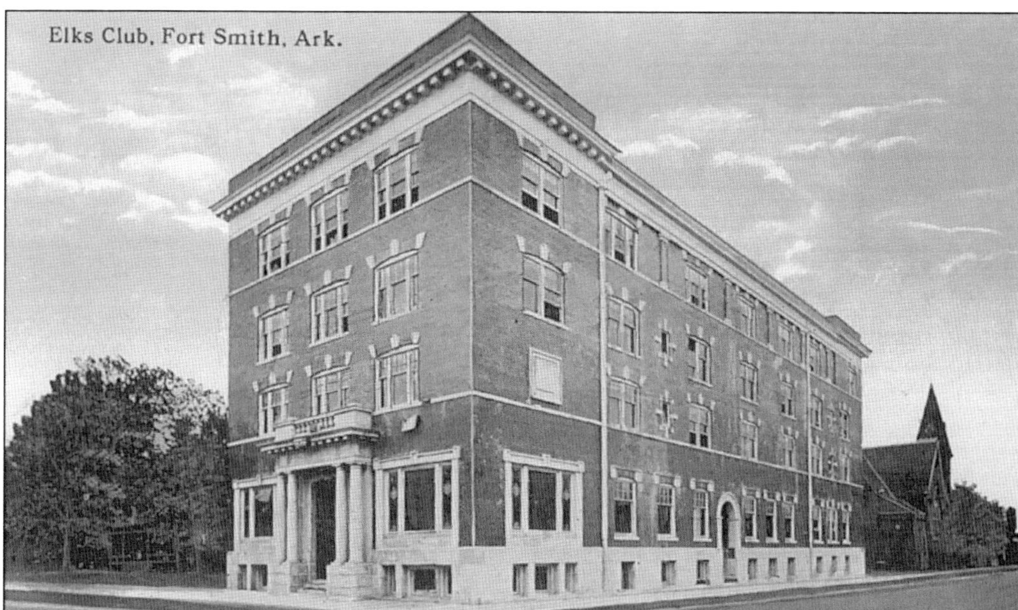

The Elks Club building, erected at 100 North Sixth Street, was built in 1908 under the design of noted local architect John Thompson Wilson Jennings. The Elks eventually vacated the building, and it went through a series of owners and uses, including being used as a hotel during the crowded years of World War II. Today, the building houses the affairs of the Harward Barry Real Estate Agency.

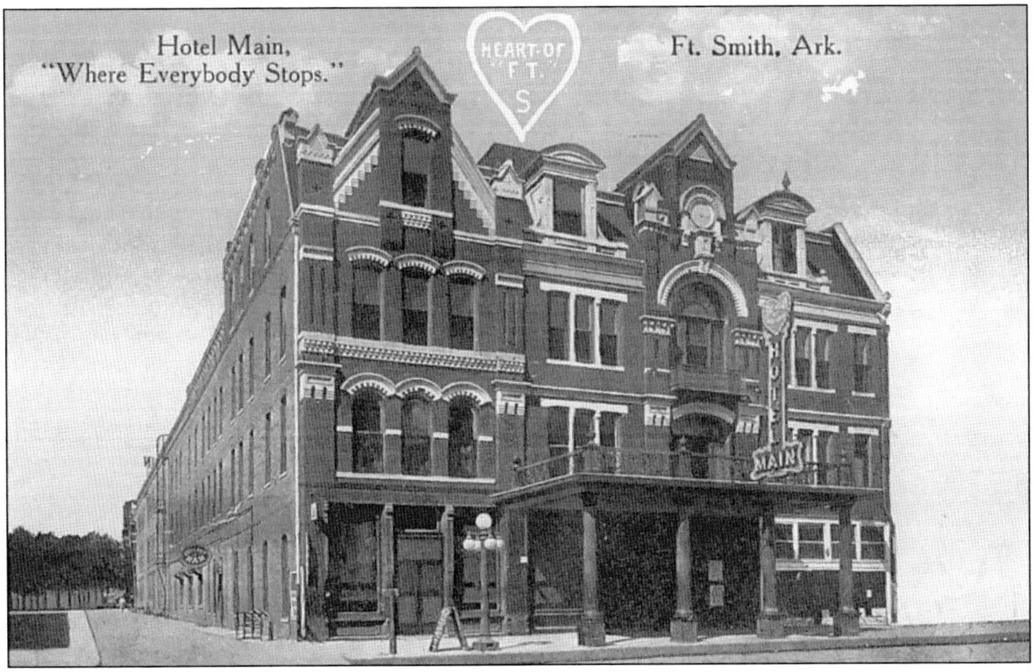

Fort Smith was still a rough frontier town in 1885 when the Hotel Main (named for its builder and Fort Smith's first civilian physician, Dr. J.H.T. Main) was erected at 608 Garrison Avenue. The following message was written on this postcard in 1915 by a hotel guest writing home to New York: "Came here from the station in an auto." The hotel advertised itself on the front of the postcard as the place "Where Everybody Stops" and the "Heart of Fort Smith," as it truly was, given its address. For a time after it opened, the hotel also housed the First National Bank, its neighbor seen adjacent in the postcard on page 21. In the *c.* 1910 postcard below, guests are seen relaxing in the lobby of the hotel, with the registration desk to the left. The hotel was torn down many years ago.

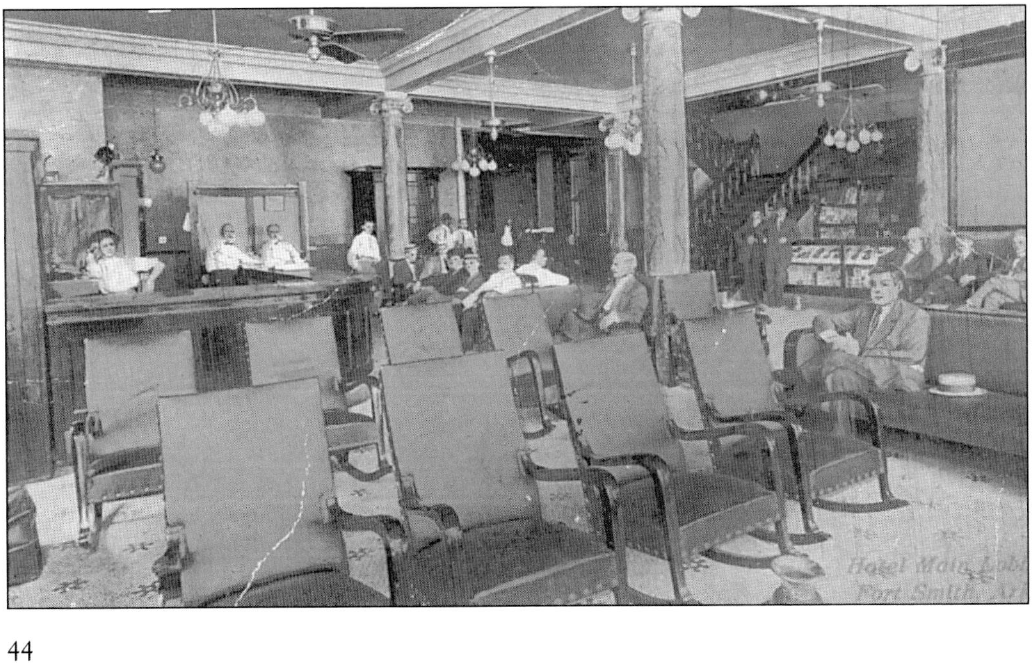

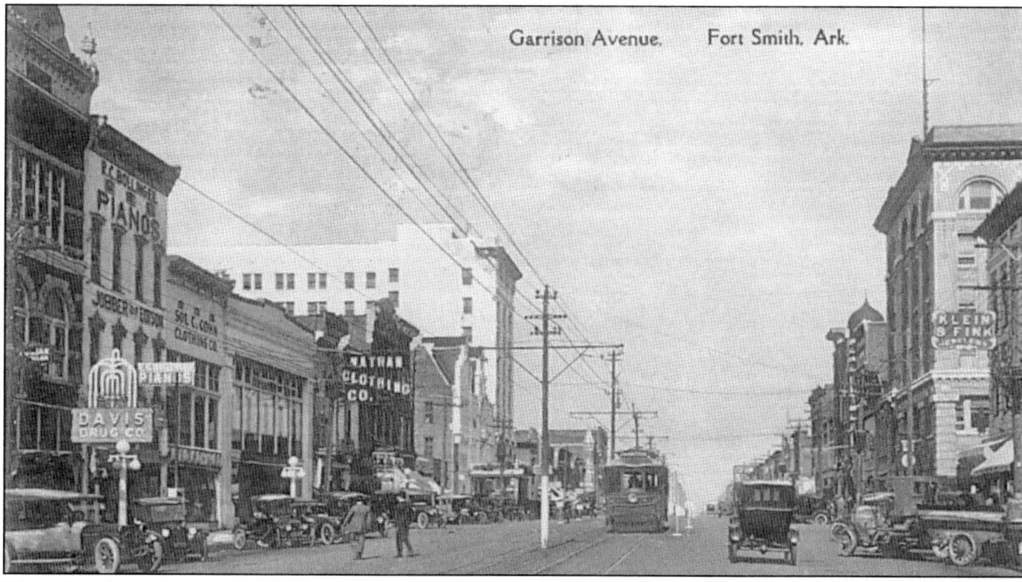

The Hotel Main's central location kept it among the lodging choices of the city for decades after its 1885 construction, even as larger and more imposing buildings were built around it. In the c. 1915 view above, the First National Bank towers just beyond the hotel. The postcard sent to Michigan bore the notation "reverse side shows one of the busy streets of the town, some live city for business, just returned from a long hike out in the country, picked cotton today." A stroll down the street from the hotel would have offered chances to shop at Davis Drug Co., R.C. Bollinger Pianos, Nathan Clothing, and Klein & Fink Jewelers, on a Garrison Avenue where automobiles were beginning to crowd the street cars. In the 1937 view below, the Hotel Main (seen to the left) still had its sign "Heart of Fort Smith" extended over the sidewalk, but the competition was closing in. Across and down the street, the Ward Hotel towered, taking business from both the Hotel Main and the Baltimore Hotel across the street to the right. Next to the Baltimore, at 617 Garrison Avenue, is the New England Cafeteria. There was a good choice of beers available nearby for Hotel Main guests, as seen to the left, including Turf Beer, which is advertised on a sign. Though the Hotel Main is gone today, damaged by fire and eventually razed by the neighboring bank, the Donoho-Merry building, with its arched entrance to the left, still stands today. It houses the Chamber of Commerce.

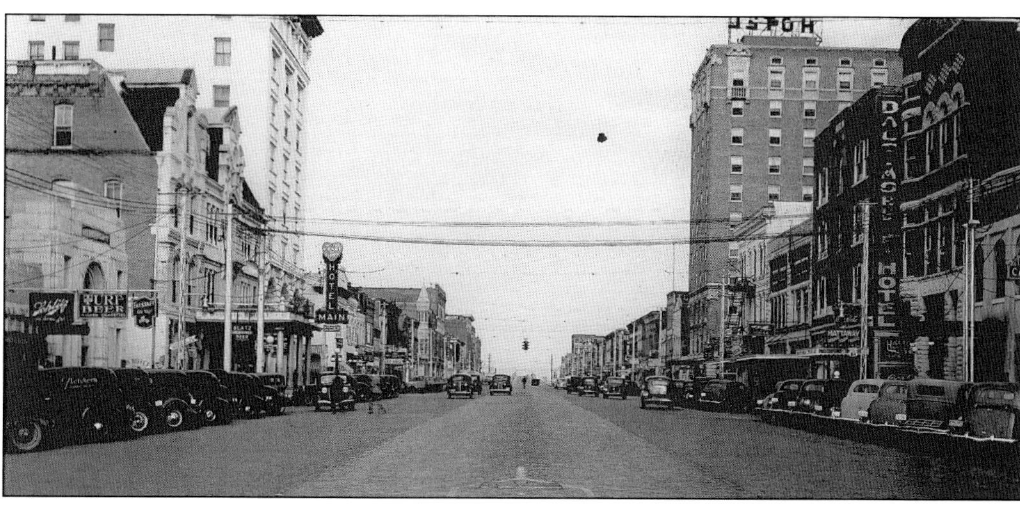

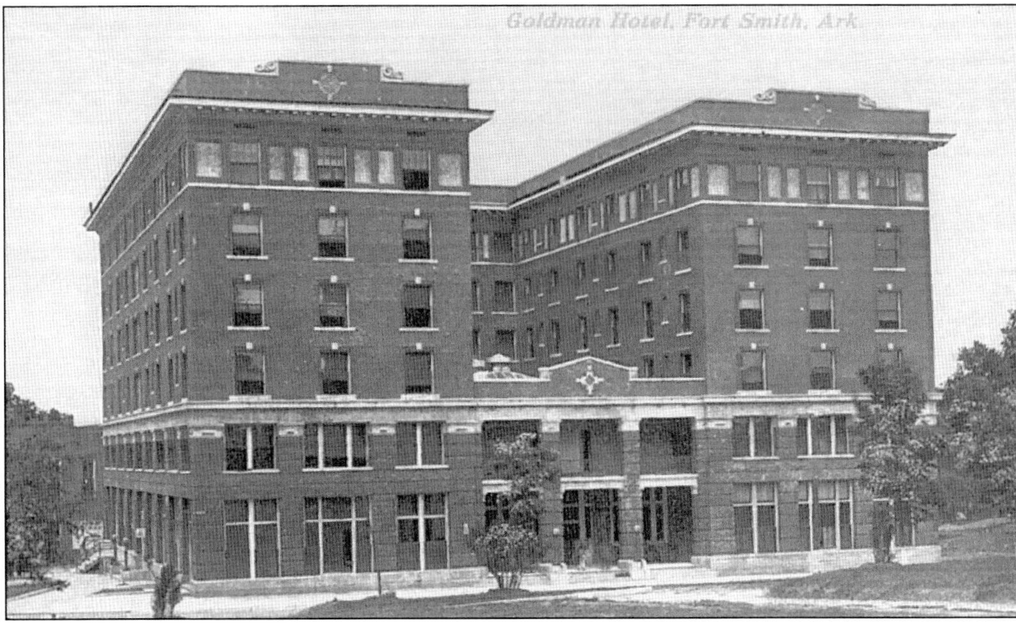

With the erection of the Goldman Hotel, the Hotel Main lost its place for good as Fort Smith's first choice in lodging. Construction began in 1908 on the six-story hotel located at the head of Garrison Avenue, fronting Thirteenth Street. Problems quickly arose for the Sebastian Hotel Company when their bank account ran dry after only two floors were finished. The Southwestern Hotel Company (which also acquired the famed Hotel Marion in Little Rock) formed a partnership with Lesser Goldman, a St. Louis Cotton Broker, and took over the new enterprise. The elegant hotel was completed in 1911, with Goldman's name on the building in exchange for his financing. The front of the hotel, facing Thirteenth Street, is seen just after completion around 1912. The postcard below shows the Garrison Avenue entrance to the hotel around 1920.

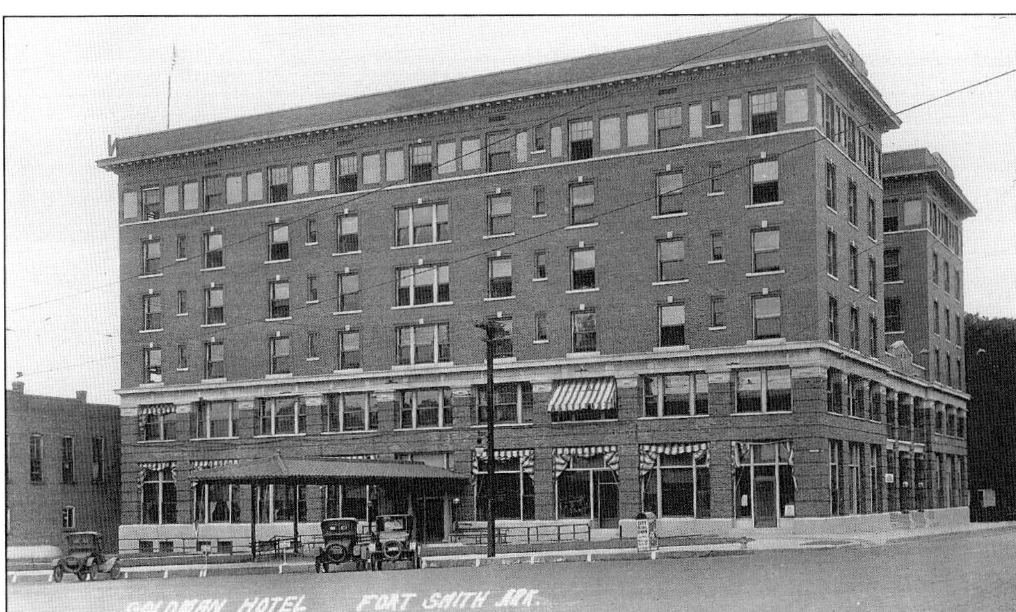

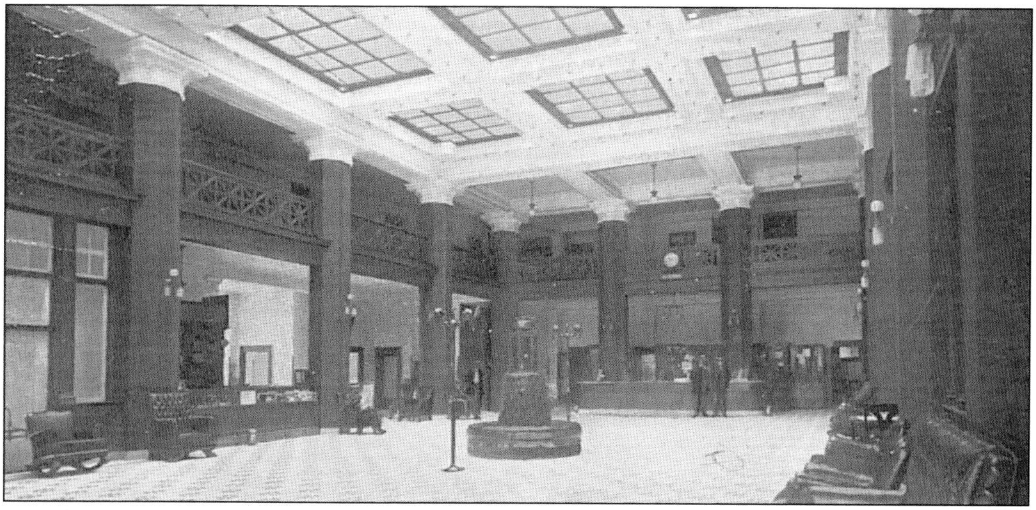

Seen here *c.* 1915, the Goldman Hotel remained the center of Fort Smith society for some four decades, as the wealthy and famous passed through this soaring lobby, with its skylights and fine furnishings. Guests over the years included President and Mrs. Harry Truman, Eleanor Roosevelt, and sports heroes like Mickey Mantle and Dizzy Dean. Patrons came to enjoy ballroom dancing and fine dinners served by tuxedo-clad waiters. The Goldman was truly the place to see and be seen in Fort Smith. Like so much in life, however, the Goldman's glory faded as other lodging opened to the motoring public. It was put on the market, and the adjacent Immaculate Conception Church acquired the property, demolishing the old hotel in 1997 to make way for a parking lot.

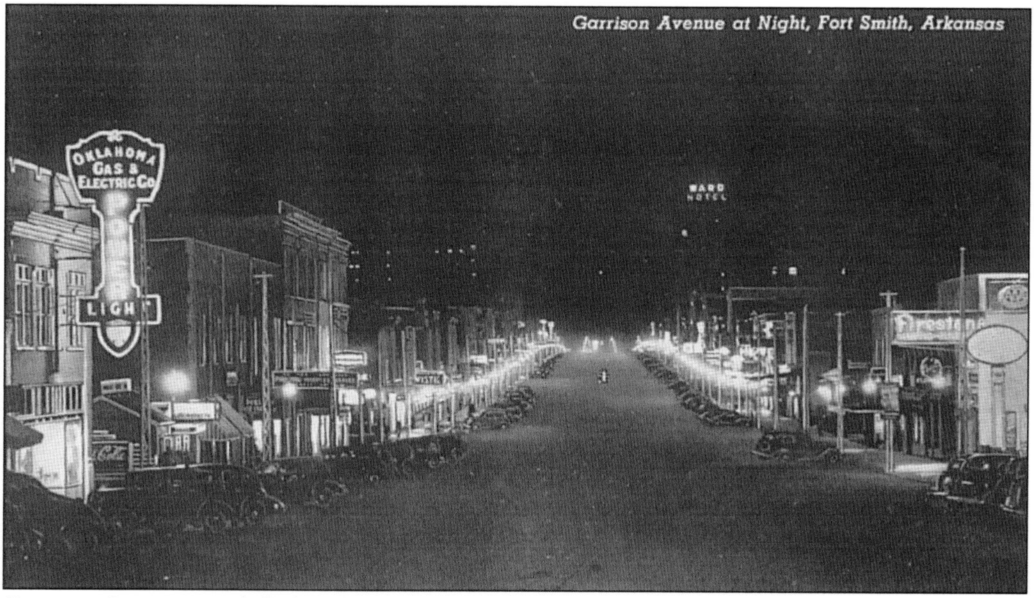

Garrison Avenue was billed as the "Great White Way," apparently because of the way the wide avenue was lit at night. This nighttime view, looking down Garrison Avenue, would have been seen by guests of the Goldman Hotel upon walking out of the canopied doorway seen in the view at the bottom of the preceding page. On the left in this view can be seen a large sign for Oklahoma Gas & Electric Company and the Firestone store to the right. In the distance, the sign for the Ward Hotel glows in the night sky.

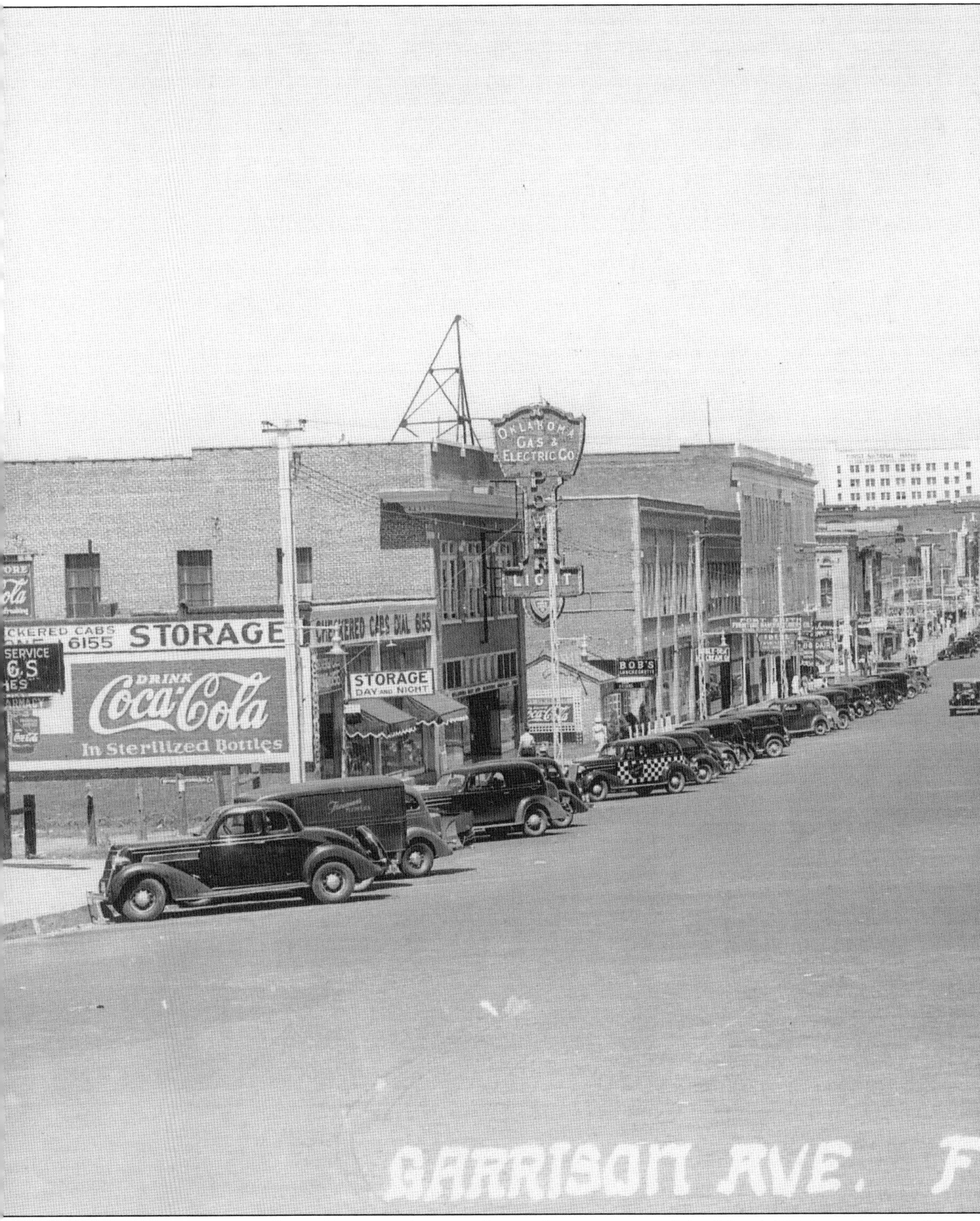

The expansive view down Garrison Avenue, from a few steps out of the Hotel Goldman just to the right, is readily apparent in this c. 1940 daytime view. A stroll downtown would have taken a visitor by many enterprises, including Happy's Auto Service next door to the hotel, Lee's Seed Store and

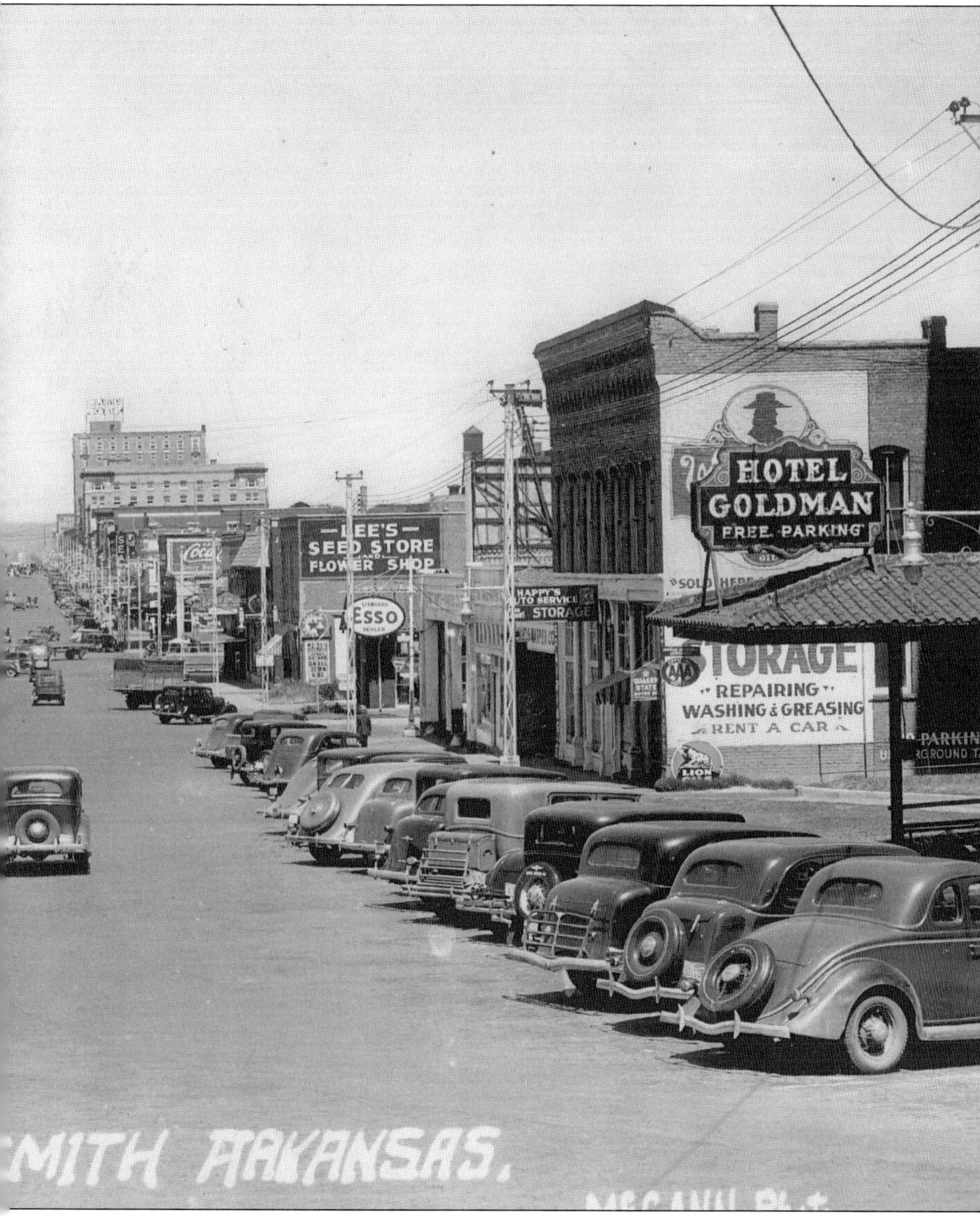

Flower Shop, and the Checkered Cab Company (left). Prominent are signs for Coca-Cola, painted on at least two buildings. The fifth car (parked on the right) has a small trunk affixed to its rear luggage rack.

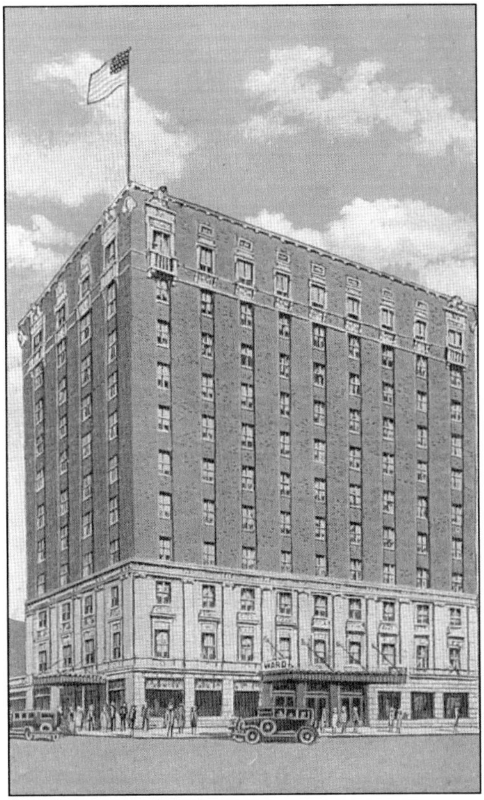

"Dear Dorothy, After much thinking and worrying I picked your name from the list of Texas—Well, here is my postcard. So please be a lady and write to me. I am a boy 14 years old, but don't let that change your mind, Your friend Bob." In 1937, young Bob DeLong had picked Dorothy Anders's name and Houston address from a list of people desiring to exchange postcards, and he sent this view of the Ward Hotel. The Ward was built in 1929, just before the Great Depression, on the Garrison Avenue site of what had been J.J. Little's clothing store. In the c. 1950 postcard below, the hotel advertised itself to be "Fort Smith's newest and finest," boasting 200 rooms with baths, circulating ice water, ceiling fans, an air-conditioned coffee shop, and free parking. The building still stands but is largely vacant, as the hotel closed a number of years ago when the motoring public shifted its loyalties to the newer facilities on the outskirts of the city.

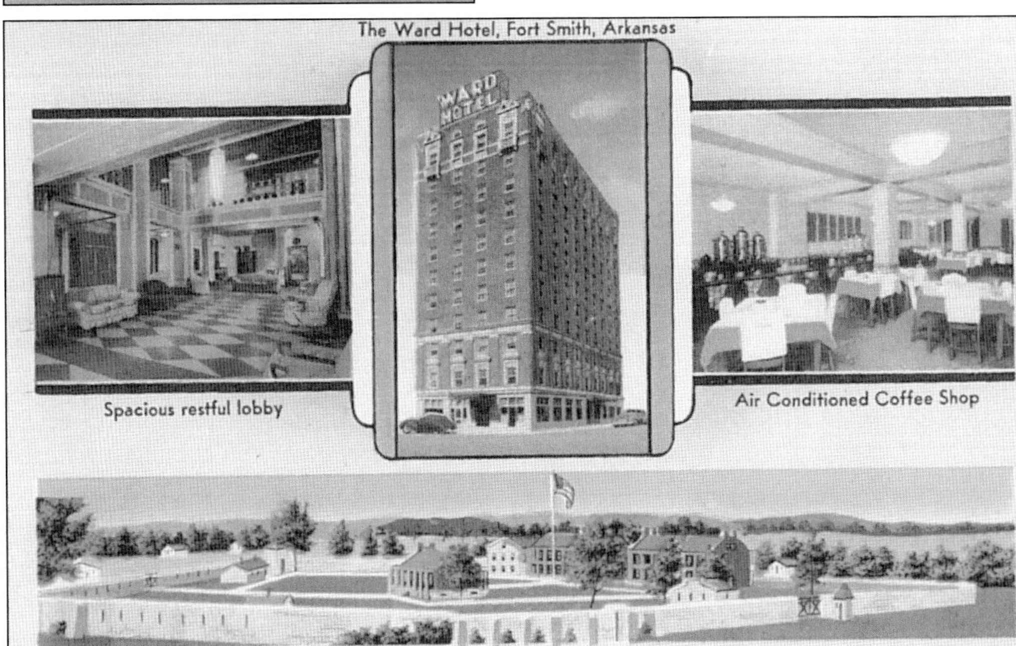

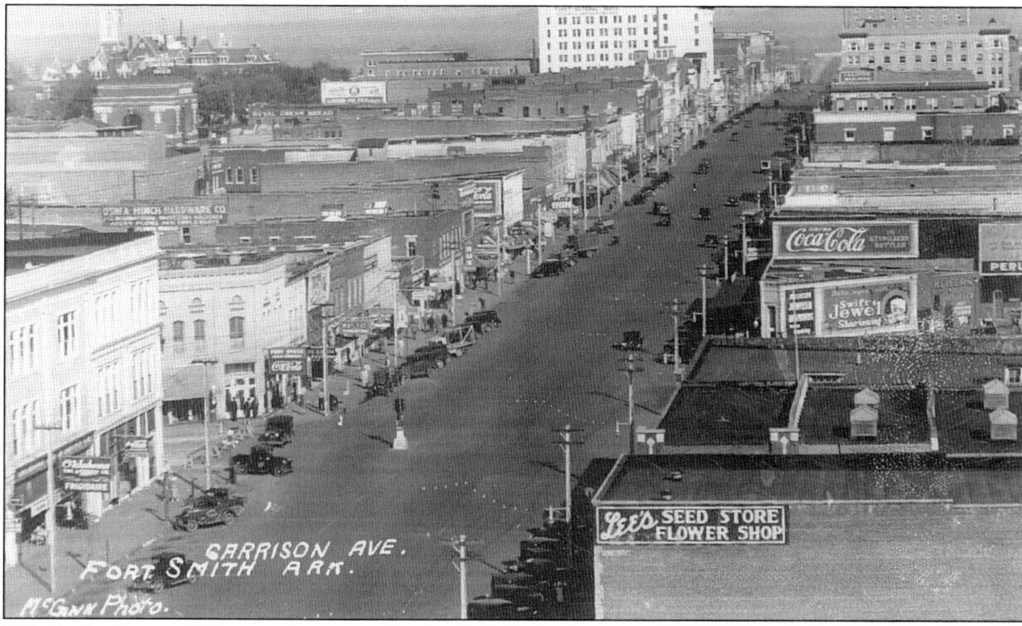

While looking up Garrison Avenue at the new Ward Hotel, now competing for guests, a photographer in 1930 stood atop the Goldman Hotel. In the far left corner of the photograph is the Sebastian County Courthouse tower with the Kansas City Southern Railroad station just below. Below, on the postcard of the same street, the sender wrote, "Aug 4, 1927, This is where we stopped—The Goldman." The hotel guest was referring to the hotel seen in the distance, to the left of Immaculate Church; the view also shows two ladies preparing to board a streetcar to the left. The sign on the building, just above the corner of the car, still advertises wagons and harnesses at a time in Fort Smith's history when even the streetcars were being forced out by the growing number of automobiles plying the wide thoroughfare.

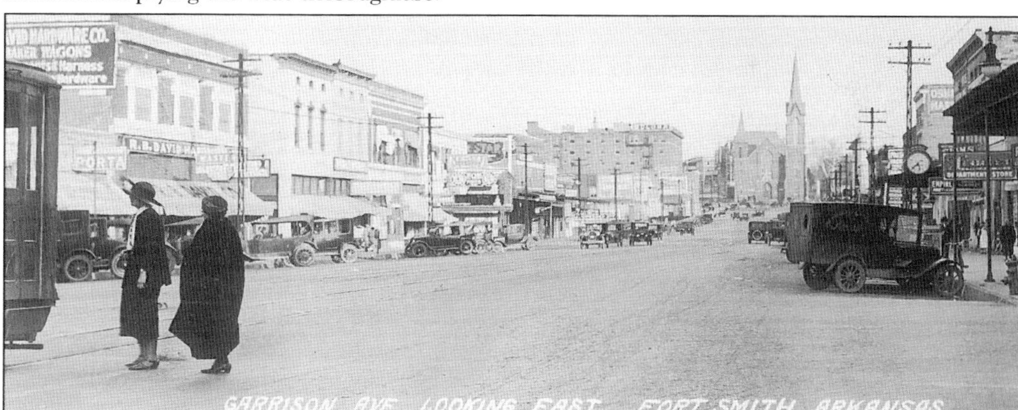

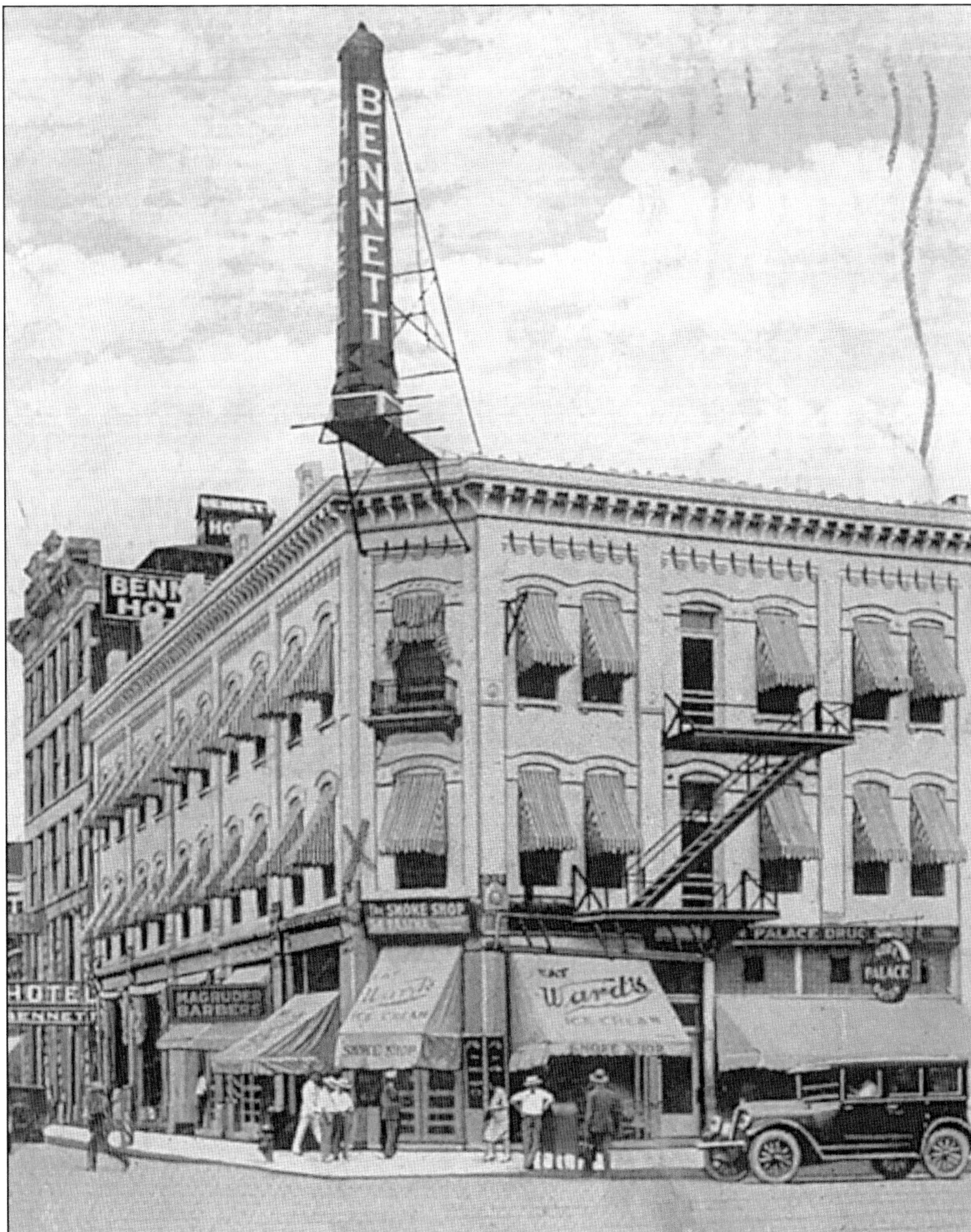

The Bennett Hotel was opened by Henry Bennett in the late 1920s at 10 North Sixth Street; it was promoted to potential guests as being "in the center of the wholesale and retail district, New & Modern [sic] in every way, running water and phone in every room, steam heated, private and connecting baths." Businesses housed on the ground floor of the hotel, seen in this 1930 view, included the Magruder Barbershop, The Smoke Shop, and Palace Drug, which operated from 1894 to 1955. Ward's Ice Cream had its own prominent awning and apparently was sold by the Smoke Shop. The ice cream was made in Fort Smith until the plant was lost in a fire. Today, the site of the hotel is a restaurant parking lot.

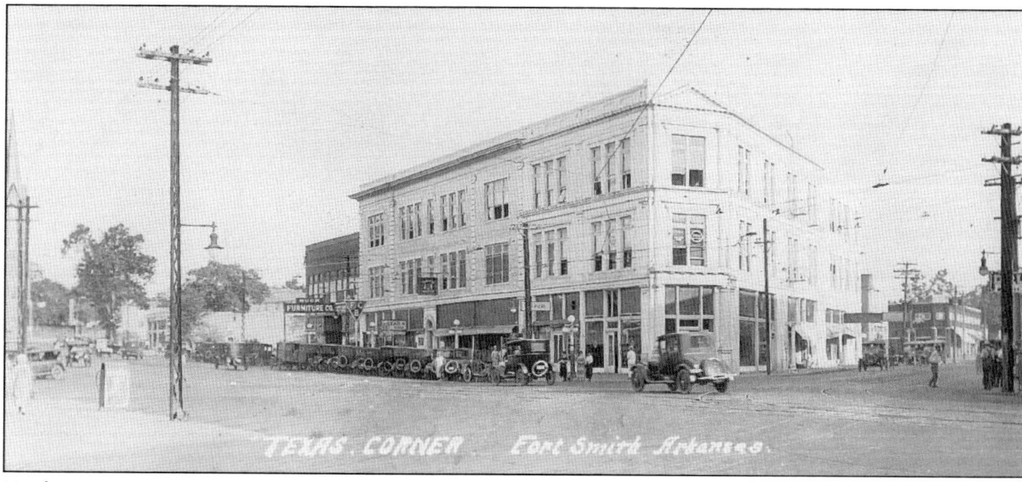

"Left St. Louis Tues., leaving here tonight, will have to work nights & Sundays for a few weeks on Interstate Commerce case. I saw the World's Series ball game Tuesday, but I don't get the thrill I used to get," were the words on a 1927 view of Fort Smith's historic "Texas Corner." The building seen here was erected at the southeast corner of Garrison & Towson around 1910 and housed a number of businesses, including Buck Furniture at the far left, Star Grocery, the Woodmen of the World Hall, and Fentress Undertaking Company. The "Texas Corner" designation came from the fact that Towson Road was once called the Texas Road, and clusters of wagons formed here for the trek toward Texas.

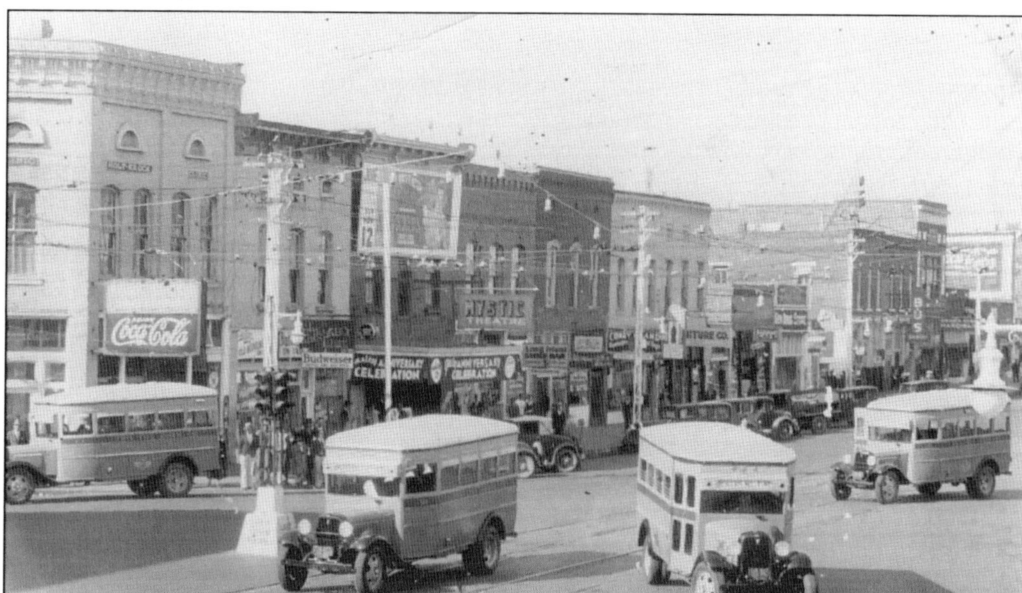

This postcard marks an important, historic turning point in Ft. Smith. On November 16, 1933, the streetcars, which ran no more, were replaced by this fleet of new buses displayed on Garrison Avenue, near the Mystic Theater. The Coca-Cola sign (just above the bus on the far left) is on a corner building housing the Holt Krock Clinic, which would grow to be the largest physician organization in western Arkansas. In the pavement of Garrison Avenue can be seen the maze of streetcar tracks still readily visible beneath the tires of the buses, arrayed like a parade of conquering invaders who had just vanquished foes of a now-bygone era.

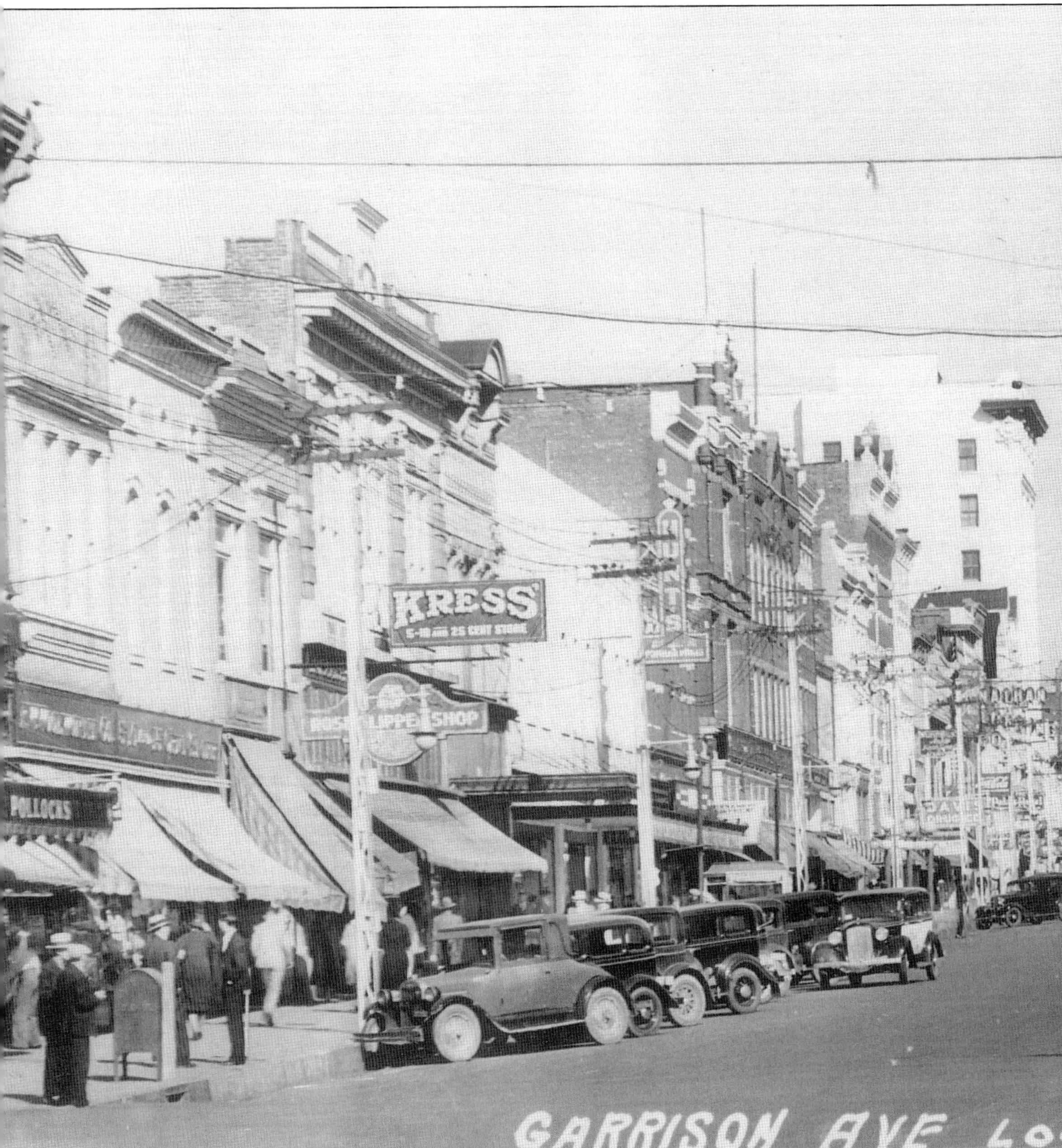

On Garrison Avenue, looking west from Ninth Street toward Oklahoma, the town was humming with activity around 1935, when the photographer shot this view from the middle of the wide street. On the left is the Kress store, an American main street institution for decades, along with Rose's Slipper Shop, Hunt's Clothing, Davis Drugs, and the First National Bank rising farther up the street. On the right side of Garrison Avenue can be seen the Ward Hotel (the tallest building), Merchant's National Bank, the Illinois Building, and Draughon's Business College (center). The

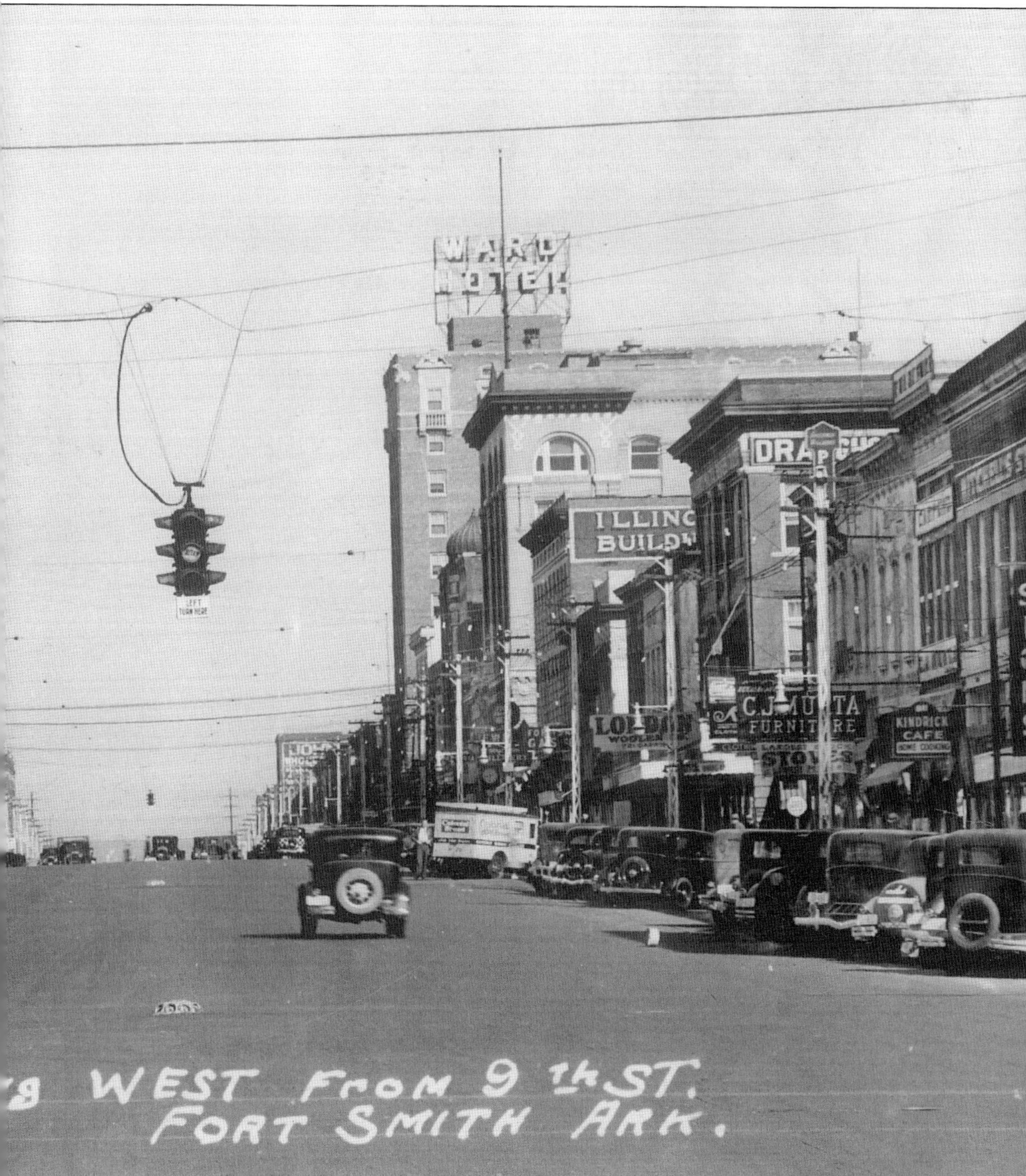

London Woolen store, Kindrick's Cafe (advertising "home cooking"), and C.J. Mutta's furniture store are also visible. By this time, the streetcar tracks had been paved over or removed, for the economy was dependent on the automobile-borne shoppers who would, in the years to come, desert downtown merchants for outlying shopping centers. While today much of the Garrison Avenue historical district survives, it is with a totally different group of tenants than those seen here.

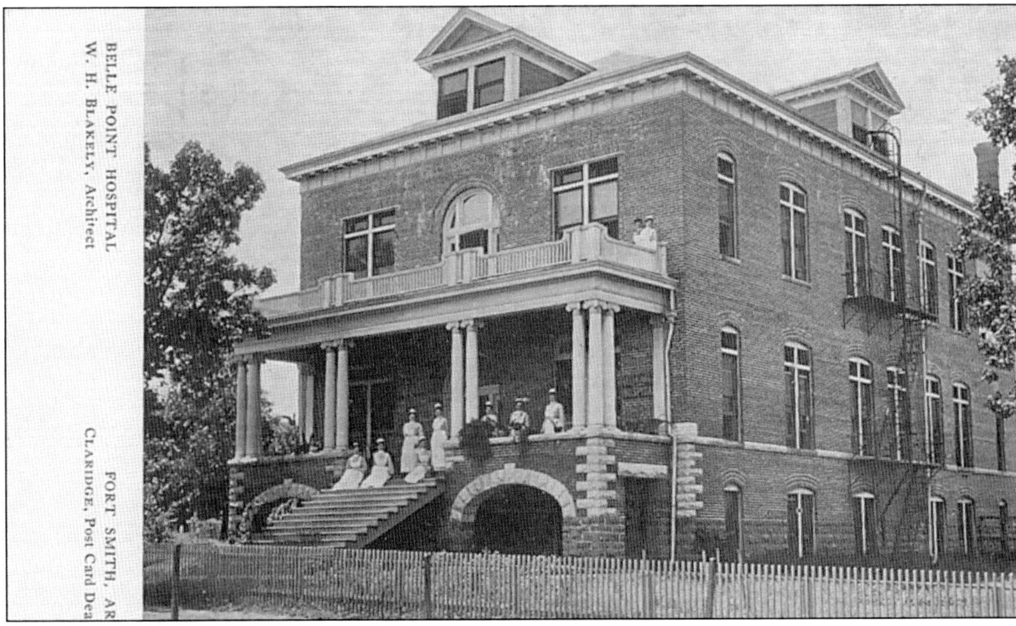

Belle Point, the area southeast of downtown Fort Smith, was home to Belle Point Hospital, a charity institution formed in 1887 as St. John's Hospital. The name was changed to Belle Point Hospital in 1899 with the merger of St. John's and the City Charity Hospital. The hospital contributed to the growth of the city; it graduated its first class of nurses in 1899, several of whom are posed on the porch in this c. 1910 postcard. By the time of the c. 1915 postcard below, the hospital at 916 South Twelfth Street had been enlarged and the name had been changed to Sparks Hospital, to honor the wife of wealthy businessman George Sparks, who bequeathed $25,000 to the institution. By 1910, Fort Smith had two hospitals but an inadequate number of beds; many surgeries were performed in the homes of patients, a less than ideal situation. That year, the posted charges at Sparks were between $2 and $4 per day for a room, $5 to $10 if use of the operating room was required, and $2 for transport in the hospital's ambulance.

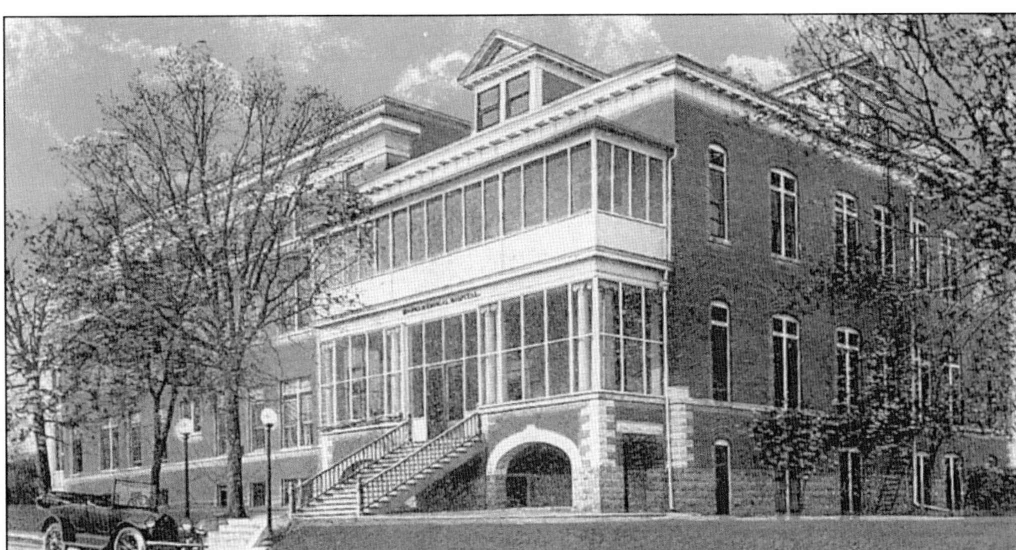

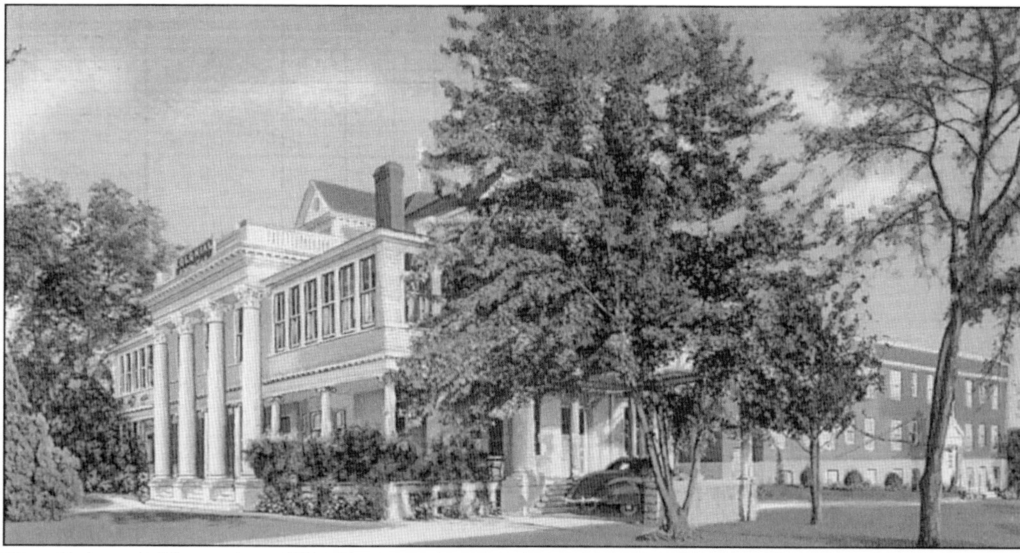

The Colonial Hospital at 1500 Dodson Avenue began as a small, private hospital staffed by two physicians, Doctors Keck and Rose, who made a specialty out of treating area coal miners. When the hospital closed in 1953, the building became the new home of the Holt-Krock Clinic. Dr. Charles Holt came to Fort Smith in 1908 and established the Holt Clinic in 1921. He created quite a stir when he, along with a few other local physicians, entered into pre-paid contracts to serve coal miners and employees of some other industries—a trend in managed care ahead of its time. Dr. Holt was joined by Dr. Fred Krock in 1928, and the clinic grew to be the largest in western Arkansas. Today, it operates out of multiple modern locations; the old Colonial Hospital building was razed years ago.

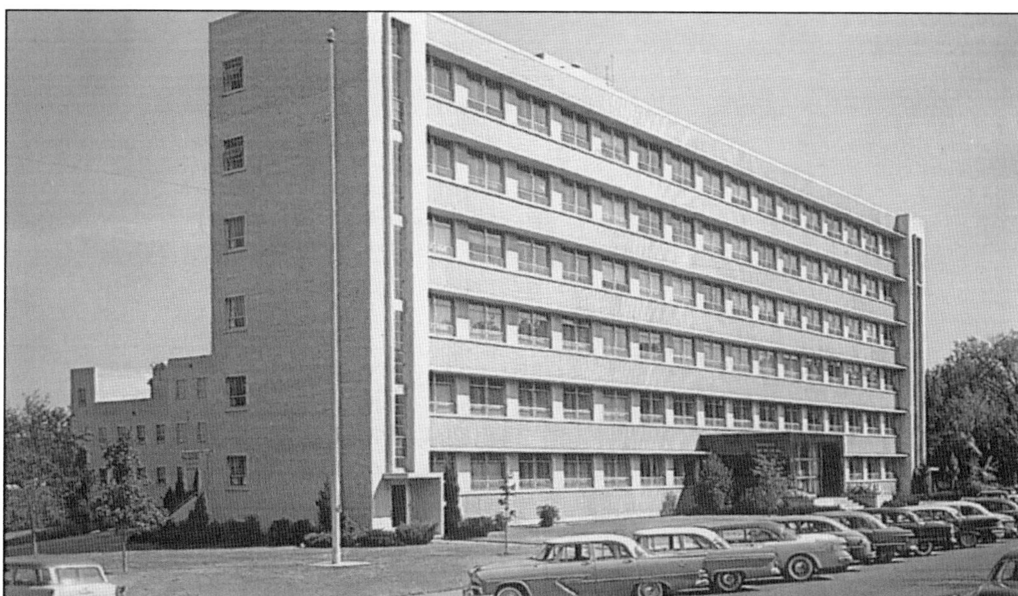

Sparks Memorial Hospital continued to grow through the years, as did its competitor, St. Edward's Mercy Medical Center. Seen in this *c.* 1955 postcard, Sparks boasted the newest hospital facility in Fort Smith at that time, having erected this building in 1953. Today, continued growth has expanded the hospital's operations over several city blocks.

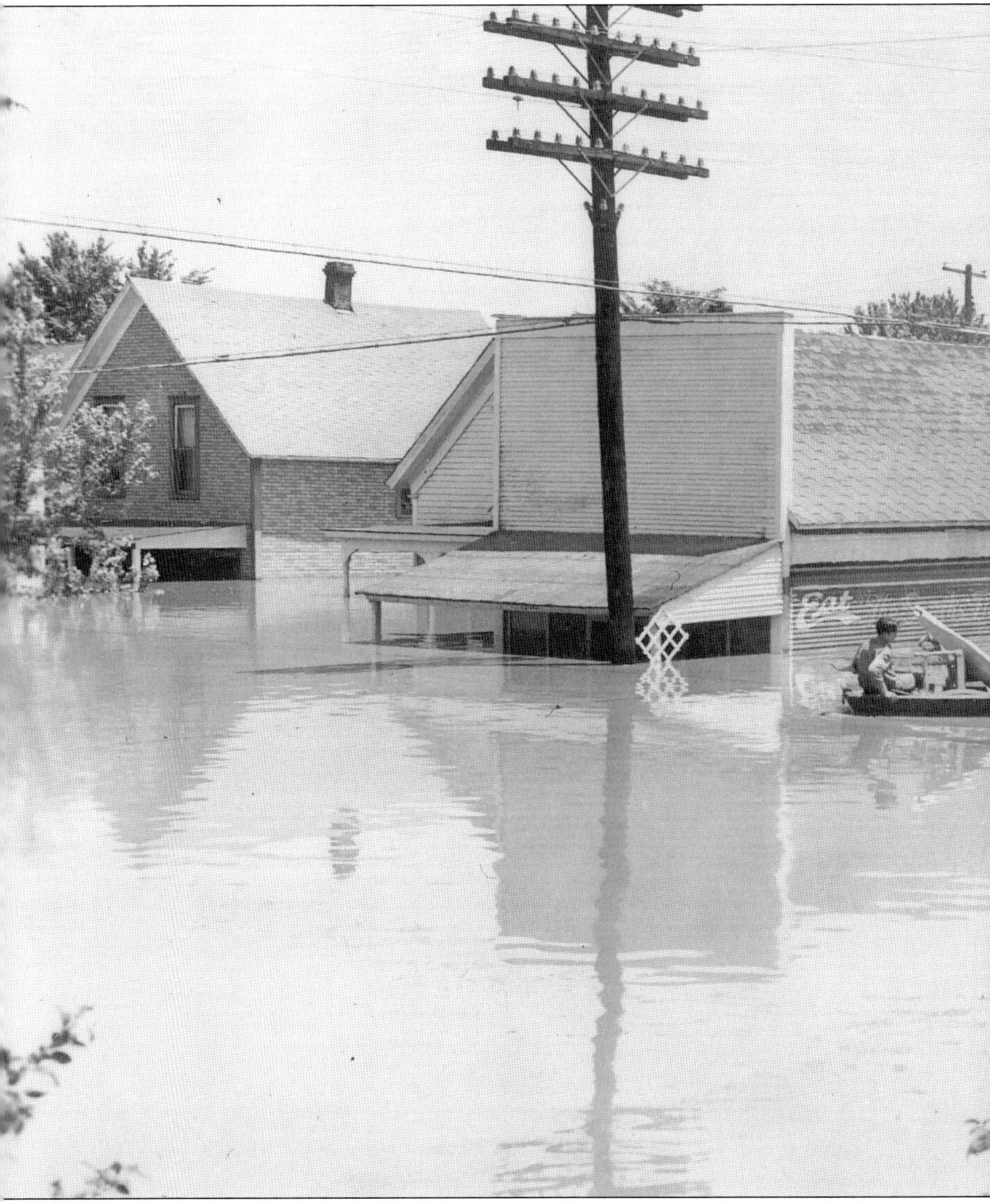

Fort Smith's location on the banks of the Arkansas River was not without its perils, despite the economic returns of river commerce. Floods were a fact of life, and one of the worst in the city's history came in May of 1943, when more than 10 inches of rain raised the river level from 8 feet to

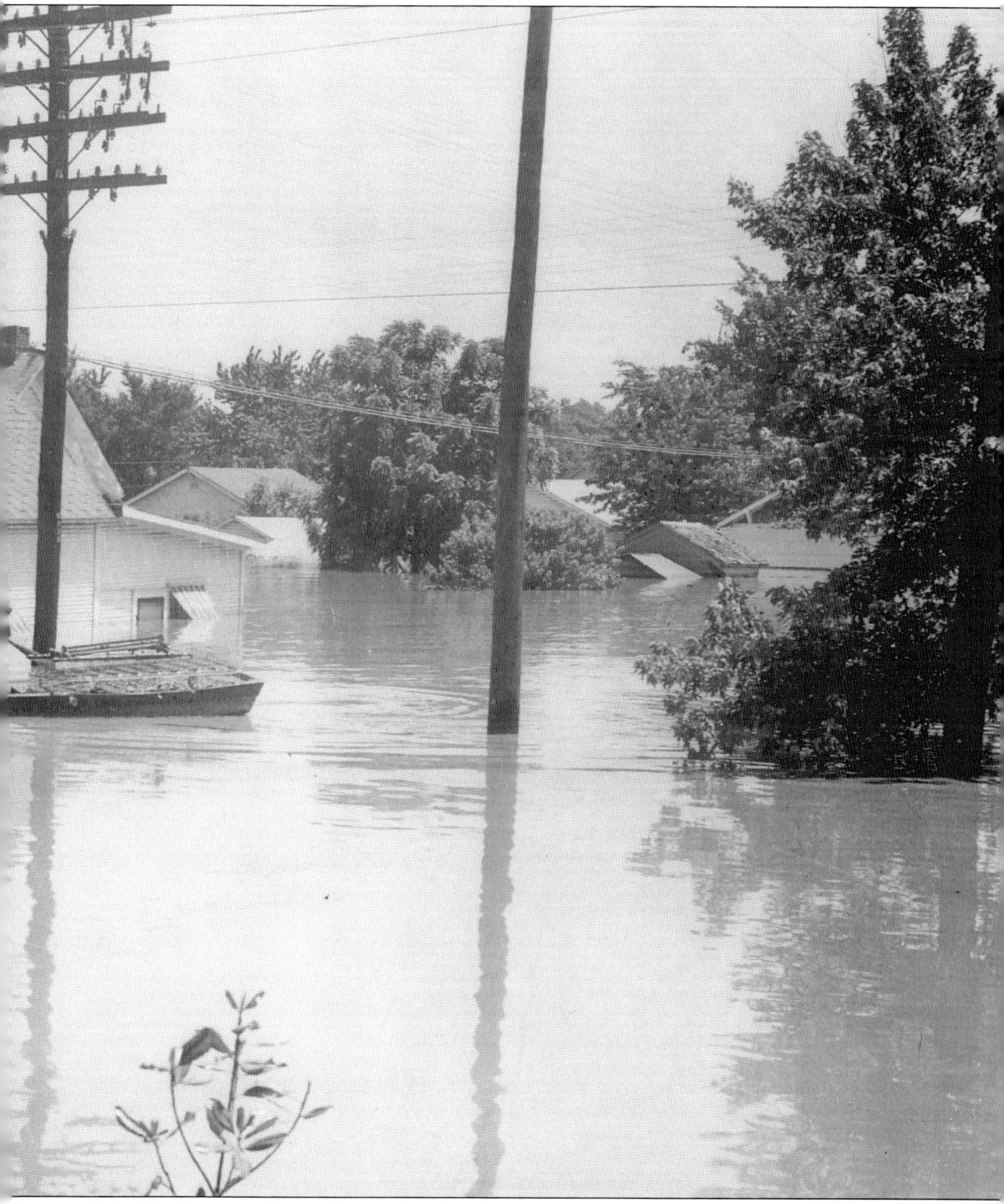

more than 41 feet within a 3-day period. Much of the north end of the city was inundated, including the small, neighborhood grocery store to the left. In the boat are two soldiers from nearby Fort Chaffee who are evacuating a woman and some of her belongings, including a set of bed springs.

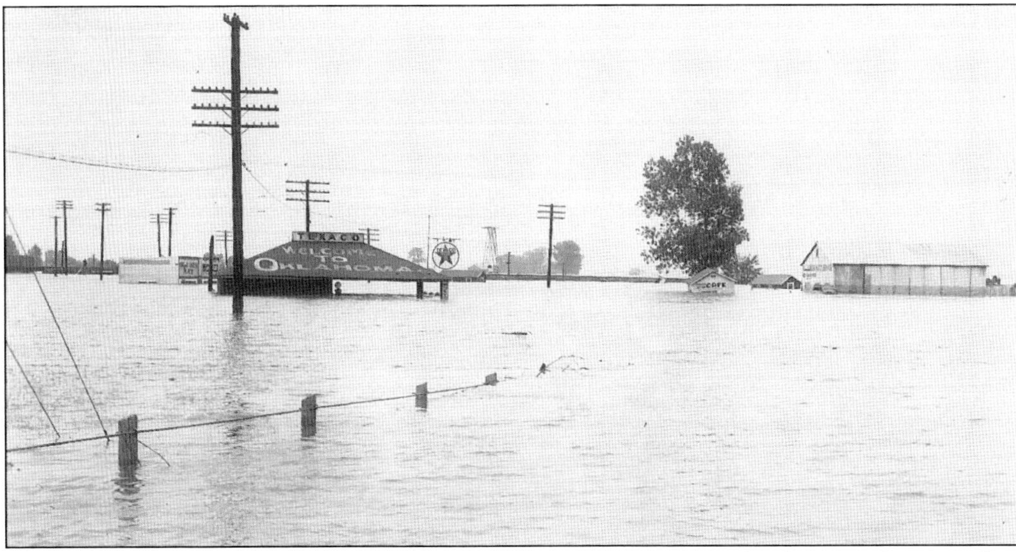

Fort Smith was almost entirely cut off by the surging Arkansas River floodwaters of 1943, a flood that spanned two states' boundaries. In the above postcard is a state-line pavilion for tourists, with a roof sign that reads "Welcome to Oklahoma," which would have normally greeted motorists crossing the bridge from Fort Smith. During the 1943 flood, the 41-foot crest of the Arkansas River almost totally isolated Fort Smith, closing all roads except those to the south of the city. On May 16th, the situation went from bad to worse when the Fort Smith end of the bridge connecting the city with Van Buren was washed out, as seen below. The U.S. Army came to the rescue as troops in training for WW II at nearby Camp Chaffee soon put their training to a real application by quickly erecting a pontoon bridge across the Arkansas River. The bridge carried a water line, foot traffic, and some emergency vehicles. Soon even the pontoon bridge was washed away, and with the loss of the water line a new crisis arose: a critical shortage of drinking water. Most water meters were shut off, and the city only allowed one house per block to run tap water, to be shared with neighbors.

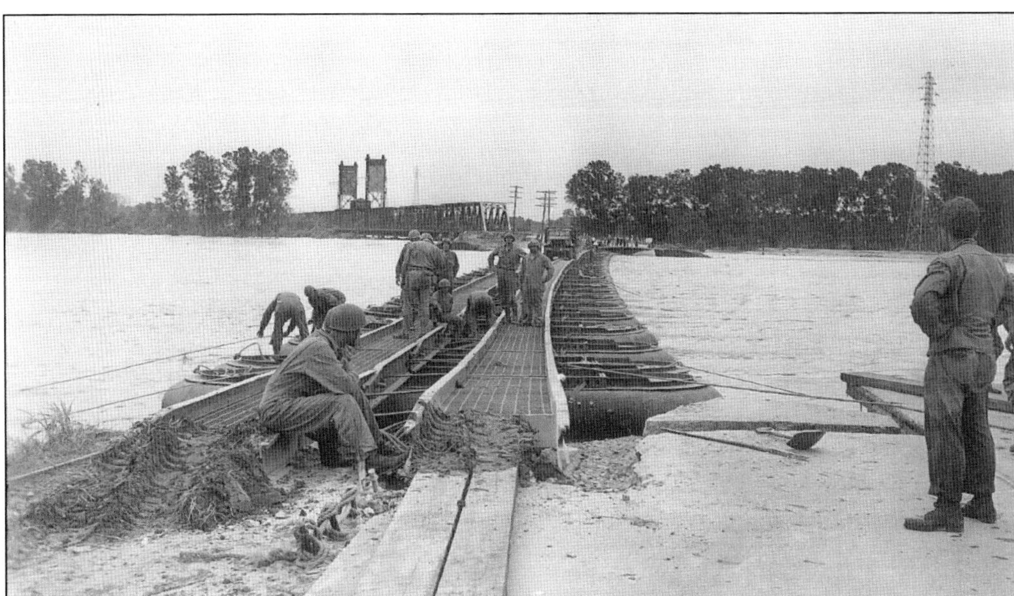

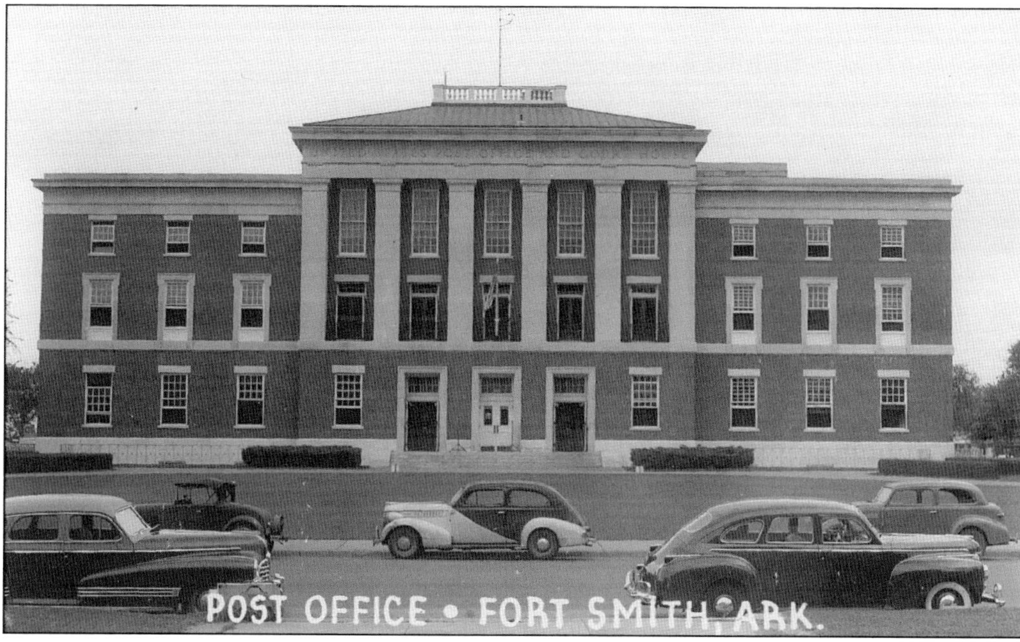

In 1937, Fort Smith acquired two handsome public buildings that will serve well into the 21st century. The post office above, seen around 1940, is now called the Isaac Parker Federal Building. Its companion structure, seen in the 1950 postcard below, has the distinction of being the only county courthouse in Arkansas constructed to serve dual purposes, both as the courthouse for the northern portion of Sebastian County and also as the Fort Smith City Hall. The WPA Moderne-style limestone building has 254 rooms and an assortment of interesting monuments on the grounds, including a statue of a Confederate soldier that was originally slated to stand in the National Cemetery a few blocks away. The U.S. Secretary of War refused to allow it at the federal cemetery unless the words "Lest we forget" were removed, a request the Confederate veterans and their supporters refused—hence the alternative home on the courthouse lawn.

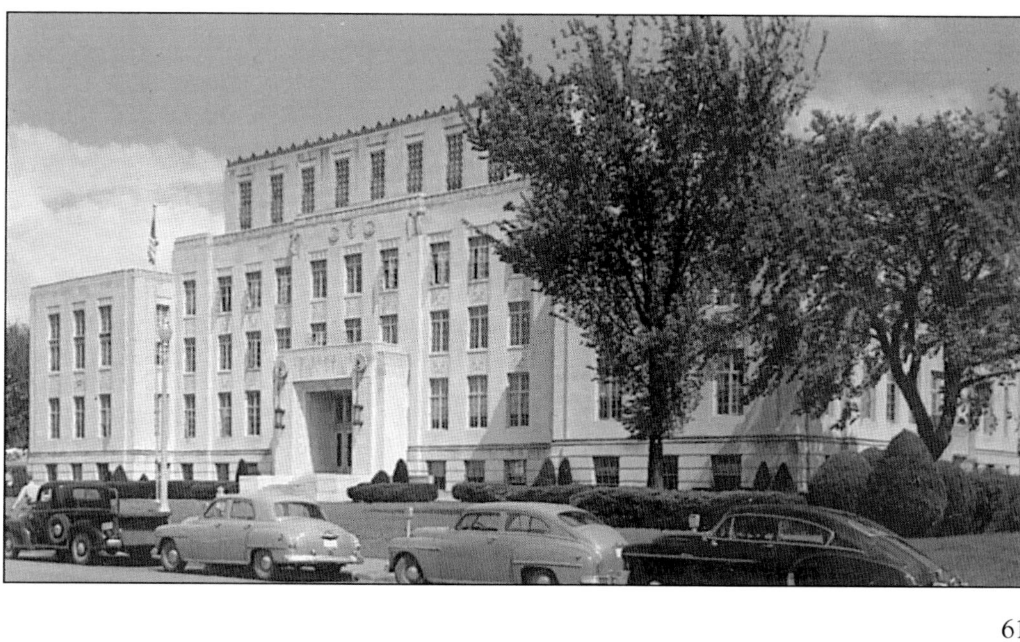

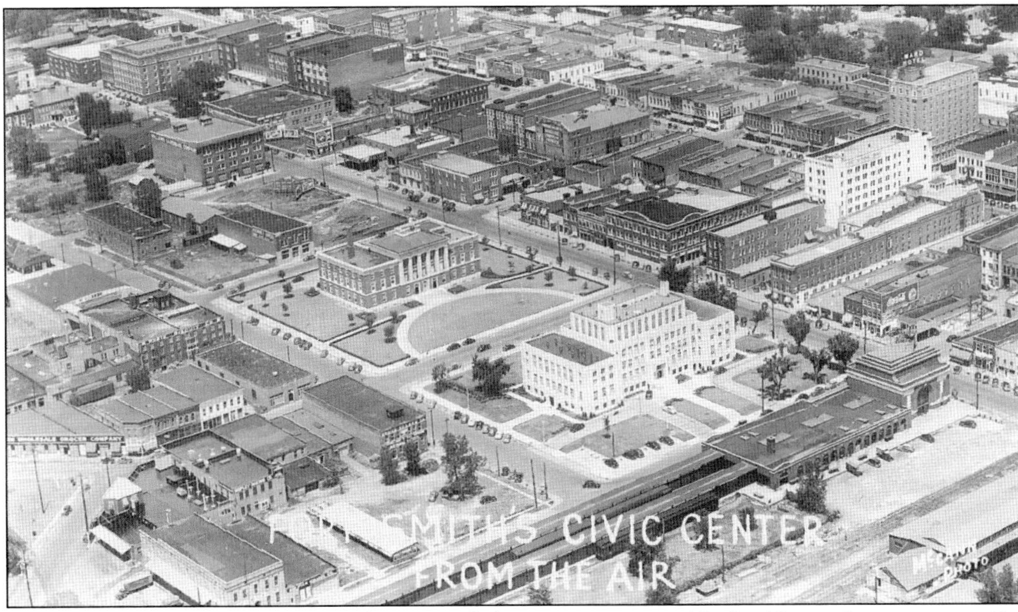

The imprint on the Fort Smith landscape made by its two major public buildings, the new post office and the City Hall/courthouse, is quite evident from this c. 1940 aerial view, which looks west toward the Arkansas River bridge (visible at the end of Garrison Avenue) in the upper left corner. Just below the City Hall building to the right is the Union Station, showing not only the main terminal (also seen on page 28) but also the expansive freight facility and covered passenger loading area stretching out behind the terminal. The upper part of the view traces Garrison and Rogers Avenues from about their midpoints, west to the river. In the upper right corner is the Ward Hotel and First National Bank. A number of the buildings seen here on both avenues are gone today.

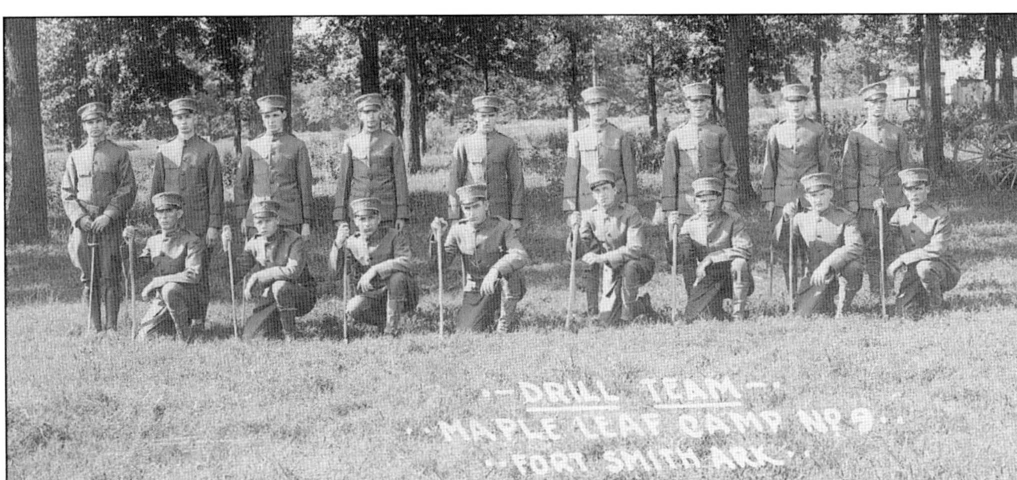

Fort Smith was a military post before it was a town, and a military presence has always been a part of its life, changing in look and purpose as the nation's defense needs evolved with history. Seen here is a local militia unit, Maple Leaf Camp Number Nine, posing for a photograph during a drill exercise. Little could these young men have known the horrors of war that the 20th century would unleash on mankind as they conducted their military exercises in 1910, a tranquil period of American history.

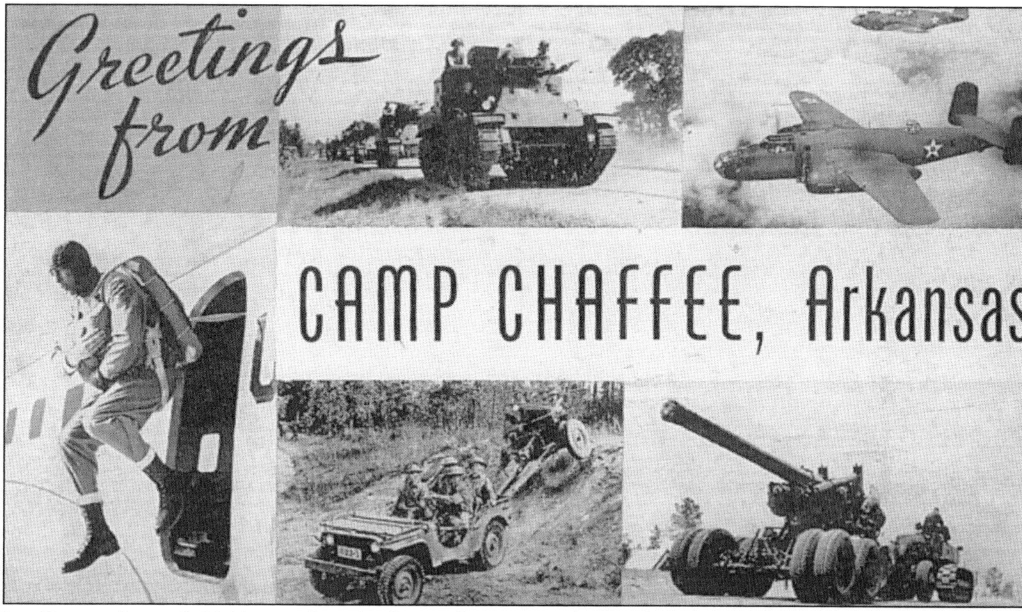

In September of 1941, as the shadow of WW II loomed, construction began on an Army training camp located just outside of Fort Smith. Built at a cost of $15 million, Camp Chaffee was named in honor of Maj. Gen. Anda R. Chaffee, first chief of the U.S. Army armored forces. The first group of 300 soldiers arrived at Camp Chaffee on December 6, 1941, and on the following day, Pearl Harbor was bombed by Japan. By April of 1942, the new base housed over 30,000 trainees. The postcard's 1943 message from Private Woodrow Wise reads as follows: "Has Mr. Powers seen any good movies lately? We have been pretty busy and still are. So long, Pvt. Woody."

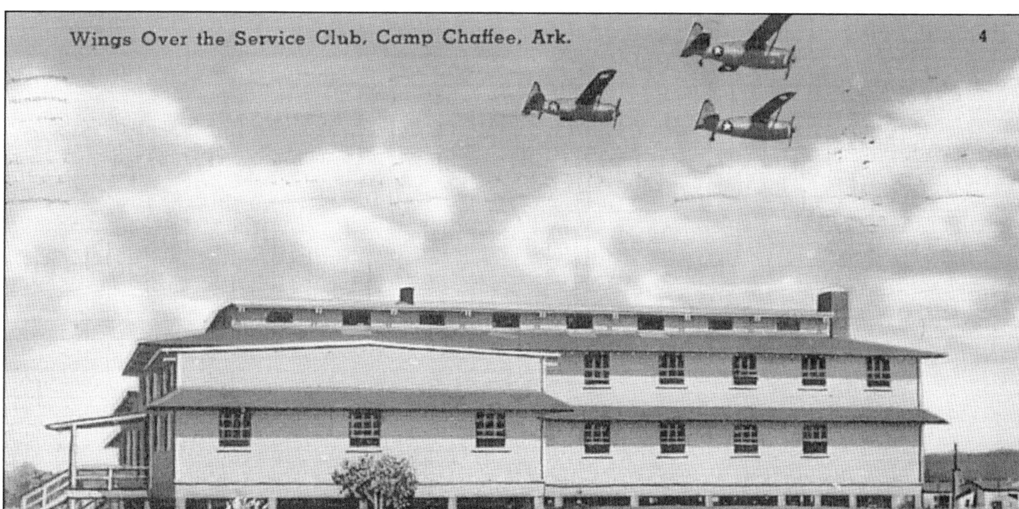

"Wings over the Service Club" is the caption on a postcard showing U.S. Army fighter planes passing over one of hundreds of white frame buildings sheltering thousands of troops, all of whom were training for the far-flung battlefields of WW II. The 1943 message from Pvt. Louis Koop to his family in Muncie, Indiana, reads as follows: "Well I am still on the truck. It is a battalion now, a small group. I am O.K., and they have learned me how to swim but water is too cold to suit me."

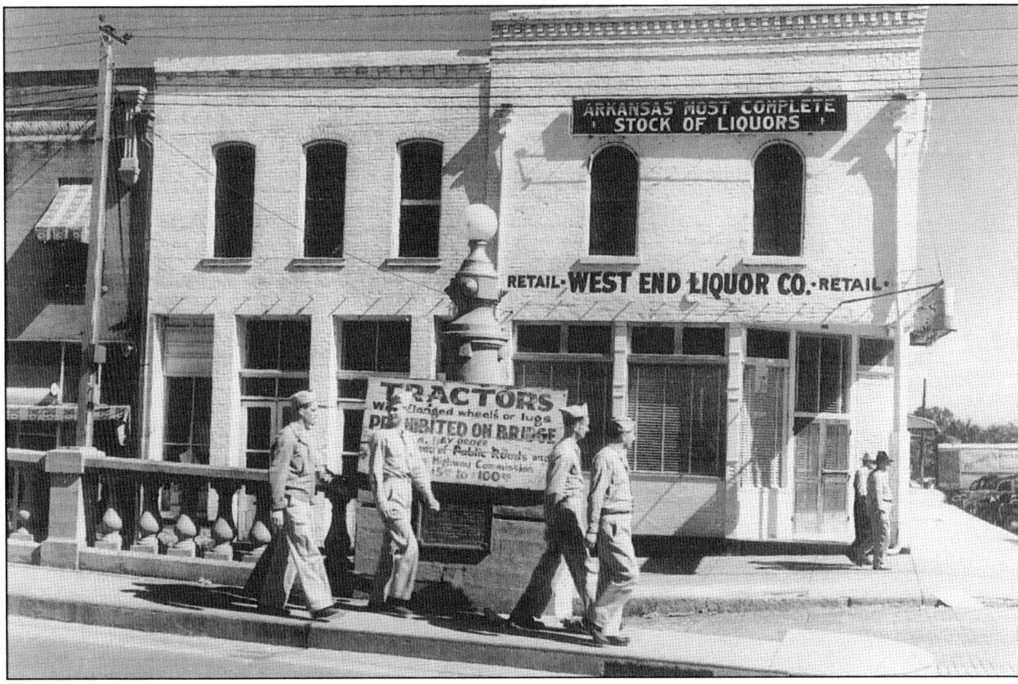

On leave in Fort Smith, soldiers from nearby Camp Chaffee are seen here coming off the Arkansas River bridge linking the city with Oklahoma. The sign on the bridge proclaimed, "Tractors with enlarged wheels or lugs prohibited on bridge." Note the West End Liquor Company, which boasted that it offered "Arkansas' most complete stock of liquors" and operated from 1938 to 1957. During the war, thousands of soldiers in training came into the city while on leave, giving a major boost the local economy, perhaps even on occasion to the West End Liquor store. The entire block of these buildings was torn down a number of years ago.

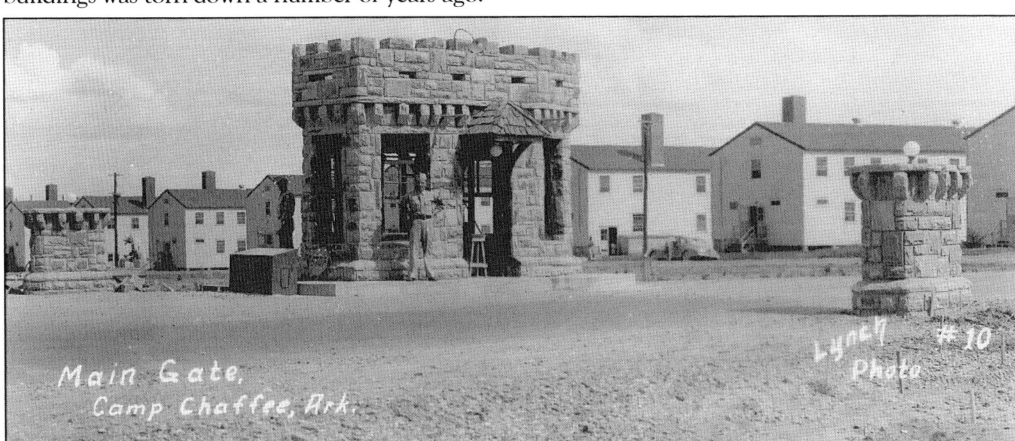

The front gate of Camp Chaffee was marked by this stone guardhouse. A sentry stands at attention in this photograph, and a long line of frame barracks is seen in the background. The gate, later relocated, was turned into a memorial to the most famous soldier from Fort Smith, Brig. Gen. William O. Darby. Brigadier General Darby formed and led across the battlefields of Europe the Army Ranger Battalion that became known as "Darby's Rangers" in exploits further made famous by a Hollywood movie. Darby was killed by enemy artillery in Europe in the closing days of the war, on April 30, 1945. He is buried in Fort Smith National Cemetery.

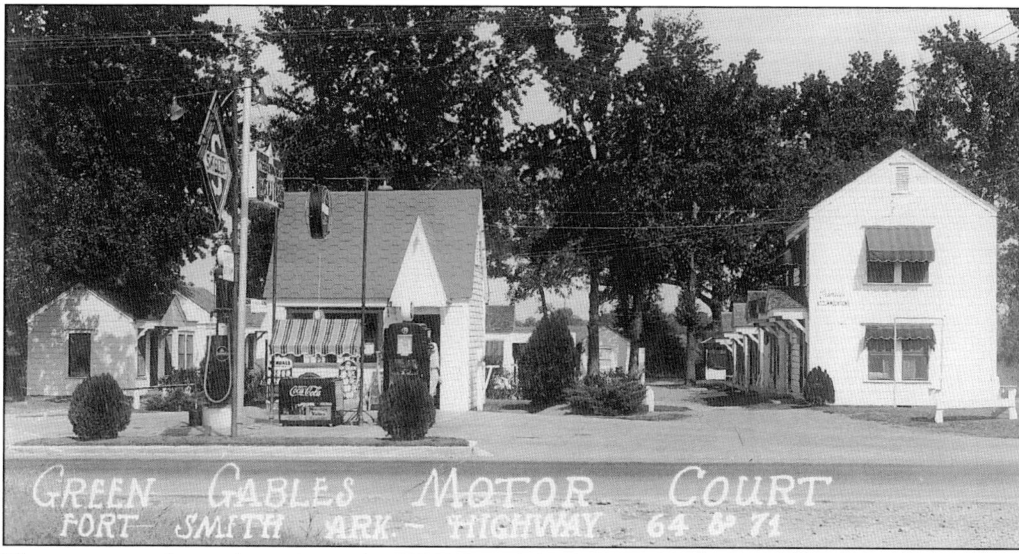

The economic boom brought on by WW II and the burgeoning number of automobiles on the area's highways gave rise to a number of "tourist courts" on the highways entering Fort Smith and offered new business to those already present. The message on the above postcard of the Green Gables Motor Court, located at the intersection of Highways 71 & 64, is "stayed here August 14, 1940." Gables adorned the front of each cabin, as well as the combination office and Skelly gas station in the front. Evident are two gas pumps from two different eras; the one to the left is a gravity-fed pump, and to the right is a newer styled electric model. Visible behind the pumps are a Coca-Cola machine and racks of motor oil. Below is a view of the Massey Tourist Court, which carried this 1940 message: "Here is one to add to your collection. We are having snow and sleet, are sliding all over town." The postcard features a map showing the court's location, which was at that time some three miles outside Fort Smith. It is gone today, and the site is occupied by the Bank of the Ozarks at 5409 Rogers Avenue.

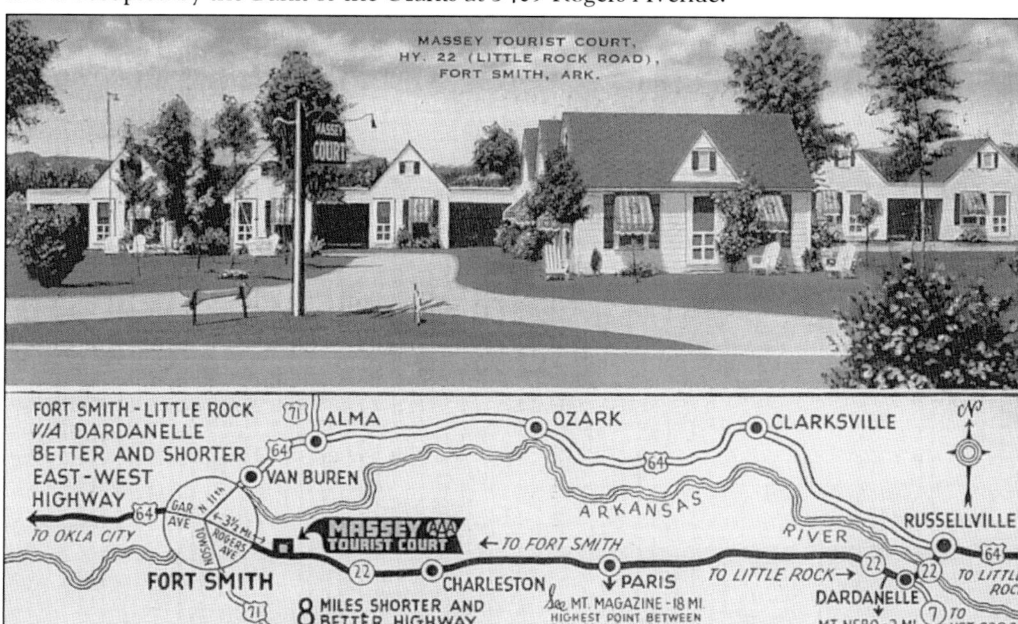

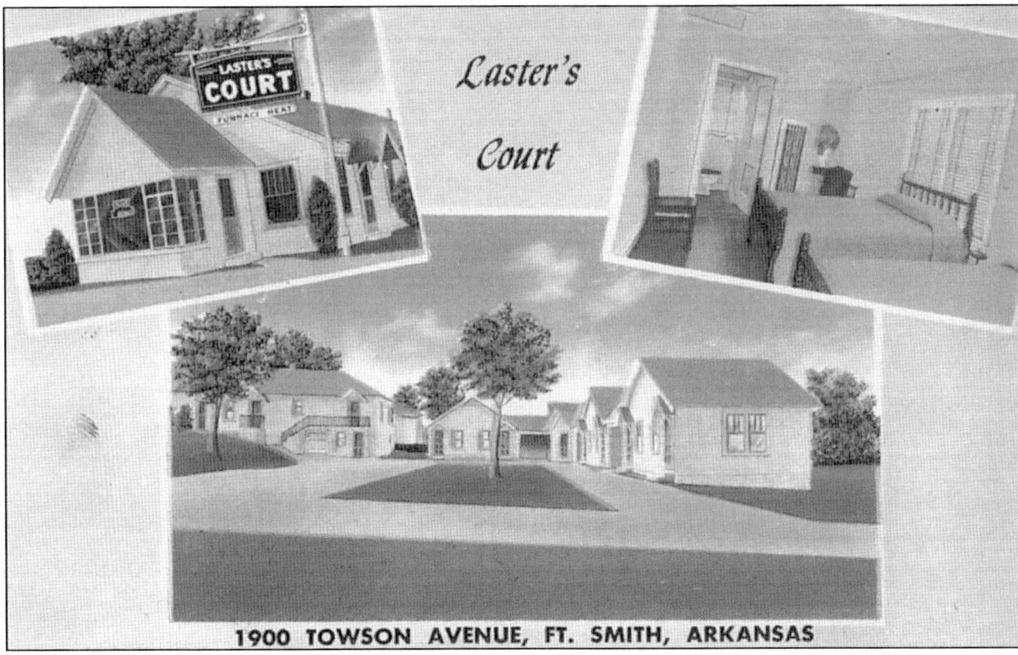

The postcard above shows the tourist court, located on Highway 71 south of the city limits, owned by Milo Laster. Laster advertised on this 1940 postcard that his business was "An outstanding Motor Court with every comfort—phone number 9769." As became common with postcards used for advertising, Mr. Laster maximized his value by putting three views on the face of the postcard. One shows the interior of a cabin with its steam heat and private bath. Today, the court is gone and Engle's Home Furnishings is located on this site.

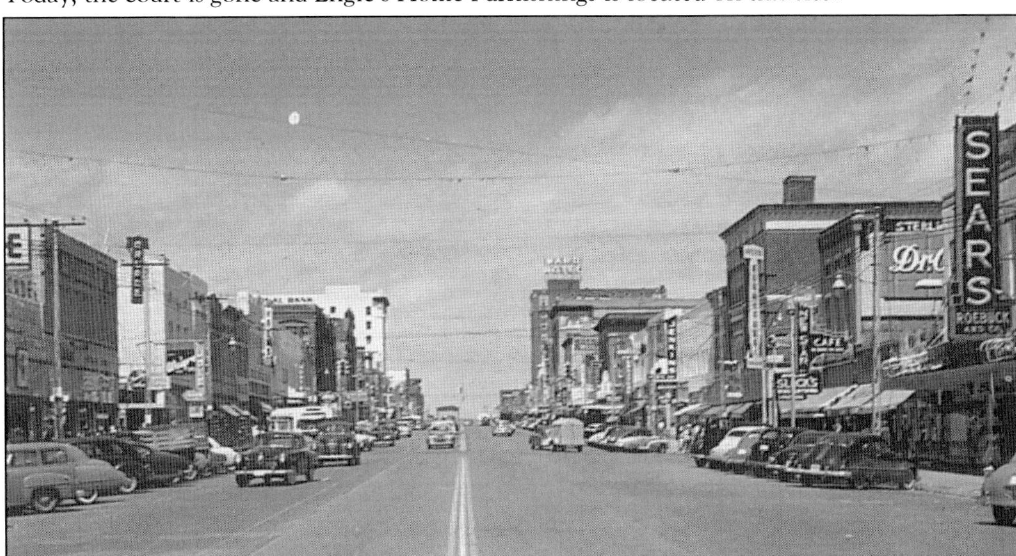

With the close of WW II, Garrison Avenue was still the booming retail center of western Arkansas. The 100-foot-wide street was lined with retailers like Sears, seen to the right. In this 1948 view can be seen many of the cars that were produced to fill the orders of post-war consumers who had done without during the war-time rationing. In the distance is the towering First National Bank on the left and the Ward Hotel on the right.

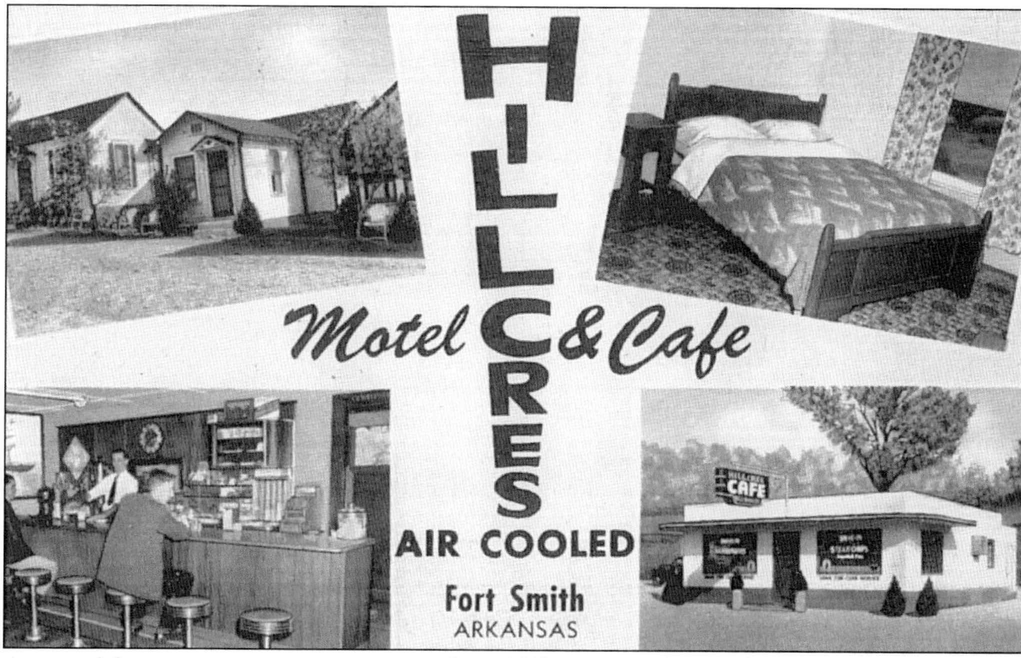

A part of the post-war economy supported the Hillcrest Motel & Cafe, located at 2500 Towson Avenue and seen here, *c.* 1950. The advertisement on the back of the postcard described 12 "modern cottages" and invited travelers to "Stop, Eat, Sleep and Gas Up." The Hillcrest is still in business today, though few such motels from that era still survive in today's franchised landscape of interstate America.

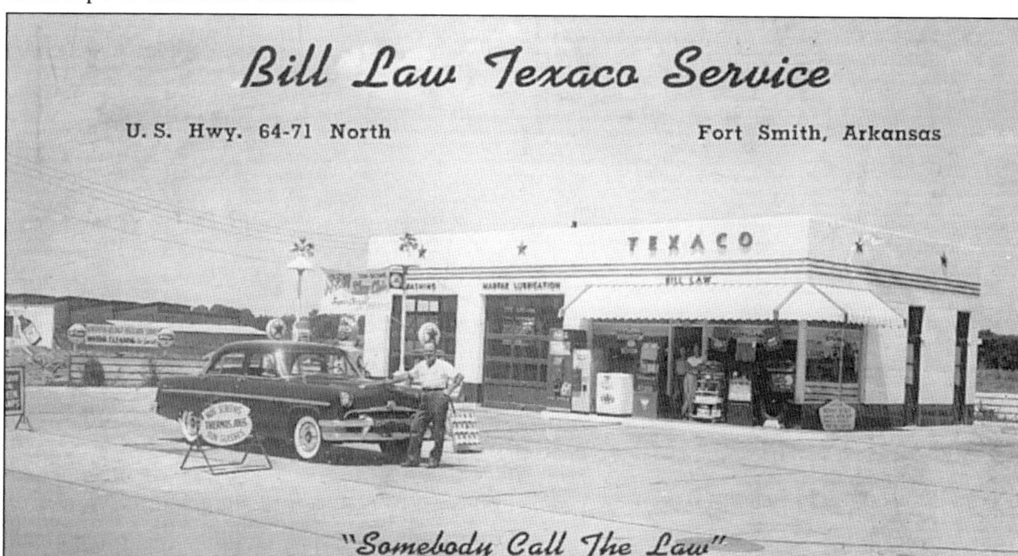

Motorists visiting Fort Smith and residents alike would have bought gas and had their cars serviced at Bill Law's Texaco on Midland Boulevard, seen here *c.* 1954. "Somebody Call The Law" was the motto of Mr. Law, presumably standing in front of a customer's car. The sign to the left of the car reads as follows: "Bug Screens, Thermos Jugs, and Sun Glasses." The station offered Green Stamps, and "New Sky Chief" gas was promoted on the banner over his two pumps. "Our Rest Rooms Are As Clean As Yours" was the promise on the back of the postcard.

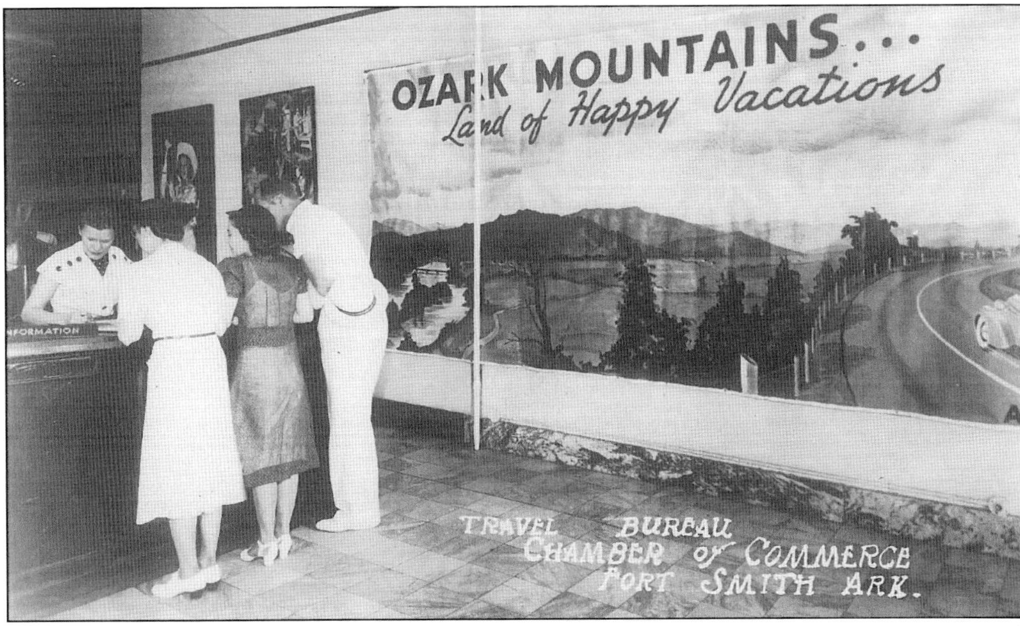

"Ozark Mountains. . . Land of Happy Vacations," proclaimed the mural at the Fort Smith Chamber of Commerce Travel Bureau desk in 1939. The campaign was part of an effort that had begun in earnest three years before, with the state's 100th birthday celebration. Private businesses and civic organizations worked to bring more tourists and their dollars to Arkansas. At the time, Arkansas carried the official nickname "The Wonder State."

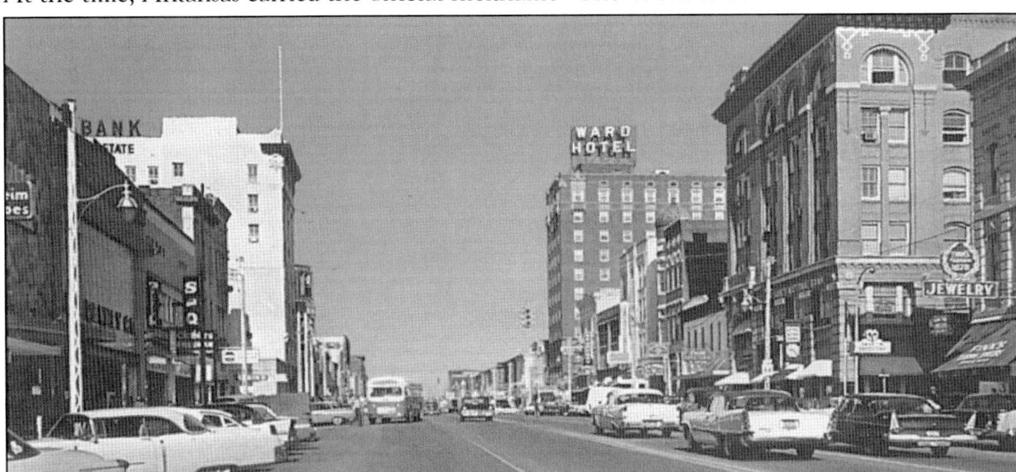

The late 1950s found Garrison Avenue busy with commerce and traffic; many of the cars are sporting tail fins. The postcard seen here bore the following message: "En route to St. Louis to report and catch a midnite plane to Hawaii on the tidal wave deal, Lucky me." The view looks west, with Merchants Bank to the left, where the bank clock shows that the picture was taken at 9:25. In the distance, a blue city bus is stopped with disembarking passengers. In the decades to follow, the grand avenue would change markedly. Some buildings have been removed, either by man or nature, and almost all the major retailers have left for outlying shopping centers. Yet the Fort Smith community has worked hard to preserve as much of its historic district as possible, and the avenue that started out as a parade route for the first fort some 175 years ago still makes a visit a worthwhile experience.

Two

Rural Settlements and Sights of Sebastian County

Geographically, Sebastian County is quite large, leading to its status as one of six Arkansas counties with two official county seats. Fort Smith, by far its largest city, is located in the northern tip of the county, a fact that long ago politically mandated its becoming a second county seat, with the first being in the southern part of the county at Greenwood. Outside of Fort Smith, the county developed into a collection of small villages and farms, the fortunes of which often rose and fell, depending on the shifting routes of railroads, timber, and coal fields. Today, the balance of the county remains a collection of small, prosperous communities that lay claim to their own postcard history.

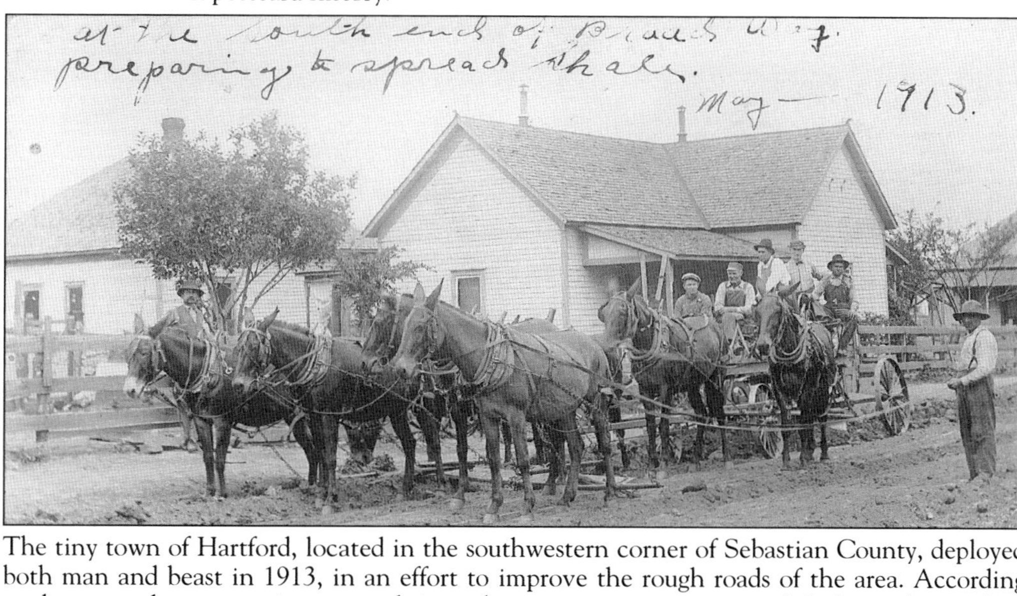

The tiny town of Hartford, located in the southwestern corner of Sebastian County, deployed both man and beast in 1913, in an effort to improve the rough roads of the area. According to the penned message, six men and six mules were preparing to spread shale on the roadbed in the hopes of helping to keep it passable after rains. At the time, responsibility for roads and highways was almost totally a local obligation, for the state had not yet begun to assume leadership in this area.

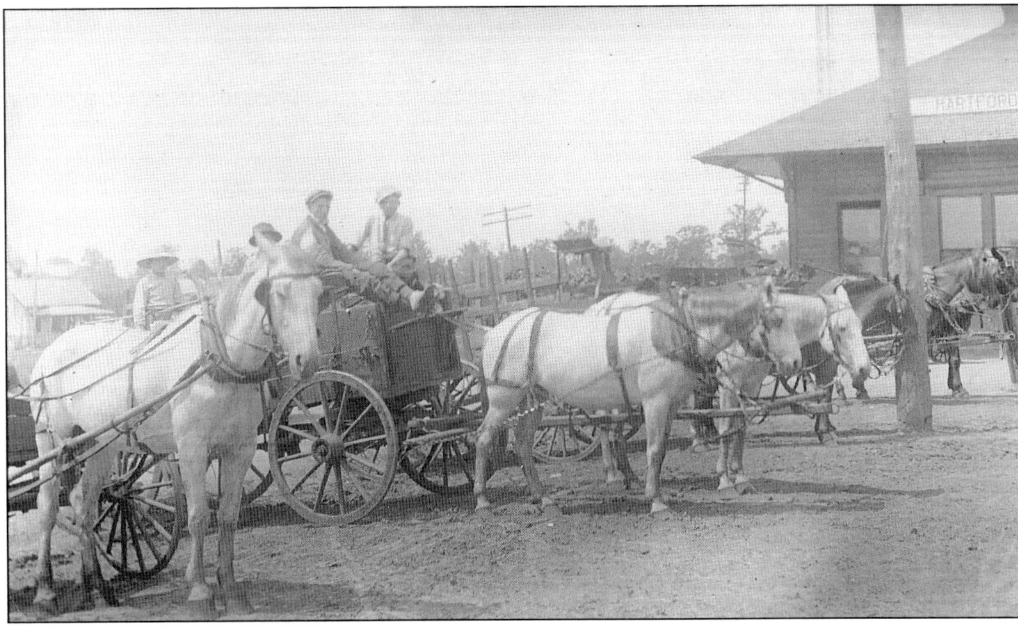

The town of Hartford came into being in what was described by early settlers as a beautiful valley between Sugarloaf and Poteau Mountains. The first settlers arrived in the 1840s and named the town Gwynn, after the man who opened the area's first coal mine. The town's name was later changed to Hartford, reportedly to honor a widow named Hart, whose name had earlier been given to a creek crossing, "Hart Ford." The Choctaw Memphis Railroad came through in the late 1800s, buying the right-of-way through town for $60. The railroad would later change hands but continue to serve Hartford through its boom times out of the depot shown in these two *c.* 1910 postcards. In the postcard above, a line of wagons waits to carry arriving freight to area merchants and farmers. The postcard below captured a view of a group of men, clearly from different steps on the economic ladder of the day. Among them are a black laborer with a handcart, two suspender-clad men, the seated man in ragged clothing and work boots, and a vested man, possibly the foreman—in contrast to the two well-dressed men to the right, wearing derby hats and ties.

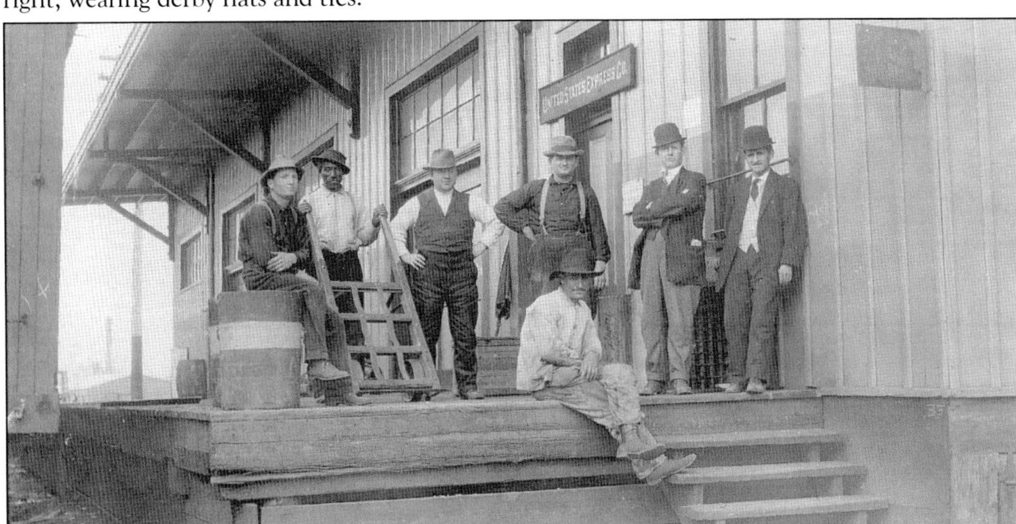

Hartford was a hard-working, coal mining settlement, but its citizens made a place for a high school, and sports for both boys and girls were an important part of the community's social fabric. Around 1910, the Hartford High School girls' basketball team posed for this shot, which was printed on postcard stock. Presumably, the young man in the center served as a coach for the team. The female players all seem to be wearing men's styled neckties with their white blouses, and all bear rather sober expressions, which is typical in photographs of the day.

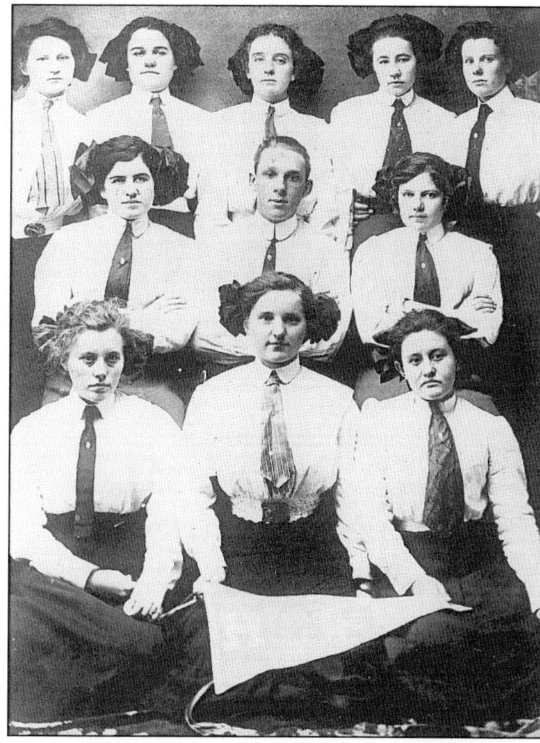

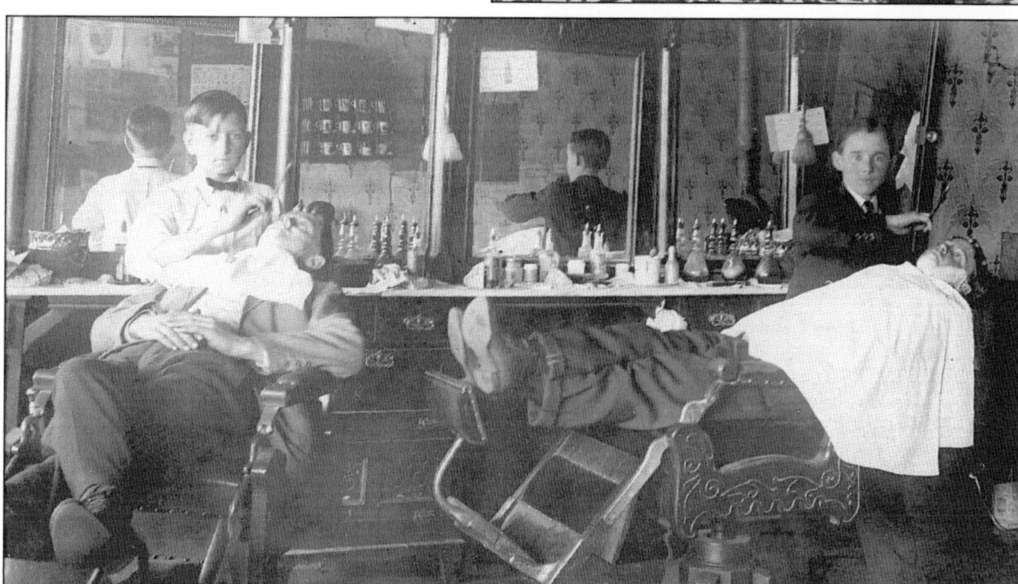

The barber shop on Hartford's Main Street was a popular spot to get a haircut and shave, as well as to discuss the town gossip, events in the coal mines, the weather, and the state of the farm crops. In this curious photograph, two young boys (seemingly too young to have been working as barbers) are posed with straight razors poised over two customers. One theory might be that the real barbers are in the chairs, while the young men posing as razor-wielding barbers might have been their sons, or simply cohorts in playing a prank for the camera. Of note are the ornate, iron barber chairs and the assorted bottles of hair oil and lotions on the counter.

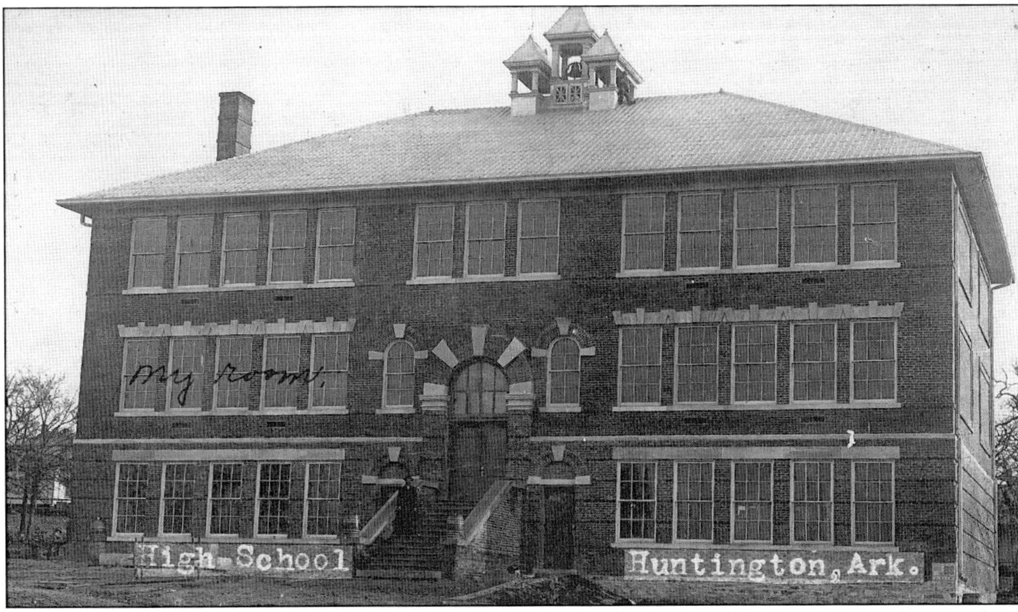

Located a few miles northeast of Hartford, the town of Huntington grew prosperous enough, as the coal mines expanded, to erect this handsome high school. A teacher mailed this postcard in 1912, noting the classroom to the left on the second floor, and writing this message: "Wonder if you people are still living? We moved into our new home three weeks ago—certainly is a beauty. Had county teachers meeting here last Sat." At that time, the average Arkansas school teacher taught a 107-day school year and earned $273 for that period.

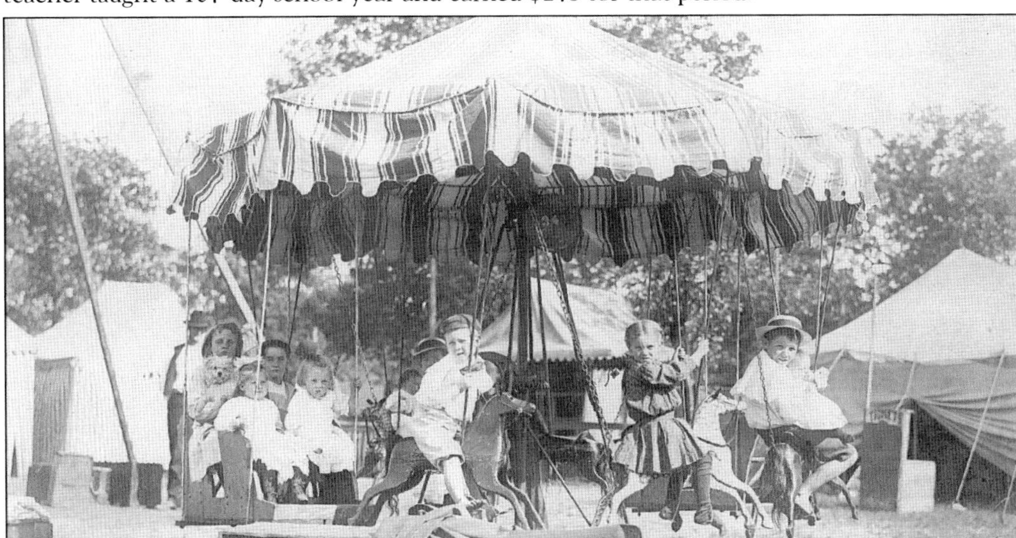

When the traveling carnival came to Huntington around 1910, it gave the local children something to think about besides school. This scene transcends the decades that have passed since a parent penciled the following message on the back of this postcard: "merygoround the carnaval [sic] was here, had a hot time, we went every night, we had 41 upstairs." This may mean they put up relatives from the countryside who came to Huntington for the occasion. The child to the right, holding an infant, is marked with an "x" and is noted on the back of the postcard to be named "Artie." The child to the left is riding with her dog.

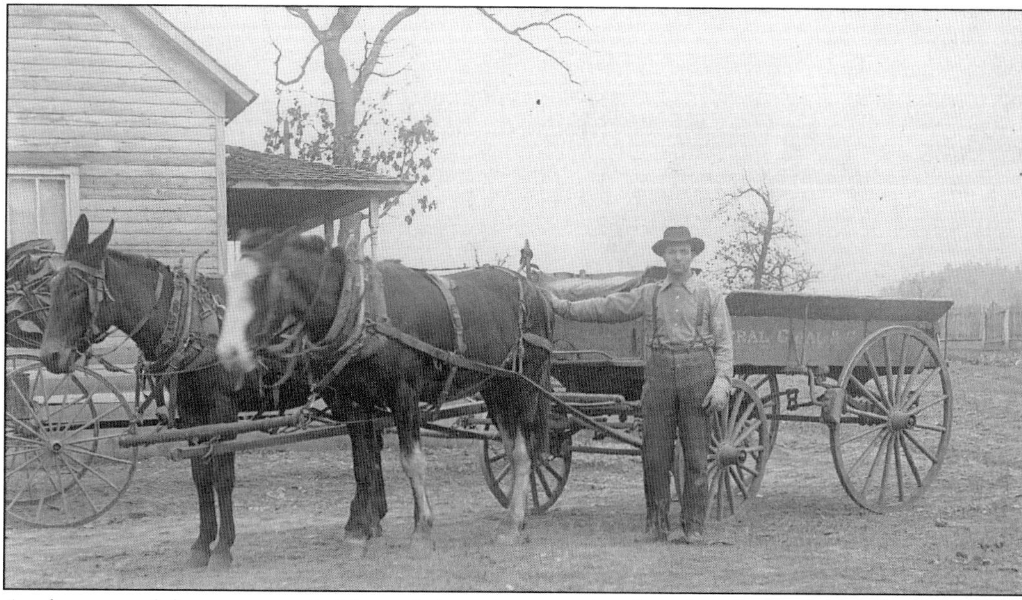

At the turn of the century, sizable coal deposits were developed in southern Sebastian County, and much of this activity centered on Hartford, spreading into eastern Oklahoma. The coal-fired economy was so good that four banks opened in Hartford to handle the business. In 1912, the Choctaw and the Midland Valley Railroad served 17 mines with 1,760 coal cars. In the above 1910 postcard, a man poses in the yard of a home, with a team hooked to a wagon belonging to the Central Coal Company. Perhaps the wagon carried supplies to mines, but it was likely used to deliver coal (which could burn the plentiful fuel for heat and cooking) to area homes. The postcard below pictures the crew of one of the Central Coal & Coke Company's mines at nearby Huntington, Arkansas. The men, many with faces caked with coal dust from their hard, dangerous work, are posed on the train tracks with their lunch buckets. Over the years, the marketable coal seams gradually played out, and by the 1950s, the mining industry was gone from the area.

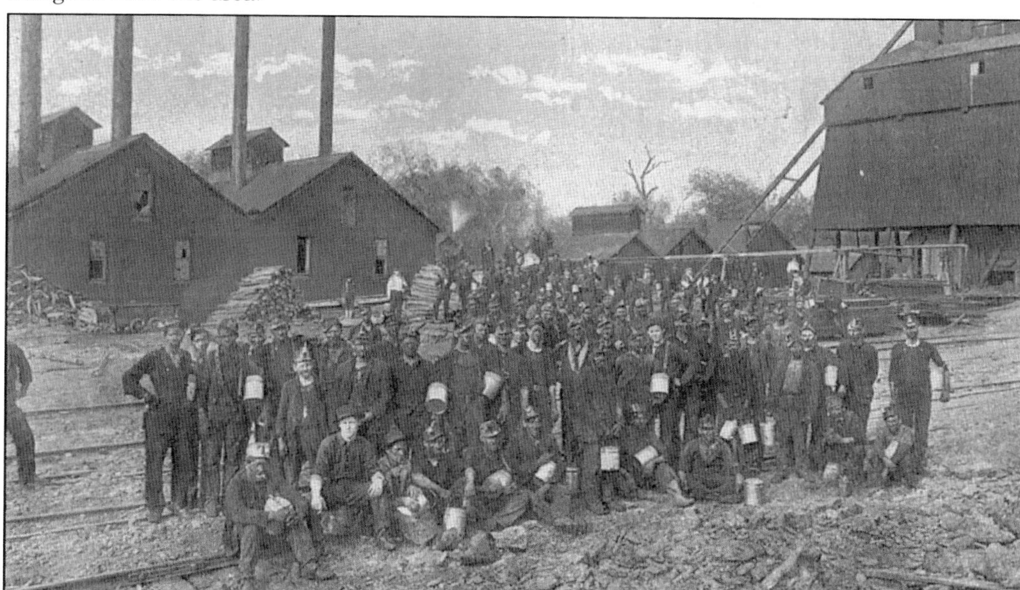

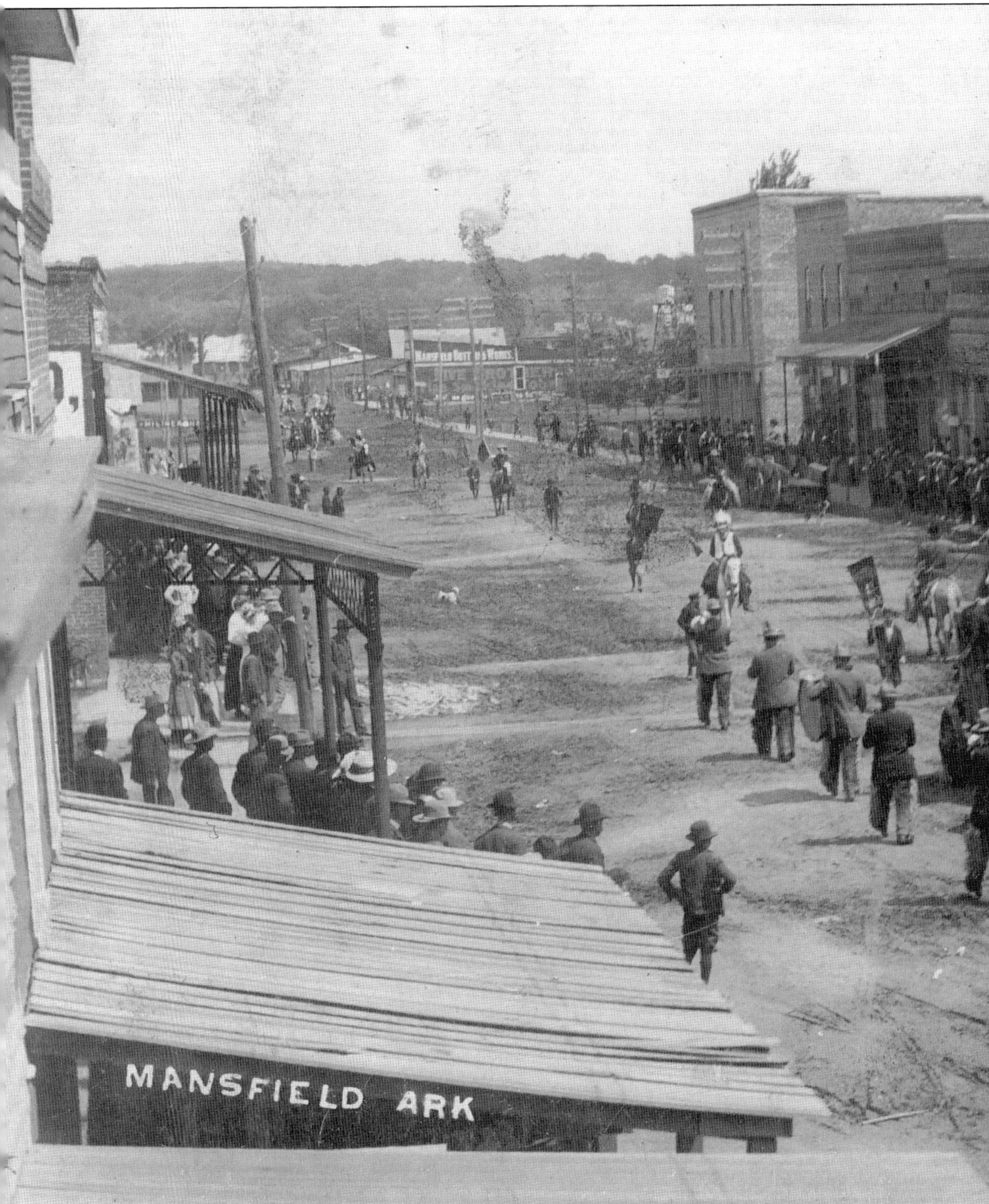

The community of Mansfield was named to honor W.W. Mansfield, a noted western Arkansas jurist who served on the state Supreme Court. On the day this c. 1910 photograph was made, a "wild west" parade was in progress, likely for a traveling show. A mounted "Indian" chief

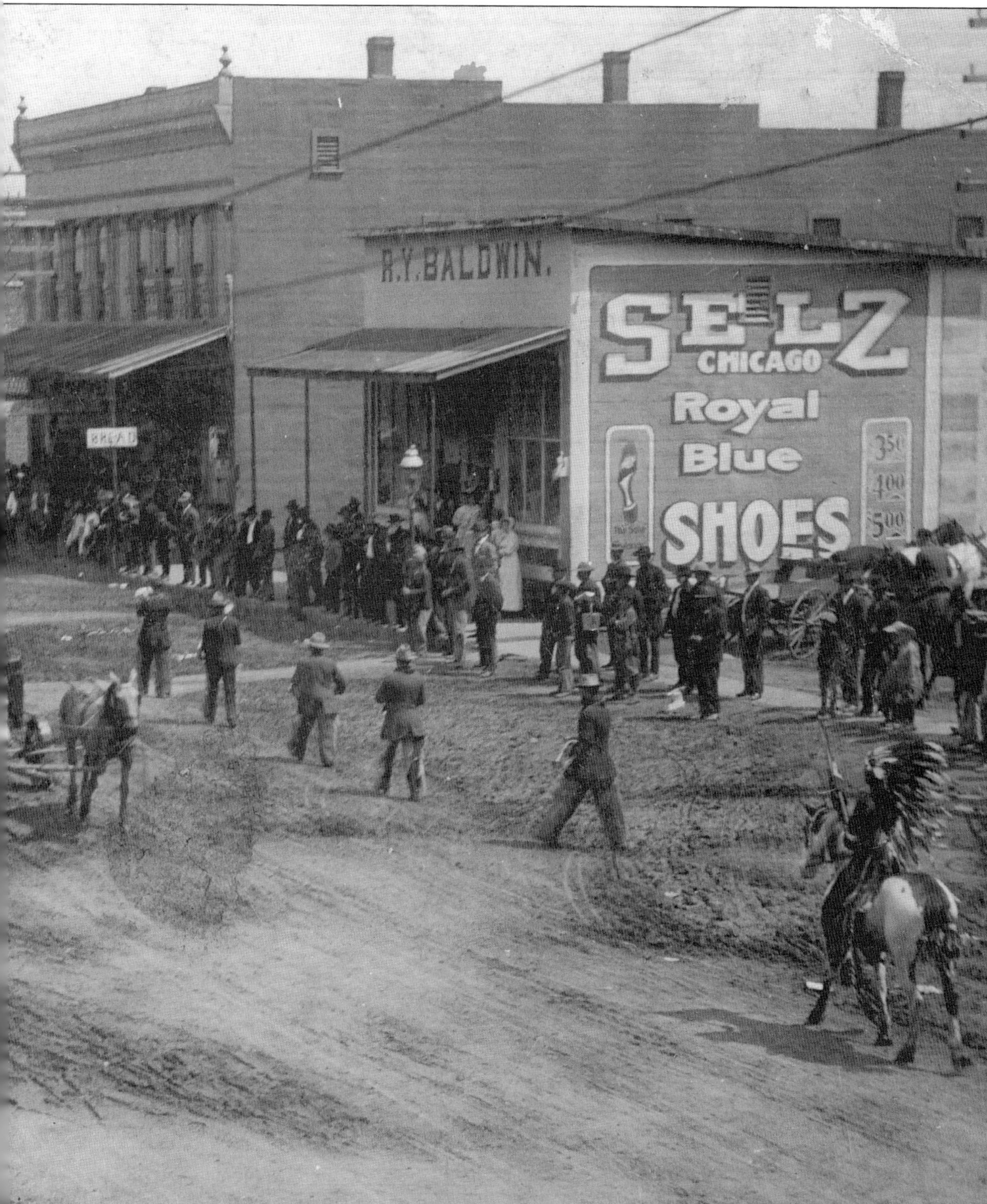

in a war headdress is seen galloping past a large sign promoting Selz Royal Blue Shoes, advertised at between $3.50 and $5 a pair. In the center of the photograph of the dusty street is a stagecoach.

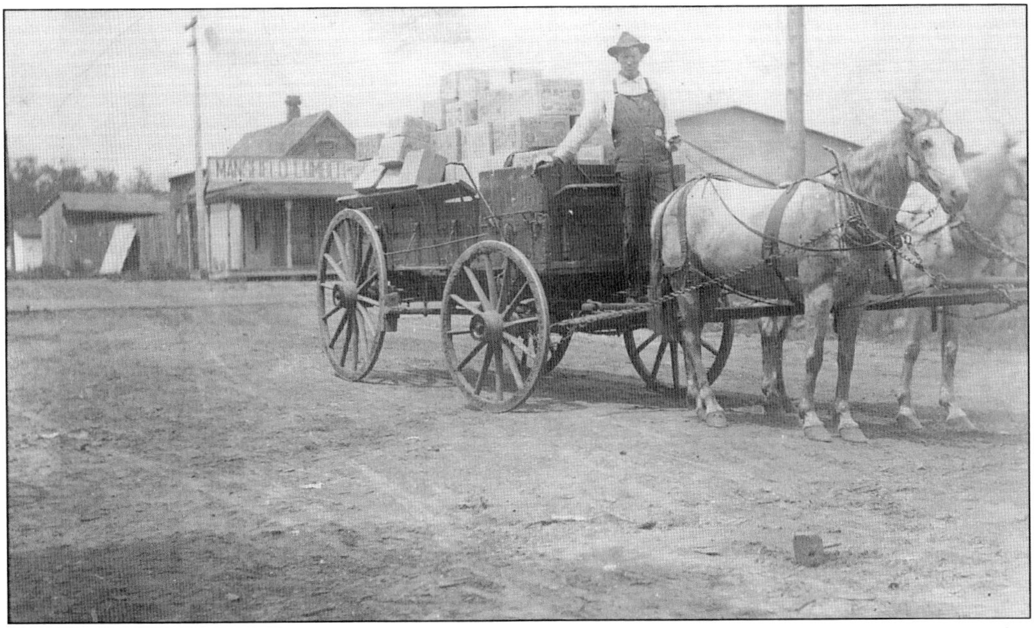

At the turn of the century, Mansfield was a distribution center for a wide area because of the Frisco Railroad spur line that reached the community. Farmers and merchants from southern Sebastian County, as well as neighboring Scott and Logan counties, used the rail station to ship and receive goods. One beneficiary was the man seen in this c. 1910 postcard, likely a farmer or perhaps a store owner's employee, who is hauling a load of new Ball fruit jars that had recently been off-loaded from a train.

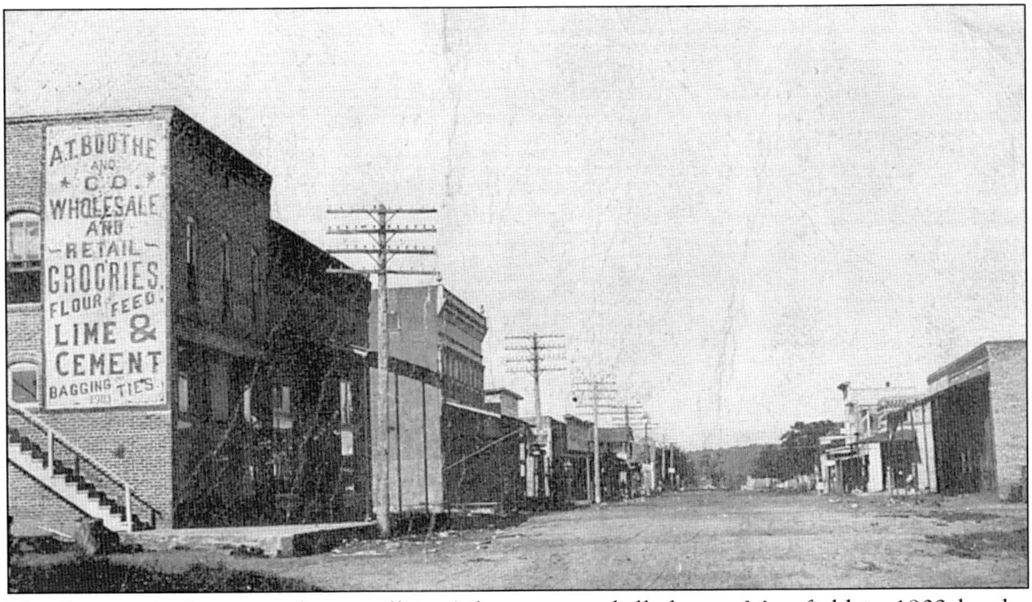

The first-producing natural gas well in Arkansas was drilled near Mansfield in 1902 by the Choctaw Oil and Gas Co., a development that brought the town its first industry, the Choctaw Pressed Brick Co. This postcard shows a view of the dirt Main Street, before the production of natural gas began to boost the local economy. Among the major businesses at the time was A.T. Boothe and Co., a wholesale and retail grocer located in the building to the left.

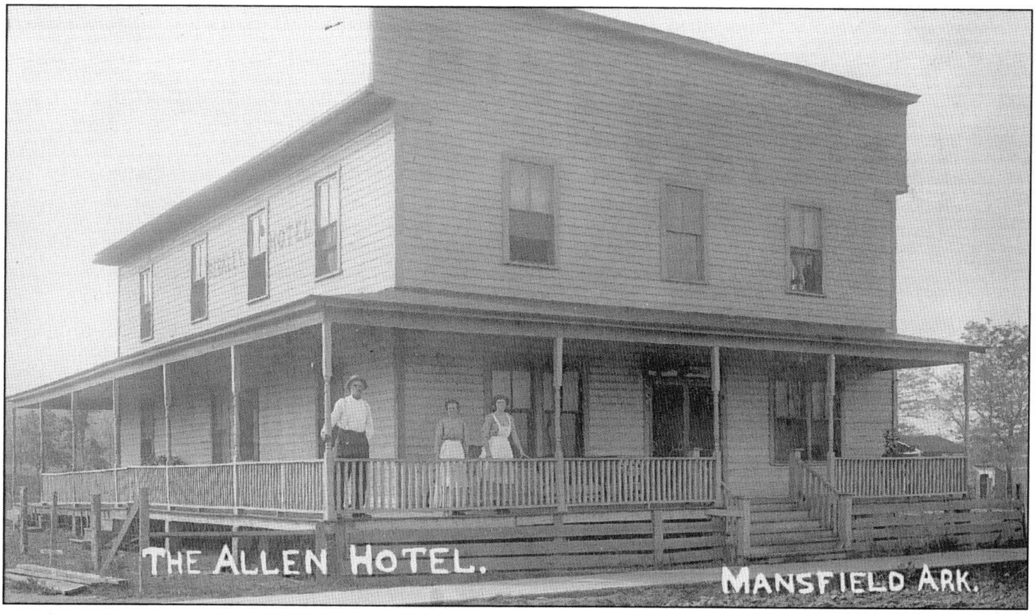

By the turn of the century, Mansfield (seen here *c.* 1910) was a busy rail and coal center that supported the shipment of thousands of bales of cotton a year, along with a thriving business community that included two hotels. One of these lodging places was the Allen Hotel, apparently having been named the Berkley Hotel in the recent past, as that is the name still painted on the side of the building. Rooms at the hotel were less than a dollar a night, perhaps including meals. The structure was built close to the street, with a sidewalk running in front of the steps. The bottom of the porch is closed in, with rough lumber to keep animals from taking up residence beneath the hotel.

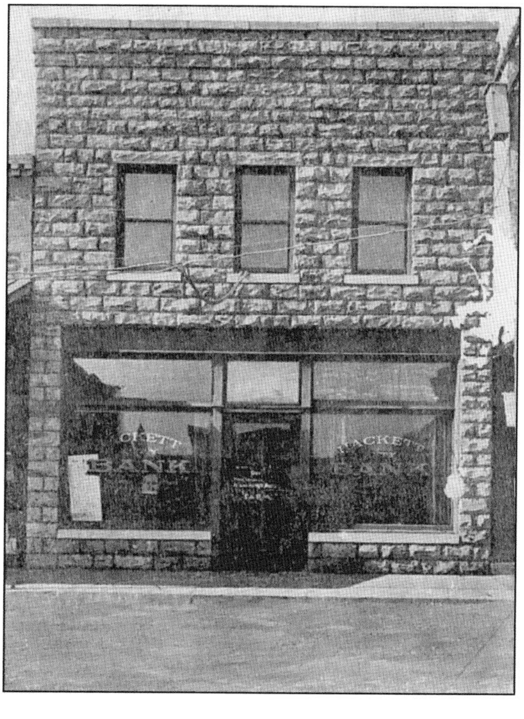

Hackett is located southwest of Fort Smith, very near the Oklahoma state line. This postcard was mailed in 1912, showing the Hackett City Bank in an era decades before huge, corporately-owned banks moved into small-town Arkansas. The stone bank building is gone today as is the entire block of buildings on that side of the main street.

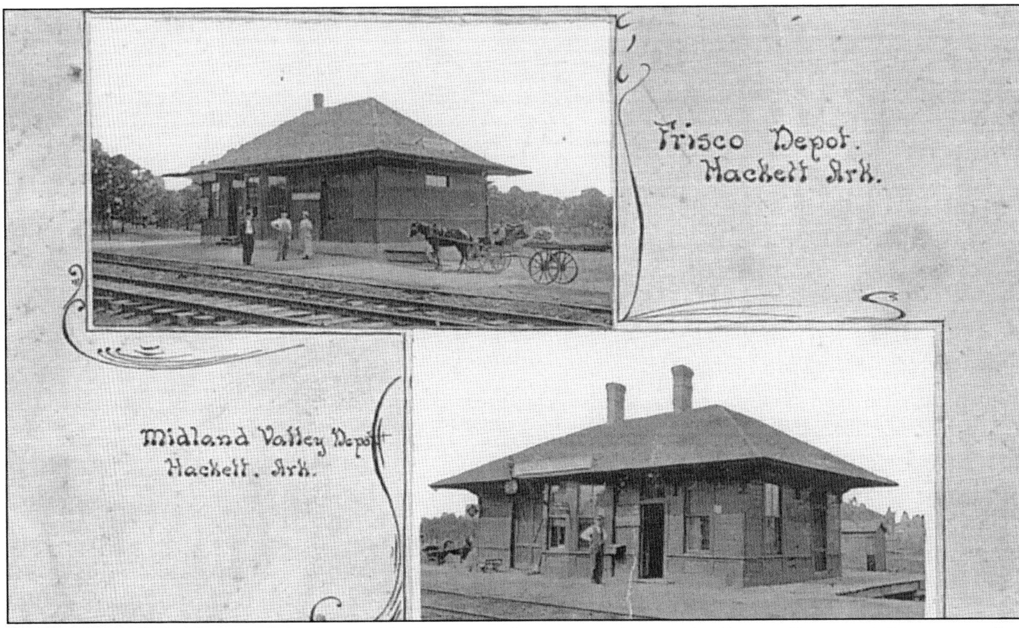

The Midland Valley Railroad put Hackett on the map when it built a rail tunnel between that community and Bonanza, Oklahoma, in order to serve the coal fields of southern Sebastian County. Completed in 1886, just over the state line in Oklahoma, the tunnel was built in large part by the labor of prisoners from Oklahoma Territory. Trains using the tunnel to get to Hackett could have pulled in to one of two train stations, a surprising feature for such a very small town. The Frisco Depot in the top photograph was removed some years ago but was restored and today serves as a home on White Bluff Road in Fort Smith. The Midland Valley Railroad depot, shown in the *c.* 1915 photograph below, was torn down after the heyday of the railroads.

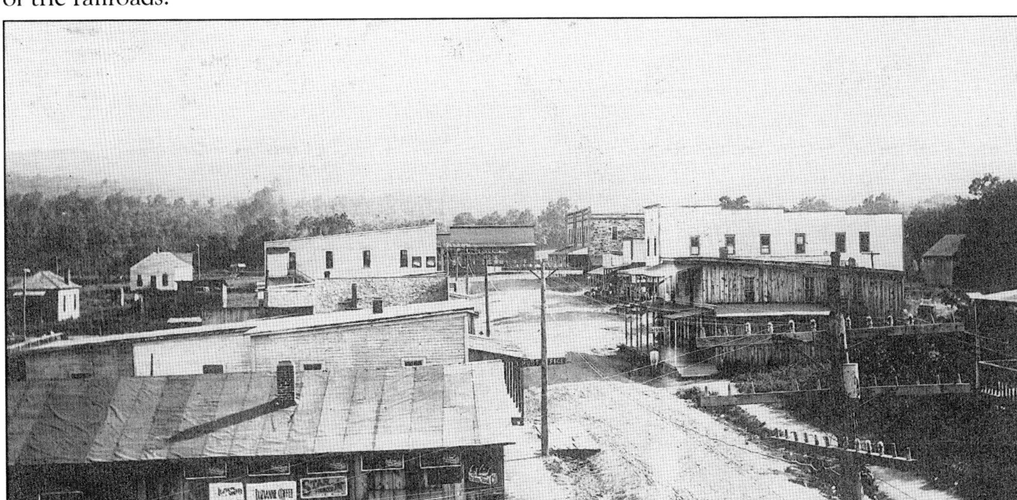

The small community of Midland sprang up between Hackett and Hartford, and for years its livelihood was tied to the coal fields and the railroad. The photographer who produced this view in 1905 stood atop a tall structure, likely a water tower, looking out over the town. The post office is the second building, just beyond the one in the foreground. Signs on the side of that building advertise Luzianne Coffee and Star Tobacco.

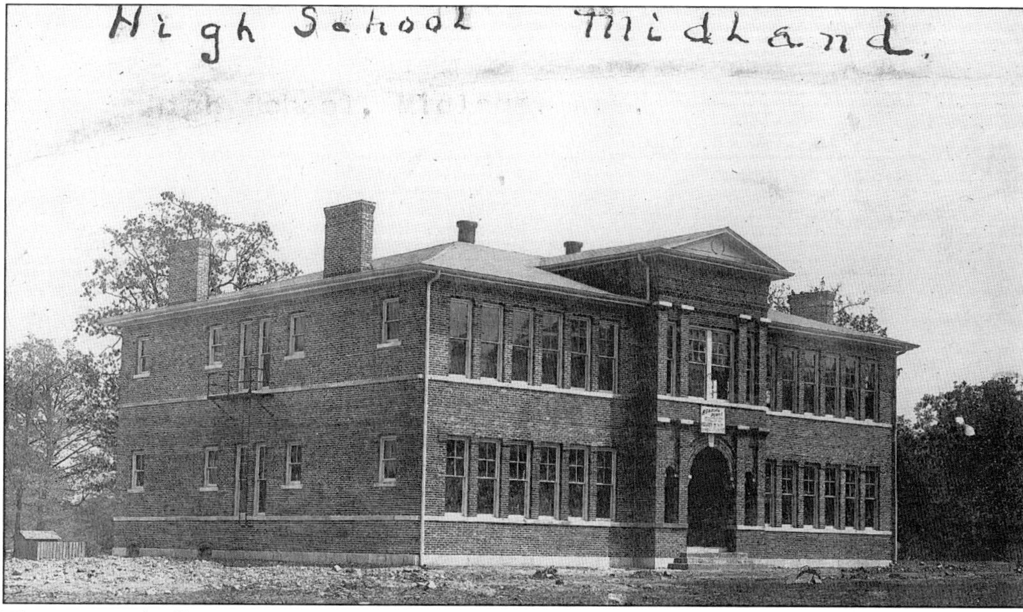

This postcard offers a view of Midland's new public school, which was just nearing completion. The sign over the arched doorway was put up by the contractor installing the boiler and "heating plant." The school had at least four chimneys, and a fire escape system is seen on the end of the building. The message on the postcard sent to Van Buren reads, "I will be going to Hackett Sunday picnicing [sic]." Today, Midland remains a very small town, and the school building no longer stands.

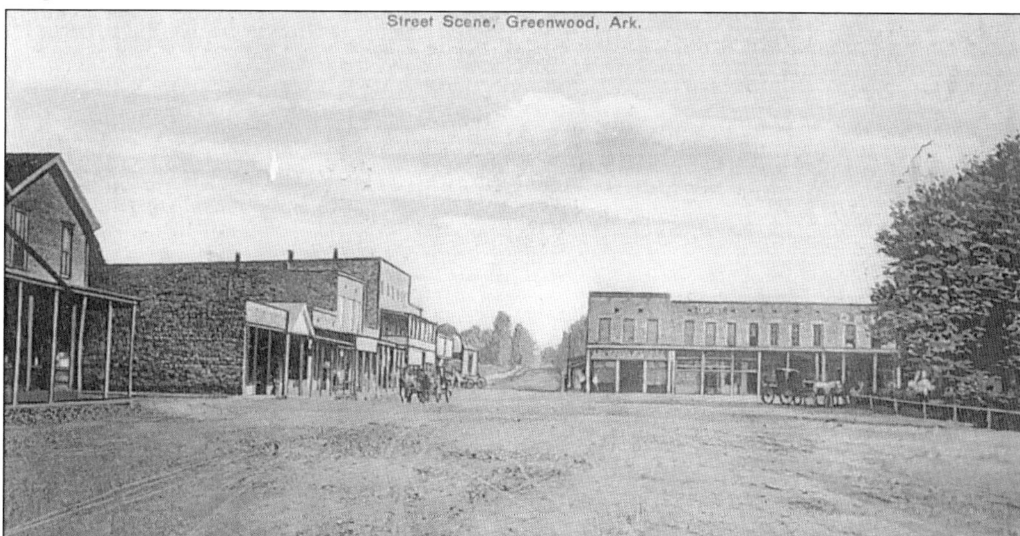

Greenwood, the county seat for southern Sebastian County, took its name from Congressman and Judge Alfred Greenwood (1811–1889). Among the politician's other careers were his service as Commissioner of Indian Affairs under President Buchanan, and as Confederate commissioner to the Choctaw Indian nation during the Civil War. The area's first county seat, Greenwood was formed in 1851 with a population of 30 people. This postcard, mailed in 1910, shows the rutted dirt street around the courthouse square. Most of the buildings are gone today, victims of fire and the hand of man.

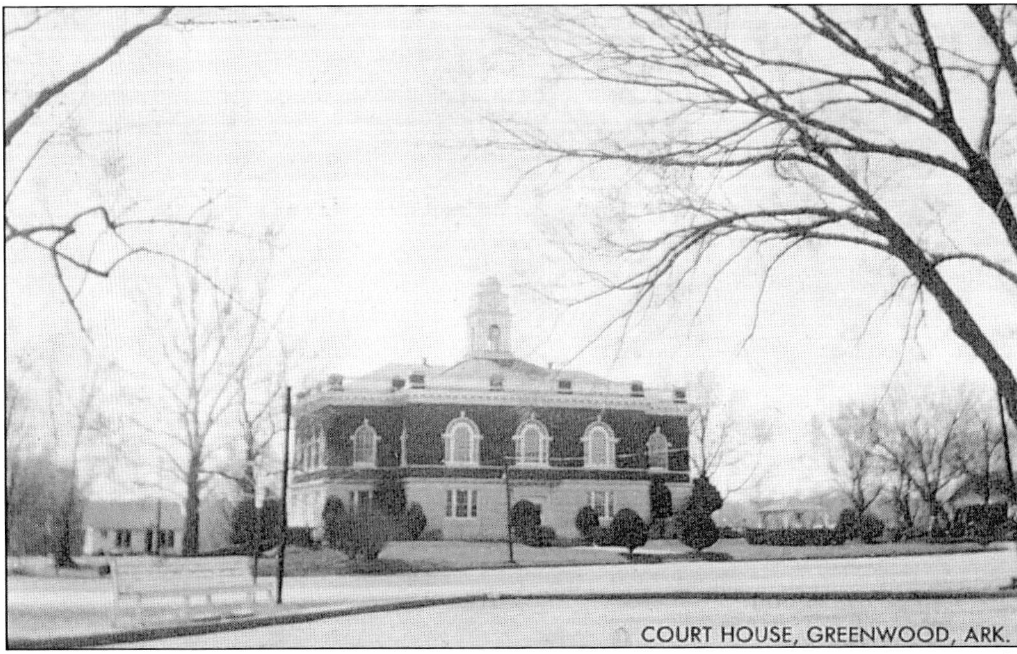

While the much larger Fort Smith to the north obtained dual county seat status after a struggle, Greenwood never relinquished the shared honor. Throughout its history, it has had five courthouses. The one shown here c. 1950 was built in 1916, but is gone today; sadly, it was destroyed along with most of the town in a 1968 tornado.

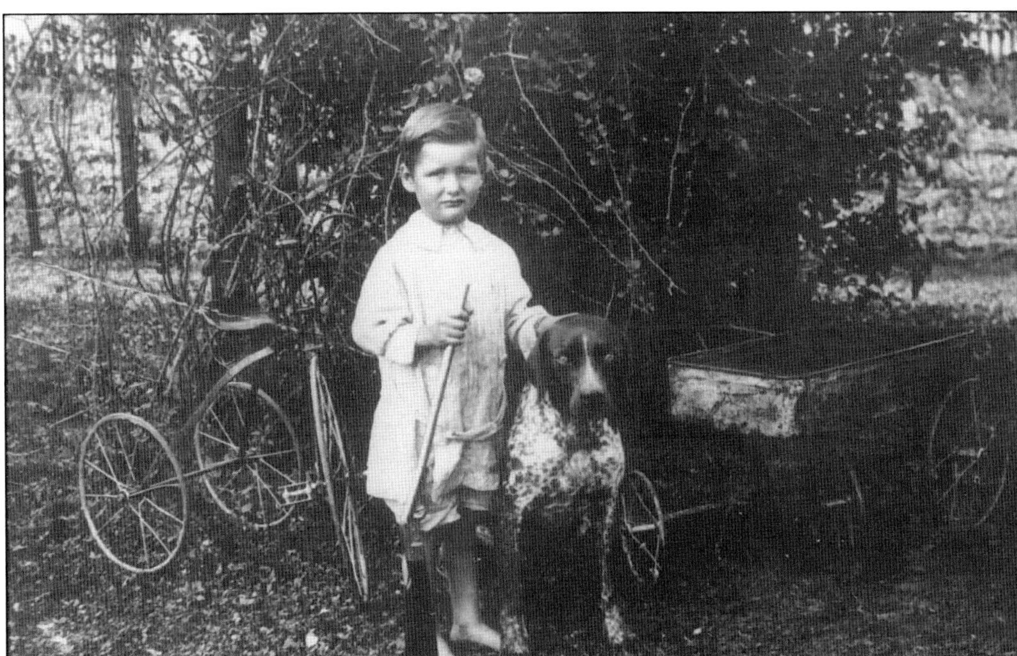

This Greenwood youngster poses in his yard beside his tricycle, with a toy rifle and hunting dog. Children and dogs have been a lure for the photographer's eye ever since the creation of the camera. Such photographs have left behind a timeless legacy of the scenes of everyday life.

Three

VAN BUREN

Crawford County was created in 1820 as the eighth of what are today 75 Arkansas counties. The huge expanse of wilderness that formed the county was named for William H. Crawford, then U.S. secretary of war. As the years passed, through the 19th and into the 20th century, Crawford County was dwarfed in size by Fort Smith, which evolved from a military post to a major city across the Arkansas River in Sebastian County. Though its towns remained small, Crawford County developed a distinct character and history that fortunately left its mark on postcards, the majority of which are views of the county seat of Van Buren.

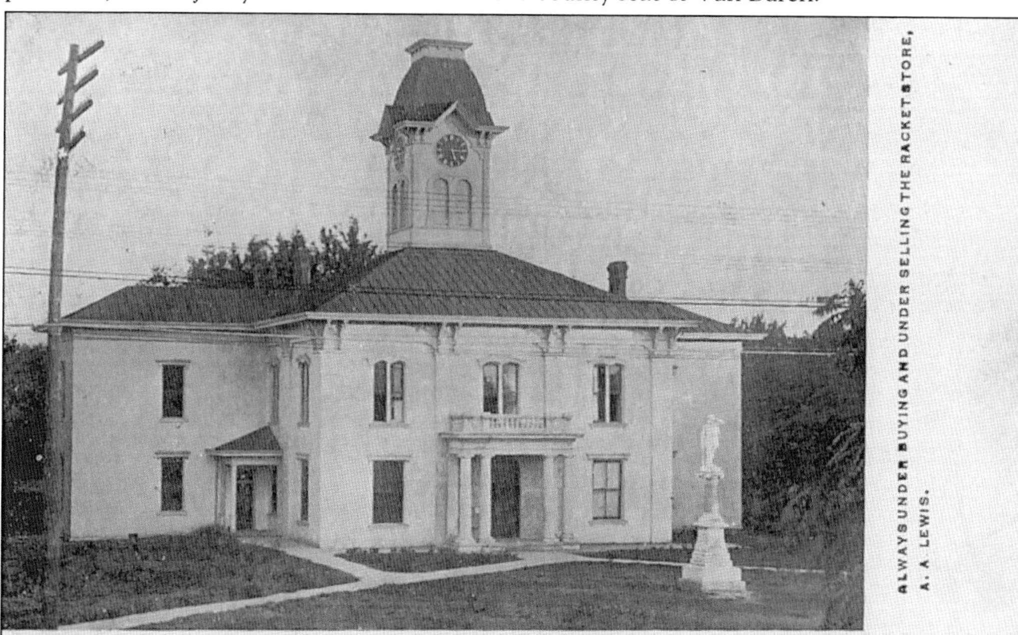

The Crawford County Courthouse, located in the county seat of Van Buren, is among the oldest such buildings still in use in Arkansas and is said to be the oldest county courthouse still in use west of the Mississippi. The building's original 22-inch bricks were first laid in 1841 and were salvaged after the fire of 1877 for construction of the present courthouse. Among the items of note on this 1905 view of the courthouse lawn are a monument to the first three Americans to die on WW I battlefields, a monument dedicated to the school teachers of the world, a sundial from the 1840s, and a monument to honor the Confederate dead. In the mid-1800s, the Butterfield Stage Route that connected St. Louis and San Francisco passed in front of the courthouse square in Van Buren, then crossed the Arkansas River by ferry a few blocks south.

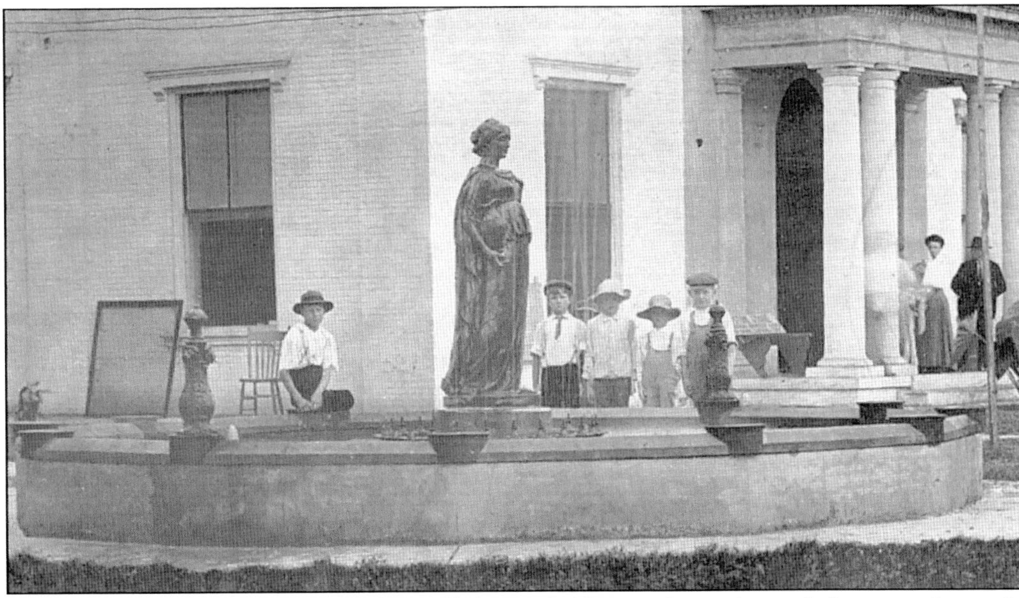

A feature of the courthouse lawn that still draws children today is the park fountain, located a few feet from the front steps. These boys, under the watchful eyes of adults to the right, surely faced the temptation to wade into the spouts of water that circled the bronze statue of a classical woman pouring from a vase. The restored landmark still welcomes visitors today.

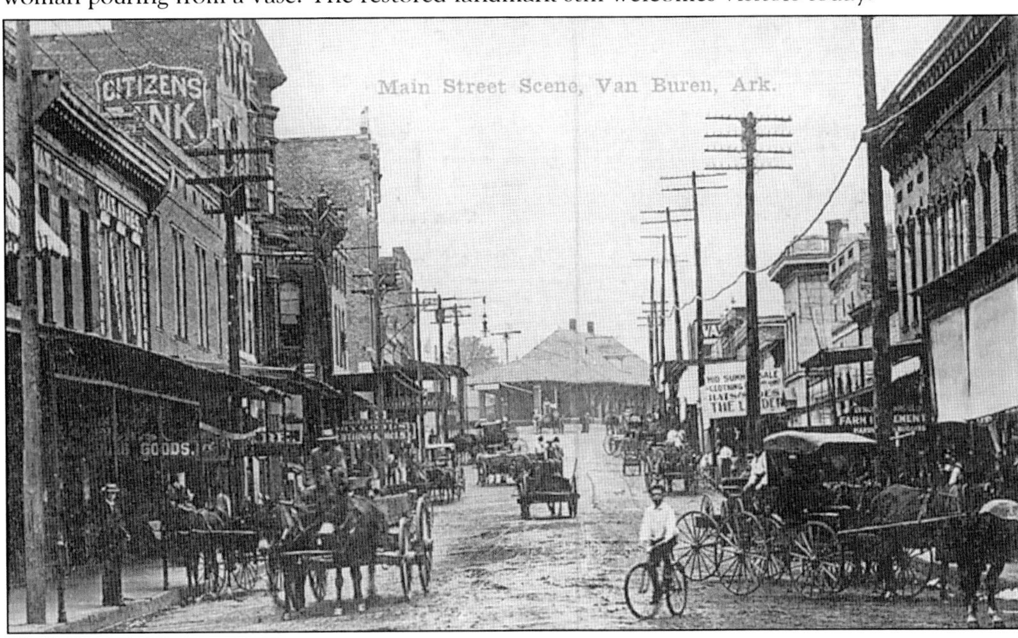

"Greetings from this burg" were the words on the back of a view of the historic Main Street of Van Buren. First settled around 1818 as Phillip's Landing, the new town that grew up on a steamboat landing soon became Van Buren, named for President Martin Van Buren. Today, along and near six blocks of Main Street, are some 70 structures listed on the National Register of Historic Places. In this c. 1900 view, the photographer clicked his shutter while standing in the middle of the street, looking toward the Frisco Railroad Depot. The scene captures a bustling business district advertising mid-summer sales, with one fixated boy on a bicycle.

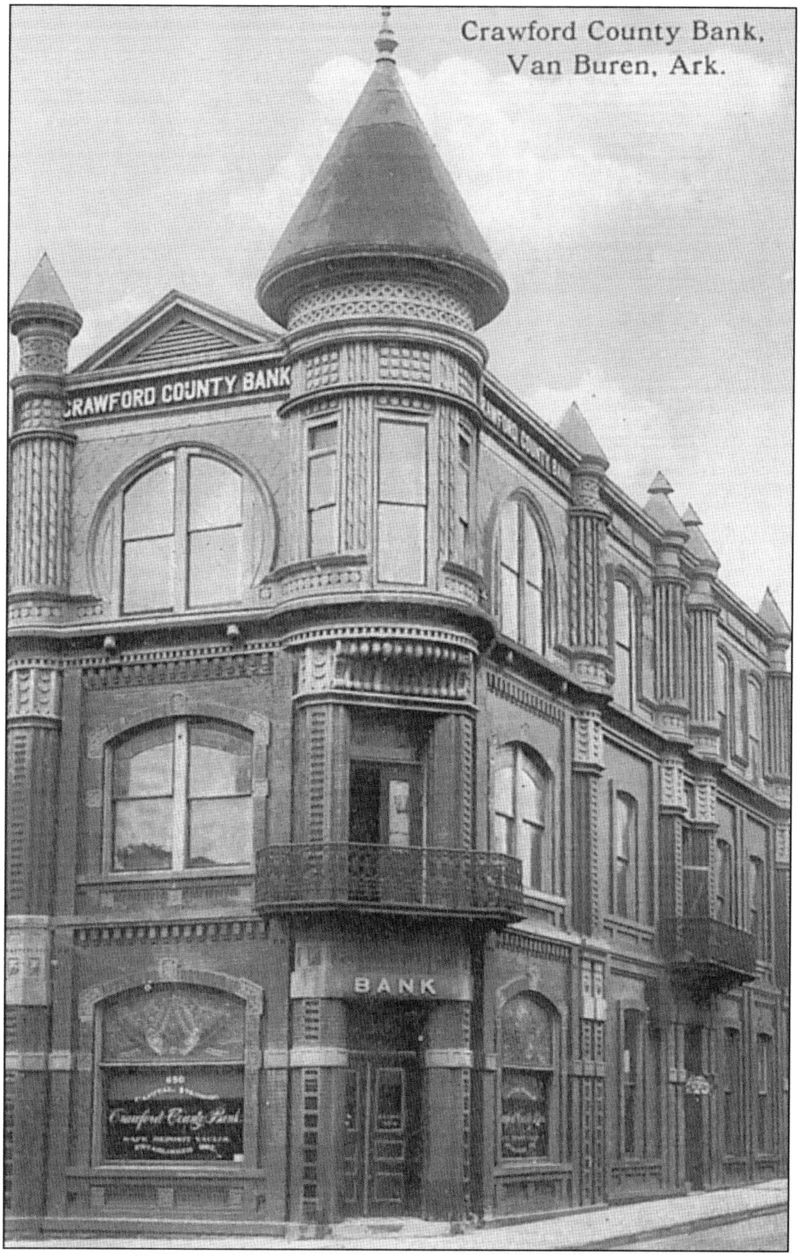

What is almost certainly modern Van Buren's most striking building, the Crawford County Bank building was erected in 1889 at 633 Main Street. The town's first bank made an intended, formidable impression with its marble mantles and lavatories and even electric lights. A dance hall flourished on the third floor in the 1920s, but it became a site of domestic violence when an angry husband gunned down a man in whose arms he found his wife. According to the Van Buren Advertising and Promotion Commission, this now-restored extravagance may have fueled the rumor that the second floor of the building is haunted by the ghost of the bank's first president. Today, the building is the crown jewel among Main Street's nationally-acclaimed collection of restored late 19th- and early-20th-century buildings and houses both a restaurant and a bed and breakfast.

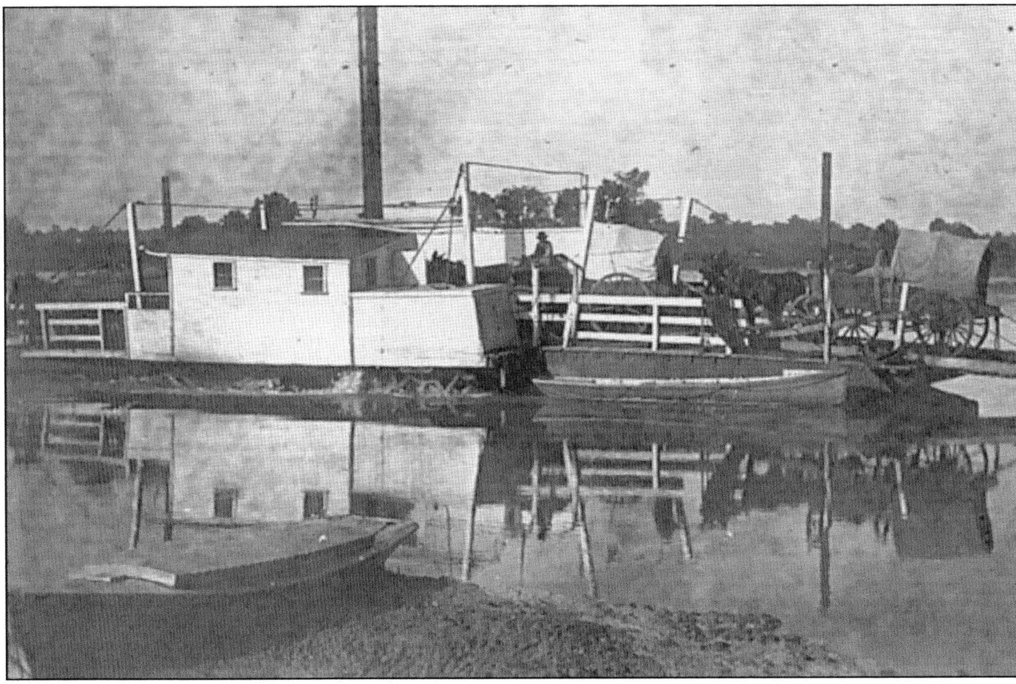

Van Buren came into being and prospered because of its prime location on the Arkansas River, across from the military post of Fort Smith. A variety of river craft docked at Van Buren, among them the ferry shown above, *c.* 1900, taking a covered wagon across the river to Fort Smith or perhaps into the Indian Territory of Oklahoma. The craft was powered by steam, which drove a paddle wheel covered by a large, wooden box seen just to the right of the cabin. Large steamboats also made calls at Van Buren, as evidenced by the image below of the *City of Muskogee*. The banner on the boat reads as follows: "Bound for Oklahoma—Biggest Oil and Gas Field in the World." The postcard was mailed in 1908, less than a year after Oklahoma had been given statehood. The grand boat, *City of Muskogee*, ended its days by serving as a converted dredge for sand and gravel until sometime around the middle of the century.

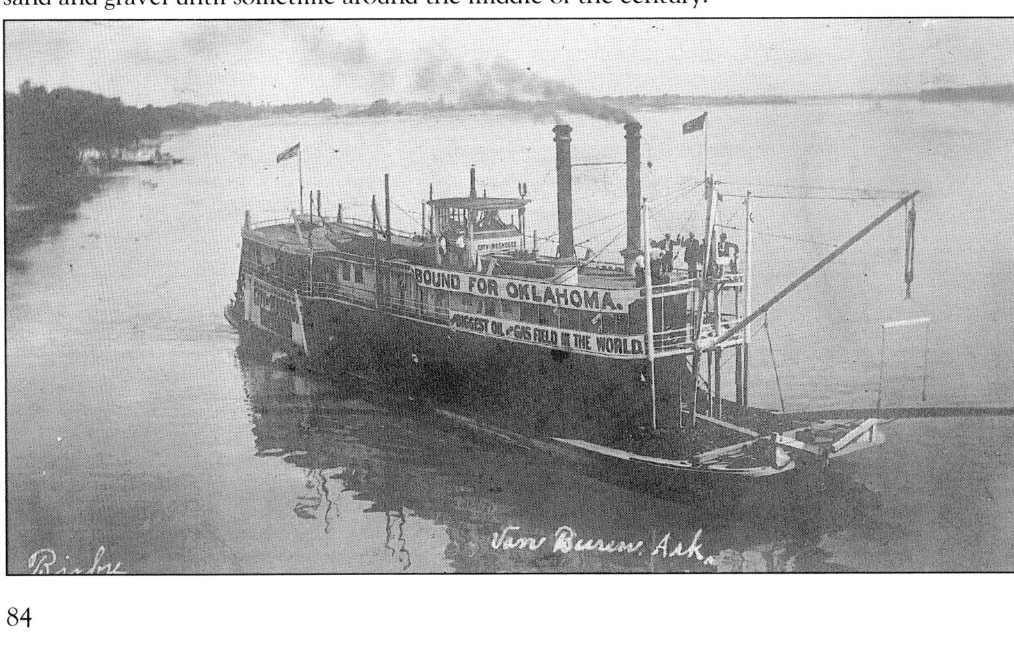

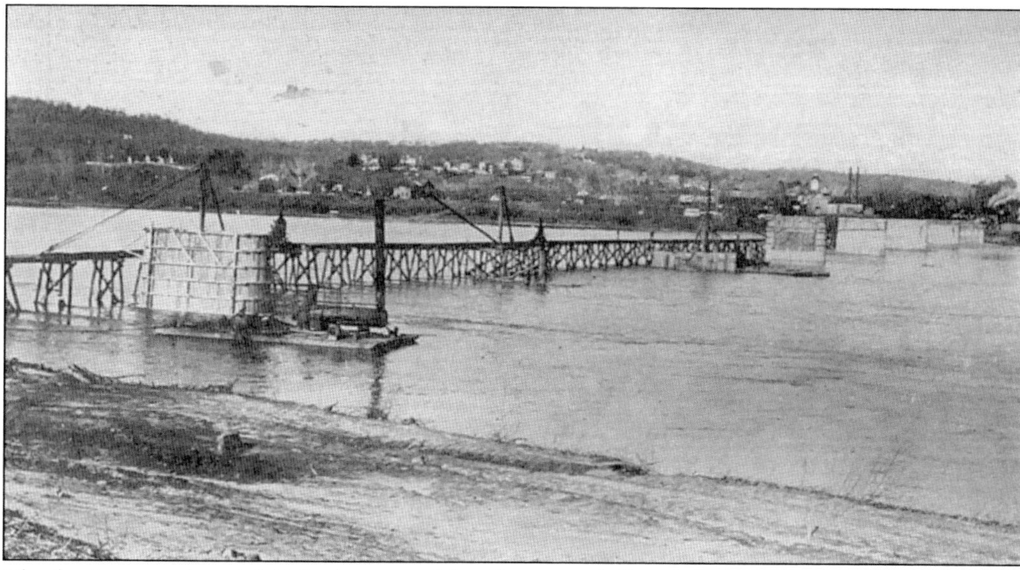

The business and social links between Van Buren and Fort Smith became much stronger in 1911, with the completion of the Van Buren Free Bridge. Under construction in the c. 1910 view above, the bridge featured seven identical spans. Any one of these could be used as a draw span if river traffic or an accident required a particular section to be raised, as seen in the 1912 view below. The multi-purpose bridge allowed two-way trolley car traffic in the center, while on either side of the tracks was space for automobiles, horse-drawn vehicles, and pedestrians. In the lower view are two airplanes that were most likely added by the photographer for greater effect. The writer of this postcard mailed in 1914 penned a tale of playing in a number of baseball games, most recently in nearby Paris and Spadra, apparently for the town of Scranton. The bridge was removed many years ago. A modern highway bridge links Fort Smith and Van Buren today.

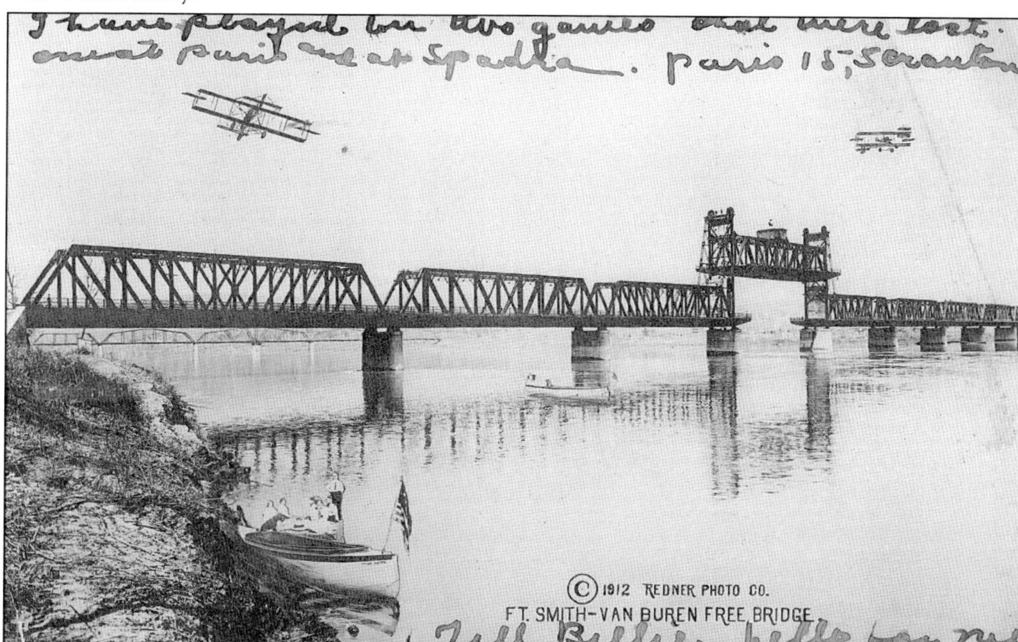

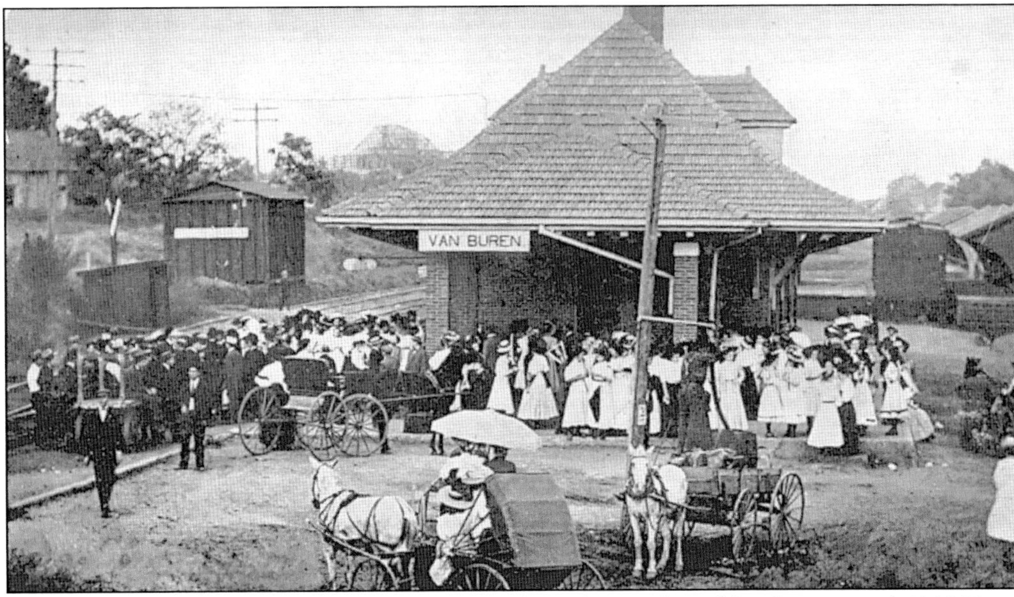

Today, Van Buren's historic district is anchored on the north end by the restored 1909 Frisco Depot, which now houses the Chamber of Commerce. The first train steamed into Van Buren in 1876 and fueled a new boom, in a town heretofore dependent on its status as a river port and stage stop. By 1882, the city was linked with St. Louis, placing the city "in the iron bands of free and uninterrupted commerce," in the words of one newspaper account. In the postcard above, the photographer caught a crowd, perhaps seeing a train off to Fayetteville and the University of Arkansas some 45 miles away. The railroad bridge below was another very welcome development for Van Buren when it was completed in 1907. Prior to that time, trains had to be ferried across the Arkansas River to Fort Smith in order to travel west. In 1908, the writer of the postcard penned this message: "Have been working hard lately, am doing engineering work for Mo. Pacific Ry. They keep me on the road most of the time. Am working between Coffeyville, Kan and Little Rock."

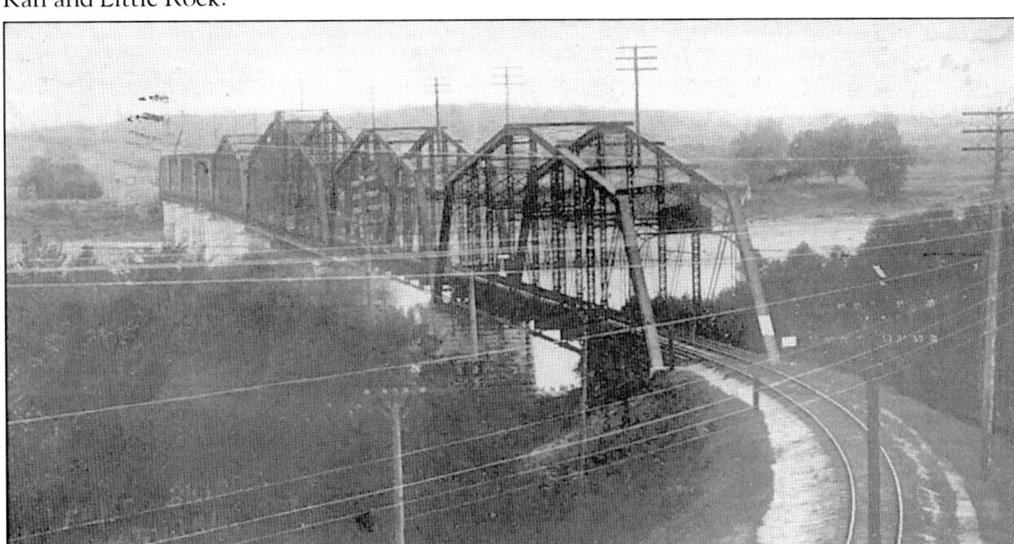

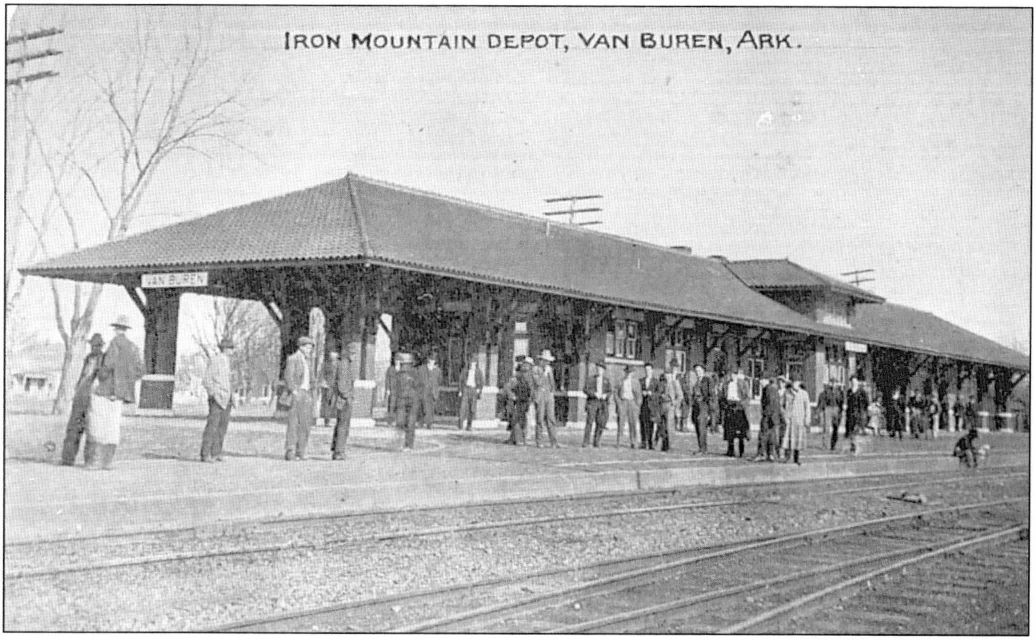

Van Buren was served not only by the Frisco Railroad but also by the St. Louis Iron Mountain & Southern, which became part of the Missouri Pacific Railroad in 1917. The above *c.* 1910 view shows a crowd of men awaiting the arrival of the train on a cold winter day. The depot no longer stands; it was removed a number of years ago. The 1907 view below shows the bustling rail yards of the St. Louis Iron Mountain & Southern that were shared with the Missouri Pacific boxcars. There are at least six steaming locomotives in the photograph, which was likely taken from atop the water tank that served the steam engines pulling in and out of the maze of iron tracks. In the distance is a cotton compress, an important shipping customer of the railroad.

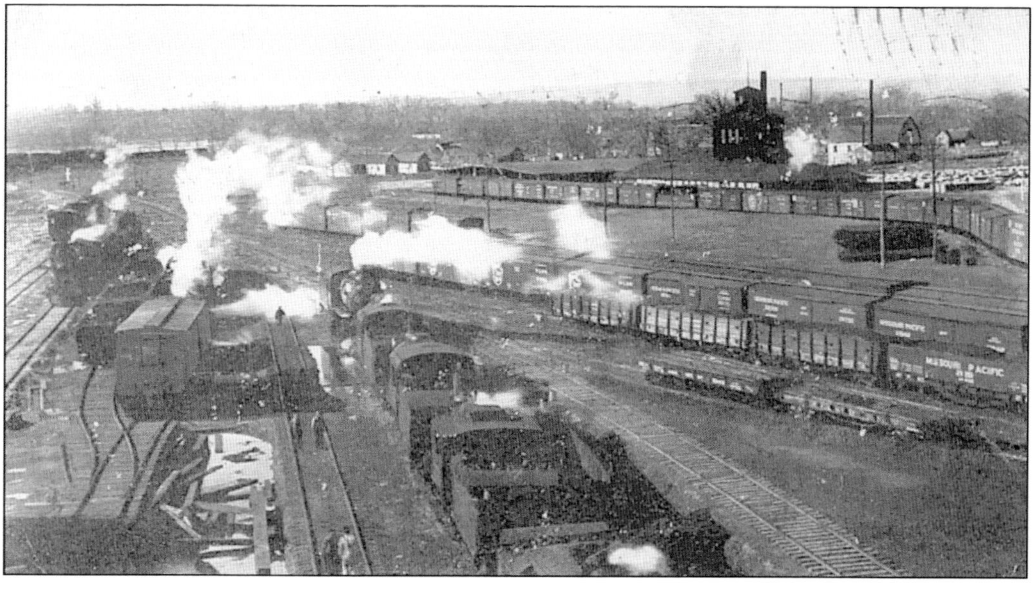

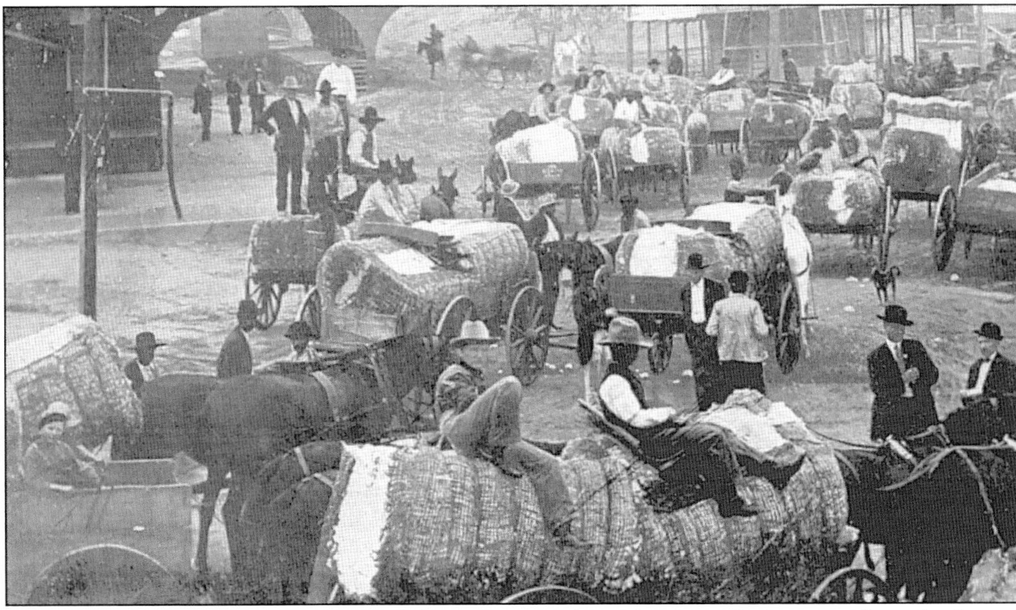

The Frisco Depot served as the backdrop to a number of postcard photographs, which were often views of farmers and their products that helped support the railroad. By 1920, according to the Arkansas Commissioner of Agriculture (a post that no longer exists), 234,000 of Crawford County's 379,000 acres were in use for farming at an average value of $38 per acre. Some 13,000 bales of cotton were produced per year in Crawford County in the years 1910–1919. As seen in this view taken of the front of the depot, much of the cotton came to be shipped on the Frisco, as farmers brought it into town to sell to waiting buyers. The 1908 view of heavy wagon traffic, with the depot to the left, was apparently sent to a collector. Its message reads as follows: "This is not exactly a Rail Road scene, hope it will please you though." In the postcard, a fruit company can be seen occupying the building in the center, while to the right (at the end of Main Street) is John Kohne's Groceries and Dry Goods Store. The store catered to the farmers gathered in the street, hoping to sell them goods in exchange for money they made selling their crops.

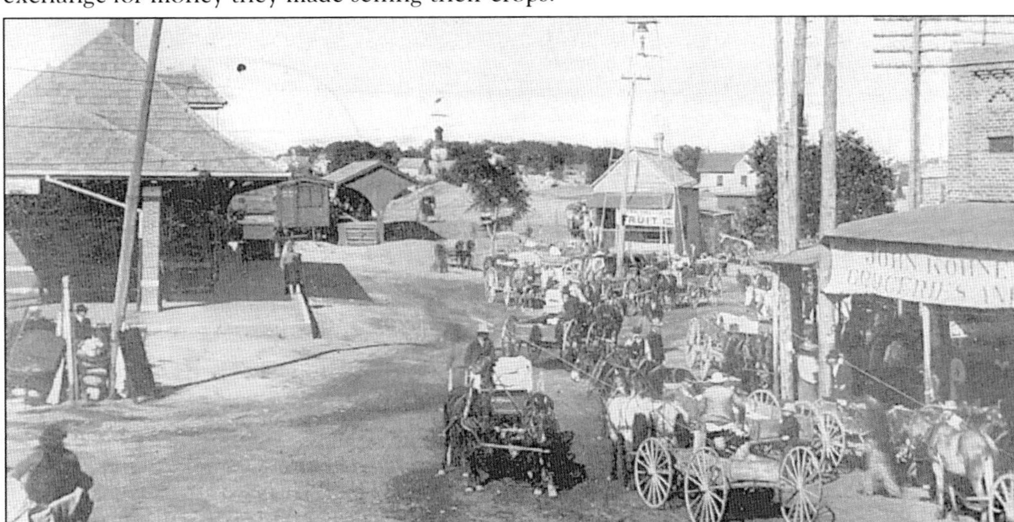

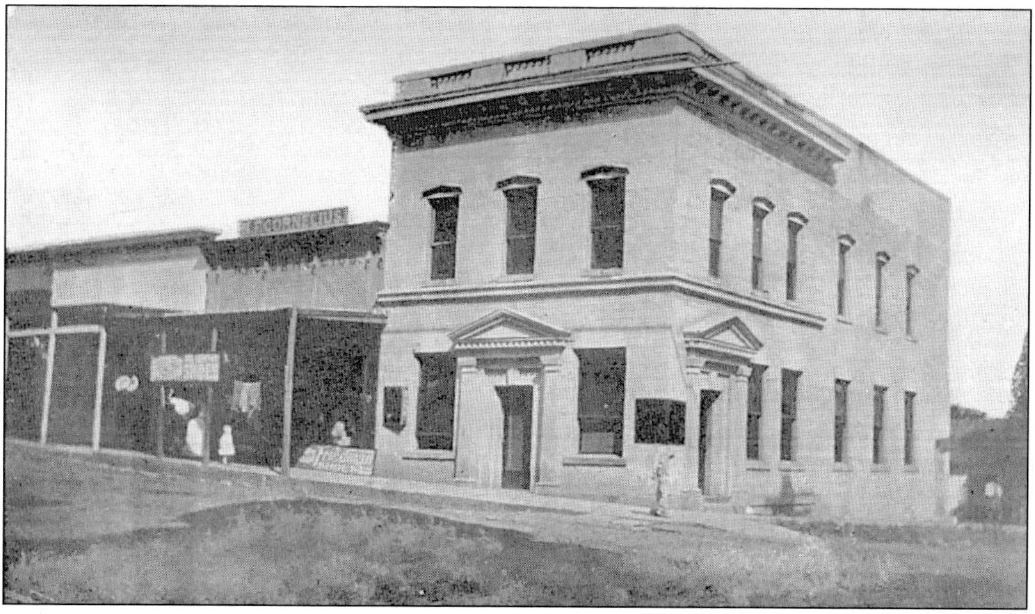

Perhaps some of the Crawford County farmers patronized the First National Bank, for which the building at 702 Main was erected in the 1880s, in the style of that era. The structure was markedly changed in 1905 to the Classical Revival style shown in these two postcards. Another remodeling in the 1990s removed these features from the building. In the 1906 postcard below, the bank building is decorated for what might have been Abraham Lincoln's birthday, as it is his picture that hangs at the top center of the building draped with patriotic bunting. The bank was located just a few blocks from the courthouse, where a stone Confederate soldier still stands sentinel on the lawn. The building presently houses antique and gift shops.

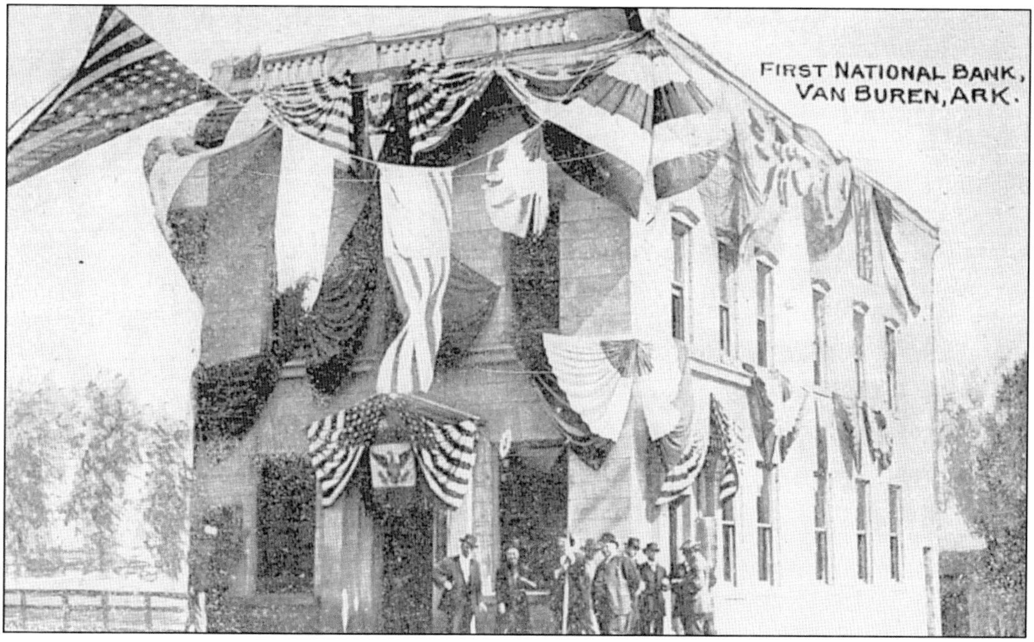

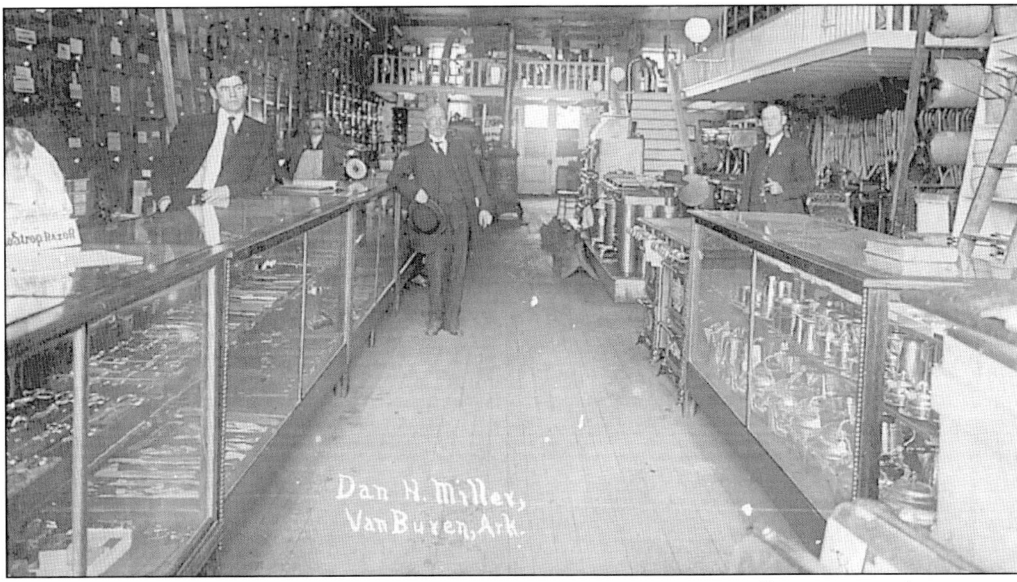

An all-purpose mercantile on Main Street was operated by Dan H. Miller, apparently posing in the center aisle of his store. Among the merchandise displayed in this *c.* 1905 image are Auto Strop Razors (left), new wood cook stoves (center), and a large selection of kettles (in the glass case at right). According to the back of the postcard, Miller's offerings also included, "John Deere plows, harrows, planters, cultivators, McCormack Mowers, International Harvester Hay Presses, Springfield and Fort Smith Wagons, runabouts, buggies, Phaeton Surries, and Farmers' Spring Wagons."

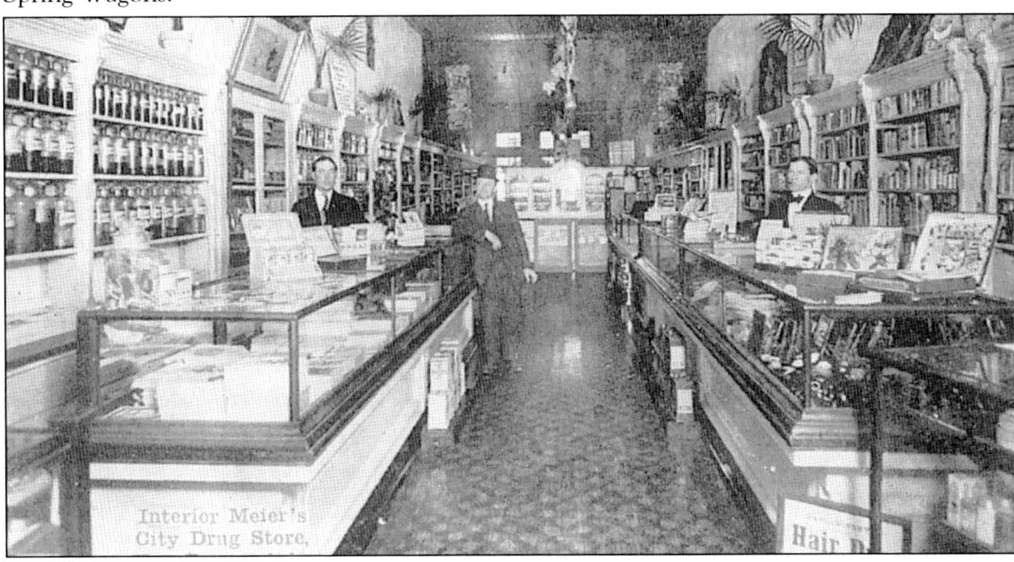

Among the most popular interior subjects for early-20th-century postcards were drug stores, in large part because the stores themselves often had the postcards made and were very often the prime retailers of the postcards. "Doc" Meier was a longtime druggist in Van Buren, and his store on the north side of the 600 block of Main is seen here, *c.* 1910. Likely it is pharmacist Meier himself standing in the center of the narrow aisle, leaning on the glass case containing cigars. The glass jars on the shelves to the left contain the ingredients for compounding drugs, while a display in the right foreground advertises hair dye.

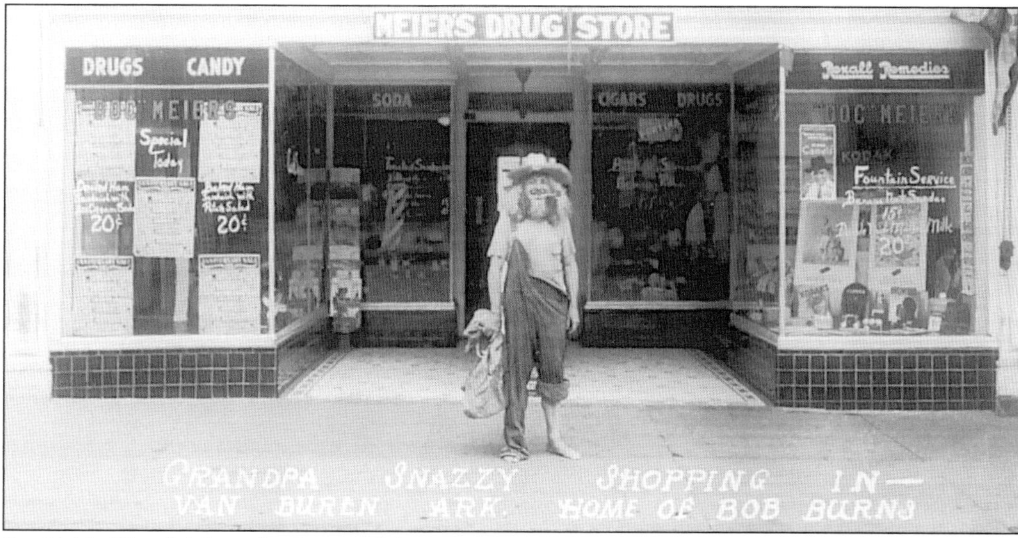

By 1940, "Doc" Meier had moved his store across Main Street and converted it to affiliate with the Rexall Drug Store company. The bearded character standing in front of the store is "Grandpa Snazzy," one of the fictional kinfolk created in the fertile radio humor of Bob Burns, a native of Van Buren who made a career in Hollywood by telling stories of his hometown. A.W. Meier, a.k.a. "Doc," was one of the real people Burns knew growing up in Van Buren, and he incorporated him into his radio humor. The window displays offer Camel cigarettes, ham sandwiches for 20¢, banana nut sundaes for 15¢, and Brownie and Kodak Cameras. Meier's store typified the small town Main Street merchant in an era before shopping centers and massive chain/discount stores forever changed the retail landscape.

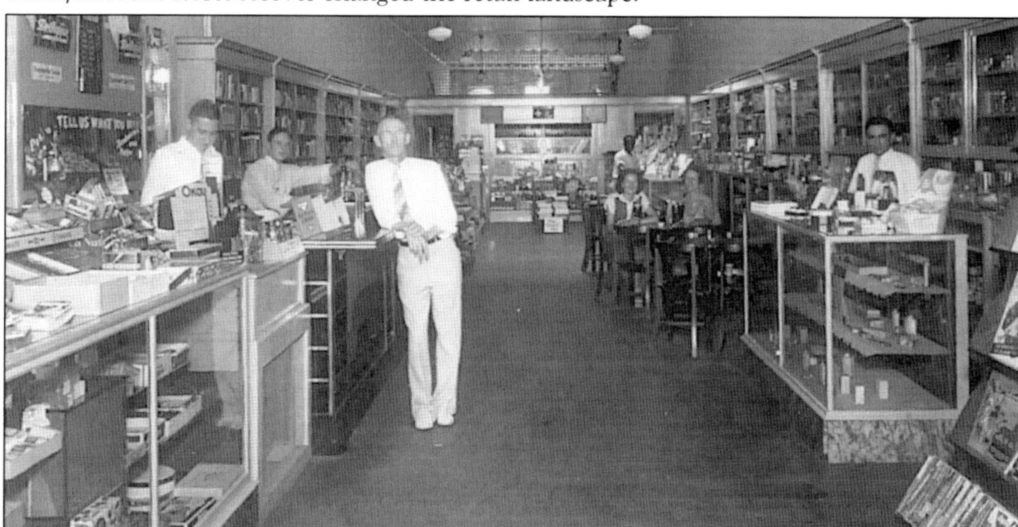

Around 1940, a much older "Doc" Meier seemed to intentionally recreate the pose that he had struck some 30 years before in the postcard seen on the previous page, except here he leans on the soda fountain instead of the cigar case. Smiling diners are seated at tables to the rear, perhaps having taken the employees up on the hand-lettered offer behind the soda fountain which reads, "Tell Us What You Want." To the right is a display of popular magazines, including *Cosmopolitan*, *Western Stories*, and horoscope magazines. Both "Doc" Meier and his business are gone today, but the building still survives.

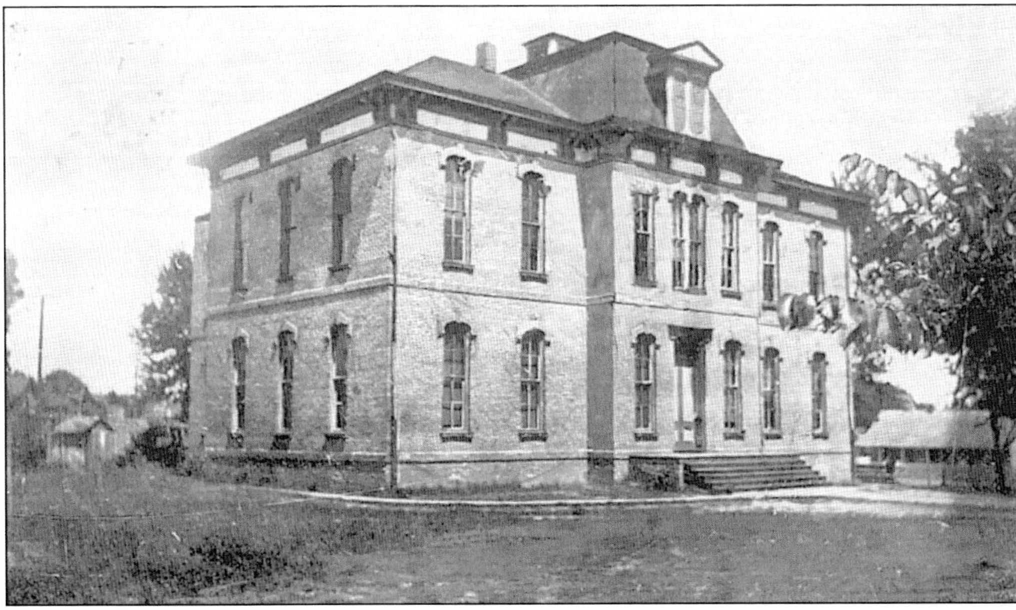

Van Buren's high school was erected *c.* 1900, when the average Arkansas schoolteacher earned $166 for a 69-day school year. The farm chores of the era, mentioned on the back of this postcard, helped keep the school year short. "We arrived all right, Papa was there to meet us, we sure had a cold old ride out, horse and Papa was sick that night. We are going to kill hogs today so you see I will have a cold old job," were the words on this 1909 postcard from a girl named Edna. When a newer high school was later built, this structure became known as the Broadway School. In the postcard below, the Broadway School athletes had won the city track meet in 1923 and were proudly posed in front of the school with their school banner and championship signs.

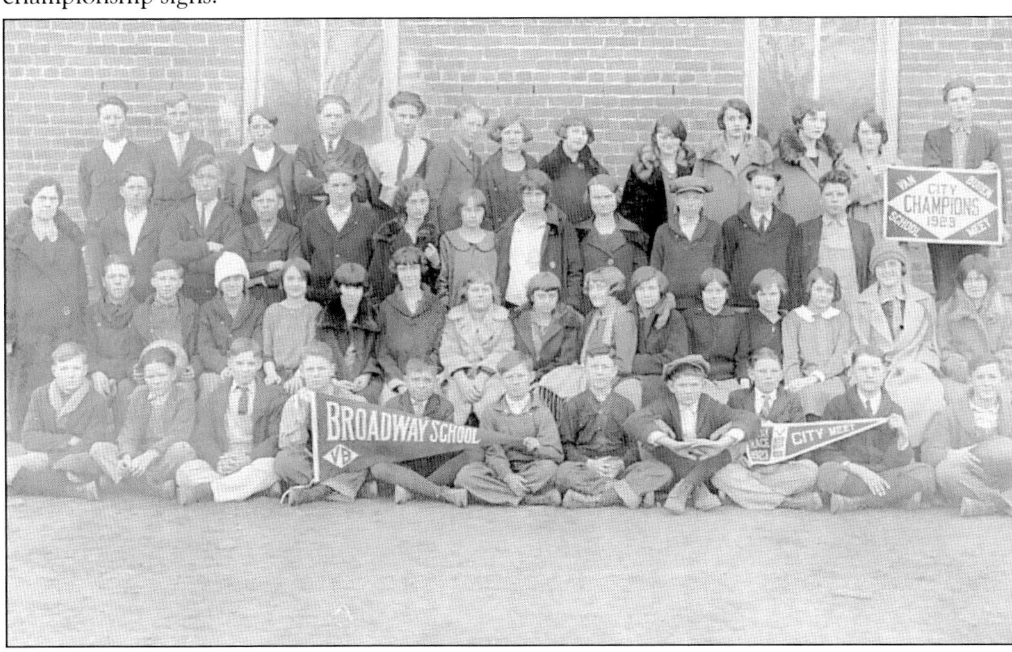

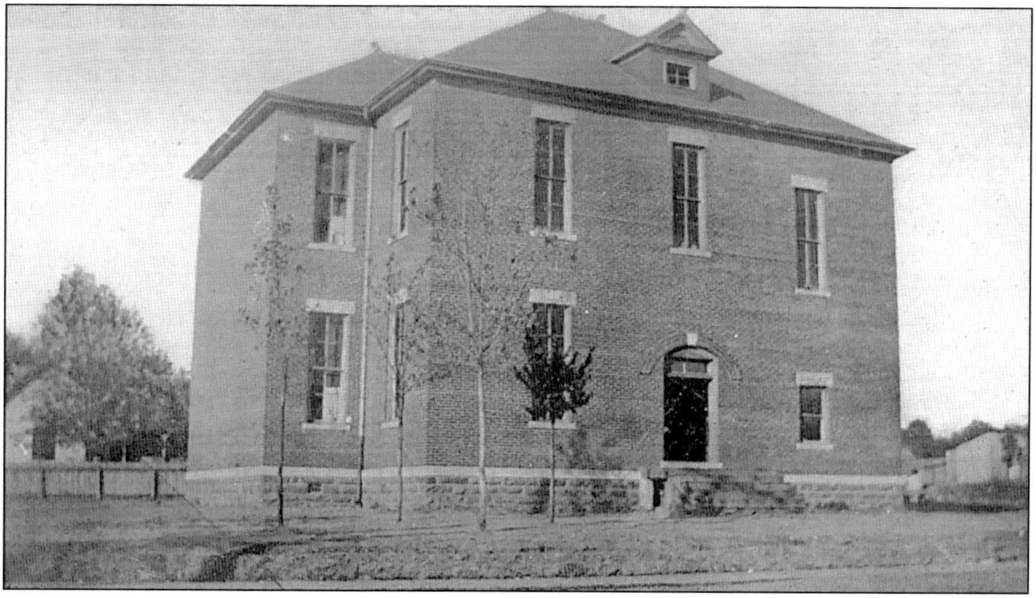

The students of Van Buren who went on to high school, in an era when many did not (compulsory education laws passed in Arkansas in 1909), would have often learned their basic "Three Rs" at Meyers Primary School, located at Thirteenth and Main Streets. The building, seen here *c.* 1905, is gone today, but the site is occupied by Jack's Motor Company.

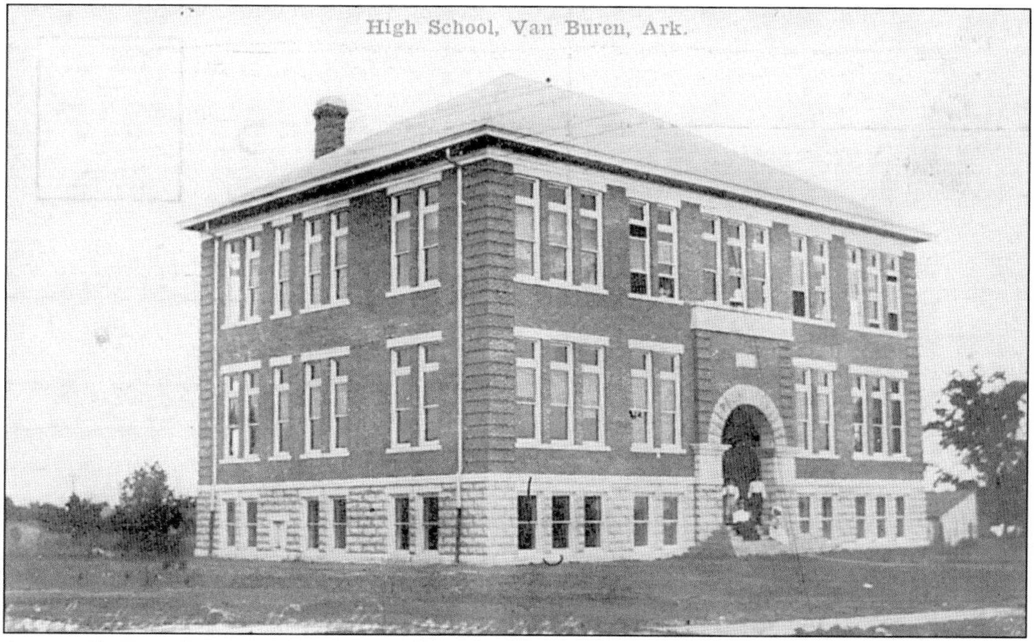

A sign of a first-class community was often its commitment to education, evident in Van Buren's erection of a new high school *c.* 1915, updating the one seen on the previous page. At that time, the state was spending approximately $15 per year, per child, to support the education of some 450,000 children, scattered throughout an incredible 5,000 independent Arkansas school districts. The building seen here served into the 1940s. The building is gone today, and the site is occupied by the Van Buren City Hall complex.

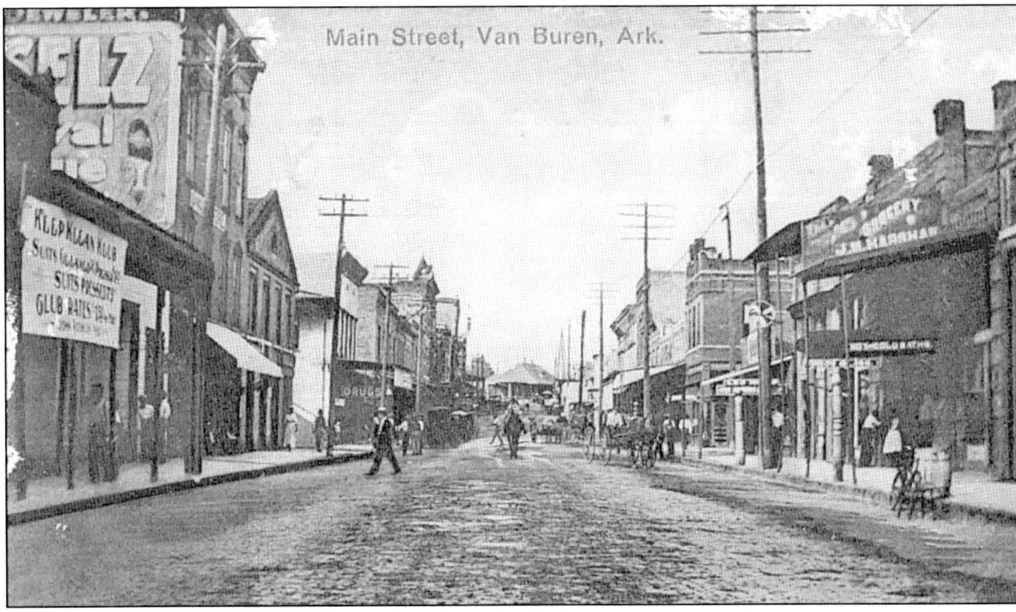

The local businessmen of means might have had their suits cleaned and pressed at the "Keep Klean Klub," which advertised on the banner to the left of this 1905 Main Street view. The Frisco Depot is seen in the distance, across the street from J.M. Harshaw's Grocery, one of several small grocery stores in the downtown area at the time. The grocery stands in stark contrast to today's large supermarkets.

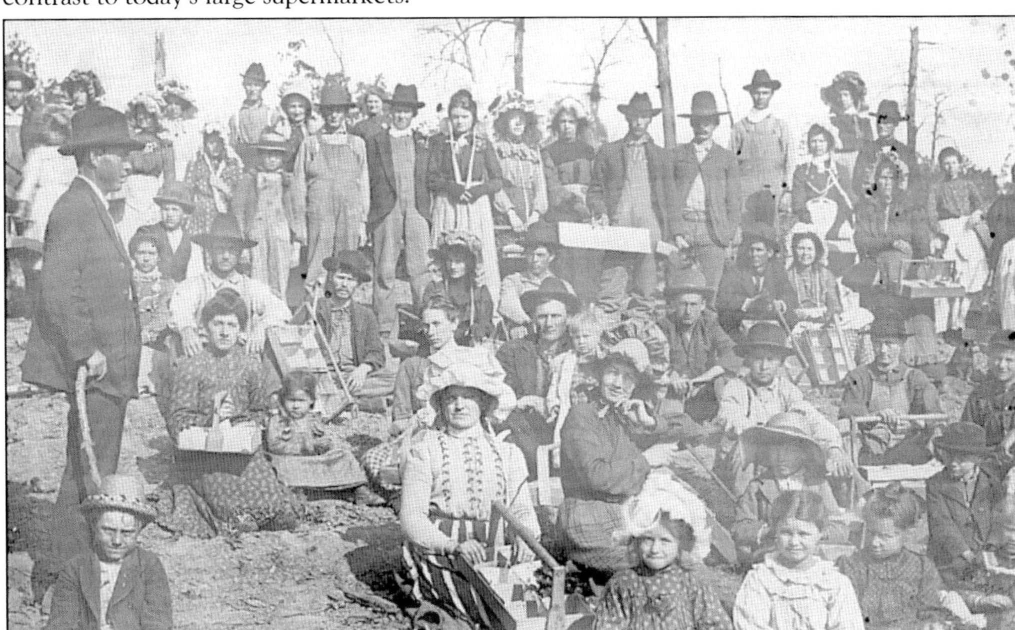

The small grocery stores of Van Buren might well have offered the product of these workers when in season. Mostly women and children were photographed preparing to pick strawberries outside of Van Buren in this *c.* 1908 postcard. For a few years, the area was known as the "Strawberry Capital of Arkansas" and shipments traveled by rail to destinations far beyond Van Buren.

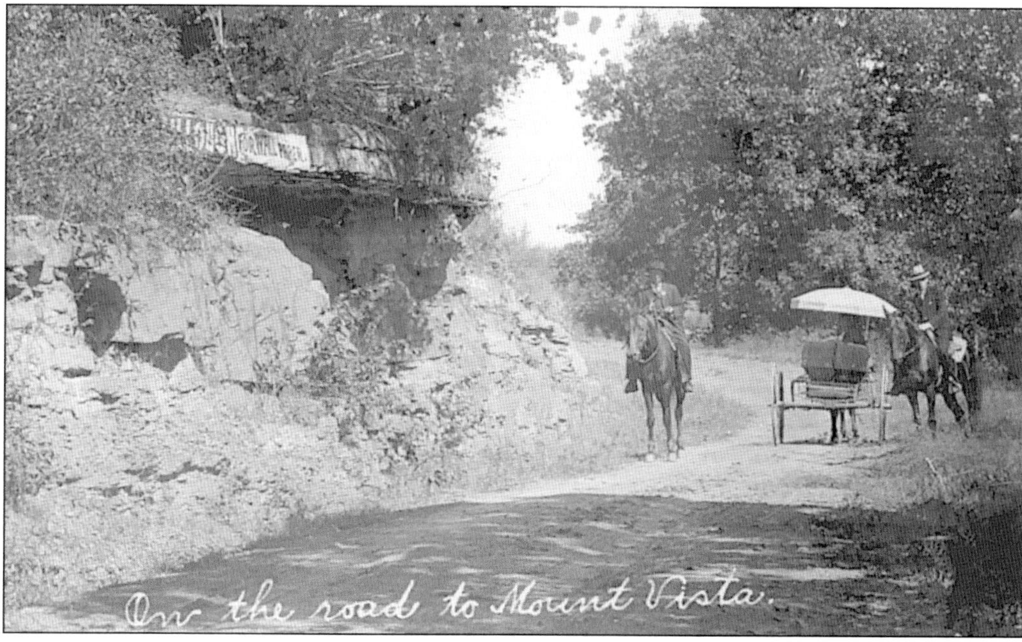

The scenic countryside on the outskirts of Van Buren provides a convenient escape for outings and a break from daily labors. As seen in the above photograph, a winding dirt wagon road led up to Mount Vista. The sender of this postcard wrote this message in 1908: "Mt. Vista is our new summer resort just a mile from town, very high and fine view. We are paving Main Street, I have just finished cleaning house." Note the advertisement for wallpaper painted on the rock ledge (to the left) and the umbrella shading the occupant of the buggy. On the 1910 postcard below is a view of the large pavilion at the summit of Mt. Vista. Its sender comments, "My hubby has been away all winter, he has a government job." Today, Mount Vista (which was hard hit by a tornado in 1996) is the site of an upscale residential area with homes overlooking the Arkansas River.

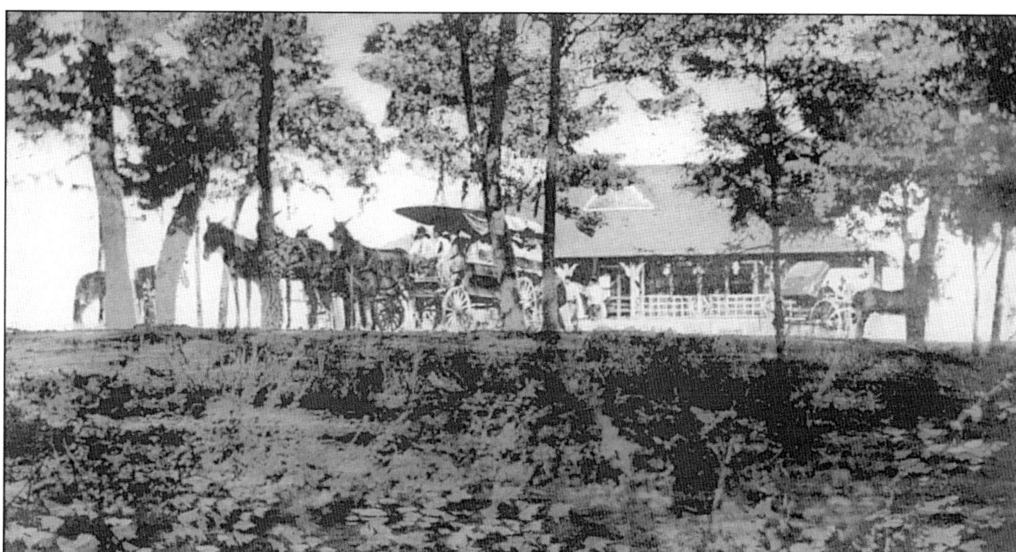

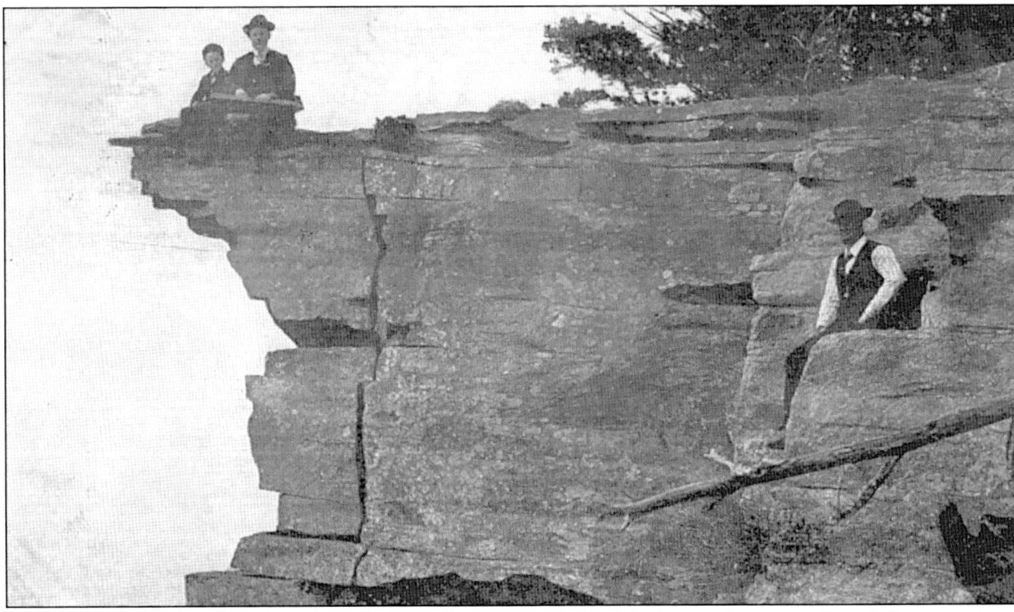

A favorite picnic spot just outside Van Buren was this bluff overlooking the Arkansas River with its precarious perch but stunning view. The postcard was mailed by a young man from Van Buren named Billy, who sent it across the river to Miss Hazel Livingston of Fort Smith. His words suggest perhaps an unwelcome courtship: "Hello Hazel, i thought i would sind you a nother view well dear have you got rested yet you said you was tyrred of me when you resed i will come to see you." It is signed "love Billy," but then Billy marked through the word "love."

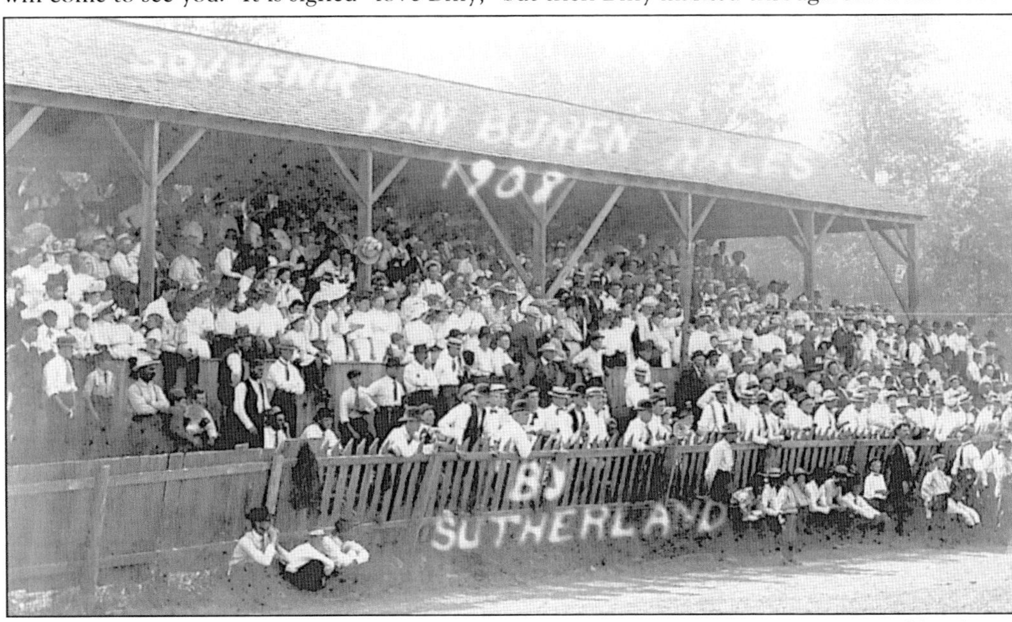

Among other diversions for spare time in Van Buren was a trip to Blakemore Field, where a packed grandstand could watch a variety of events. Apparently, this 1908 crowd is enjoying a horse race. Several of the women in the crowd appear to be studying programs of some sort, and almost all seem focused on whatever is out of the photographer's lens to the right. Today, the stadium site is occupied by Consolidated Printing at 1712 E. Main Street.

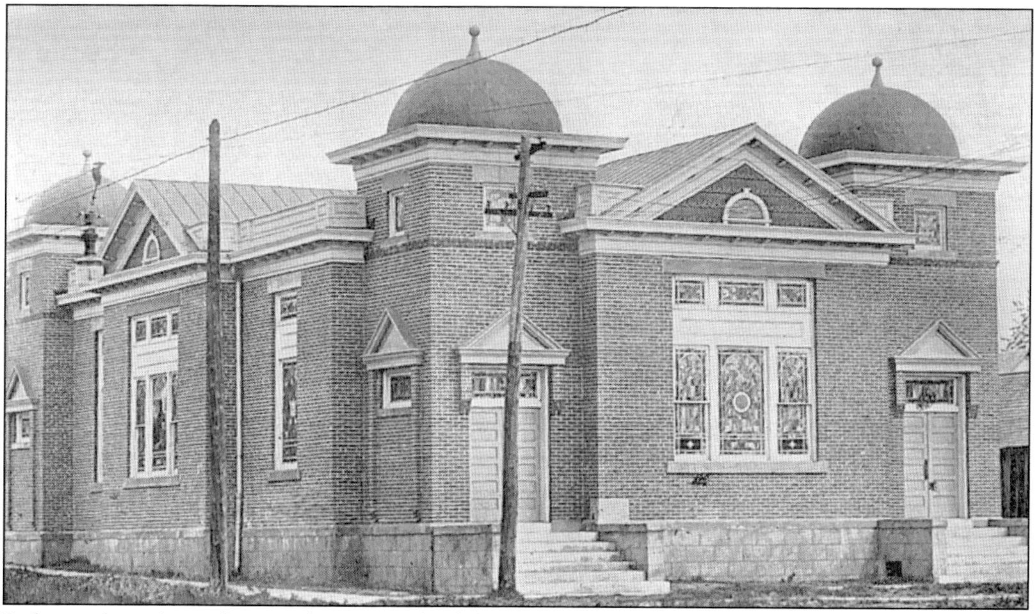

Religion has always been a fixture in the life of small-town Arkansas, and almost no town was without at least one Baptist church. The Baptist faith arrived in Arkansas with missionaries in 1817 and became the most prominent denomination throughout most of the state. Van Buren's Baptist church was erected at Eleventh and East Main Streets around the turn of the century. Having been added onto over the years, the church still stands and is in use today.

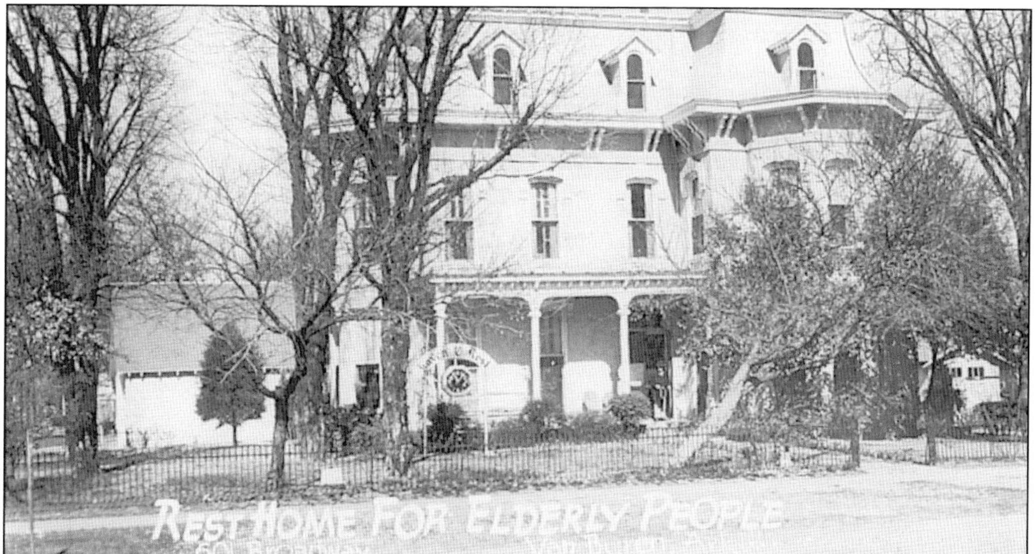

Although Van Buren had no hospital until later in the century, it did boast an early version of what today might be considered a nursing home. The "Rest Home for Elderly People" was housed in this Victorian mansion at 601 Broadway. The sign in the yard (lower center) of this c. 1920 view bears the phrase "Haven of Rest," beneath which a clock records the time as 11:05. The private enterprise would have cared for the homeless and frail elderly of modest means, in an era before government-financed social programs gave rise to Arkansas's for-profit nursing home industry of today. The home is long gone, having been replaced by a strip shopping mall.

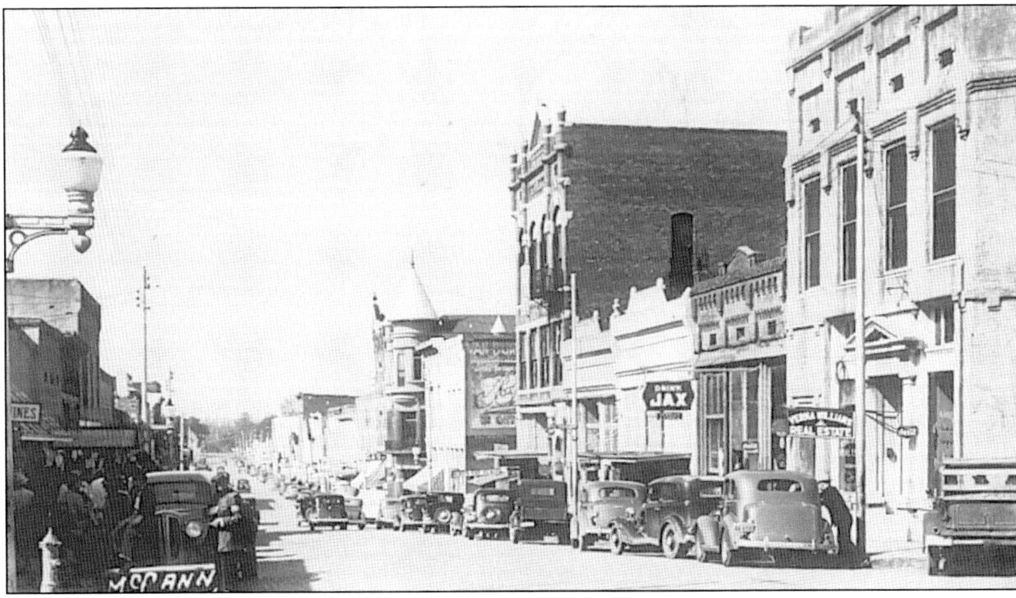

In the 1940s, the war-time economic boom, which was felt most at bustling Fort Smith across the Arkansas River, also boosted Van Buren's business community. The above postcard, mailed in 1942, shows Main Street beginning with the former First National Bank building (right) and extending down past the towered Crawford County Bank in the distance. Today, these blocks are some of the best restored and preserved Victorian Streets to be found in middle America. The wartime message from Private Meade Robinson reads as follows: "They have put us together by platoons, had nice box of Buszath's candy from the Cahills, I sure love chocolates." Seen below in the 1940s is the 600 block of Main Street, anchored by the 1905 Citizens Bank building on the corner, while farther down the block is the Jeryo-Delzell Drug Company (formerly Doc Meier's Drug), and the Rio Theater. Today, this block of buildings stands restored, with a number of new occupants.

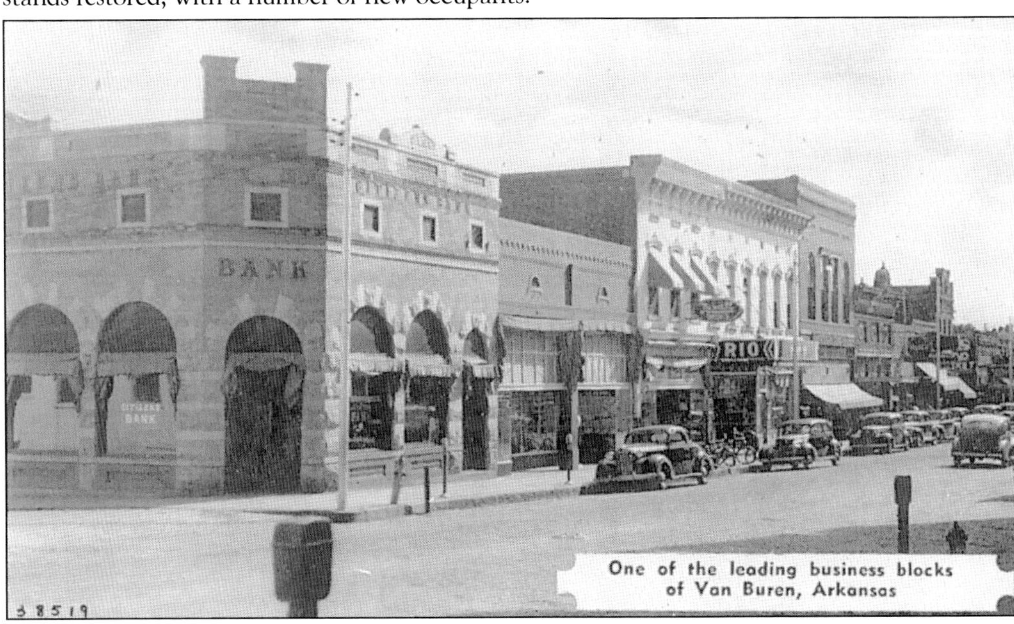

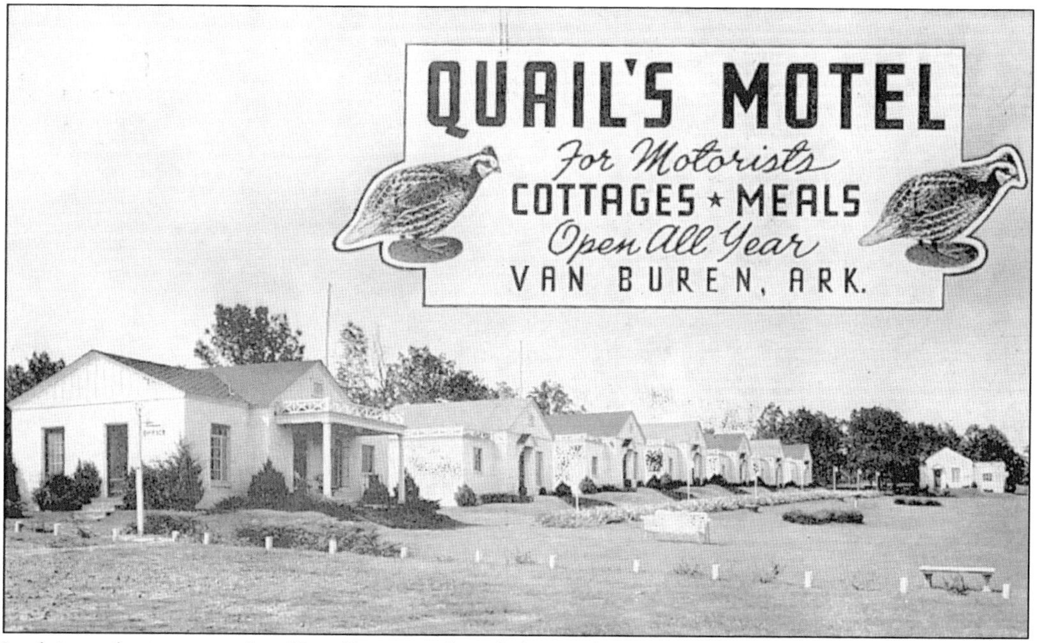

Lodging choices on the Van Buren side of the Arkansas River were much more limited than in Fort Smith. Beginning in the 1930s, Quail's Cottages on Oak Lane offered travelers accommodations in whitewashed brick cottages like the ones seen here. The motel, located on old Highway 71, offered meals at the popular Blue Dragon Tea Room, which adjoined the office shown below. The 1939 postcard's message reads as follows: "If you go to Texas by car be sure to stop here—they have such attractive cottages. We enjoyed it so much. A mockingbird's giving a concert outside our window now." Although no longer operated as a motel, the cabins are still standing today and are rented out as apartments.

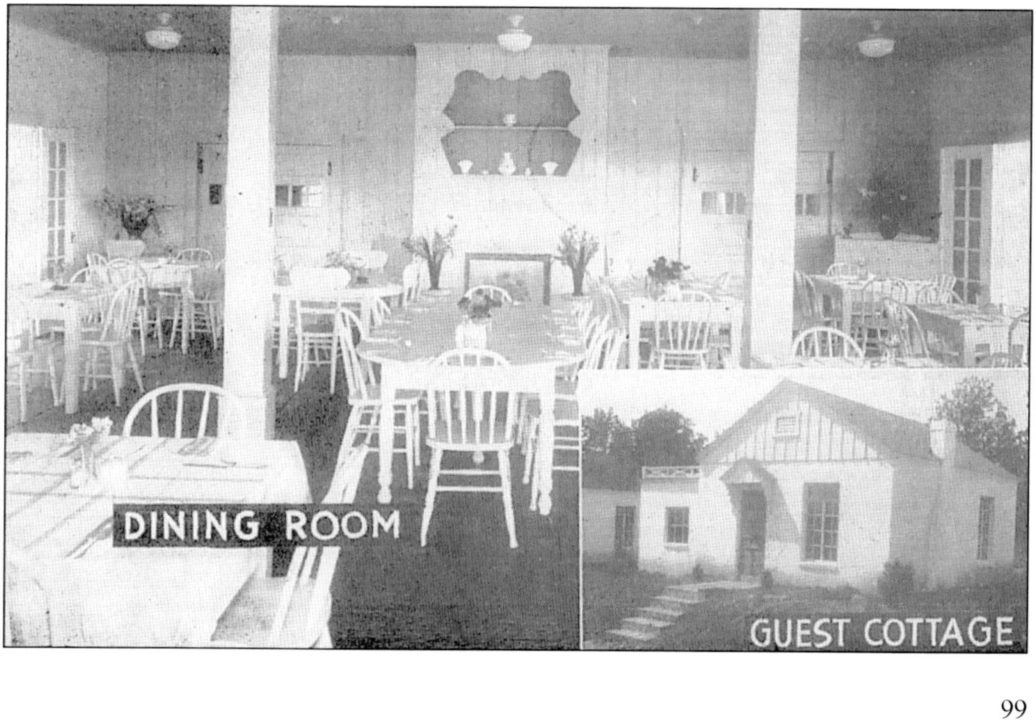

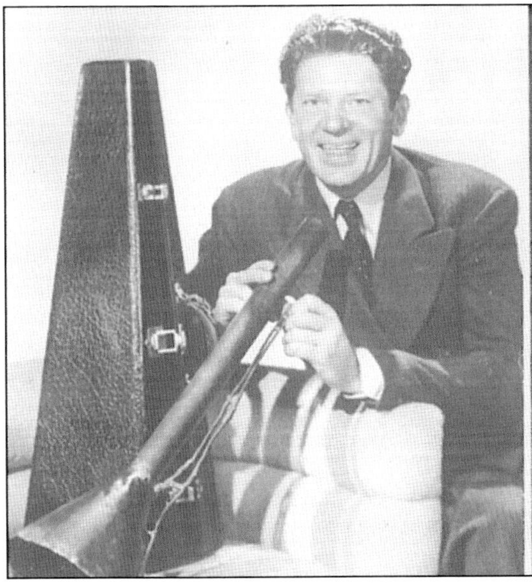

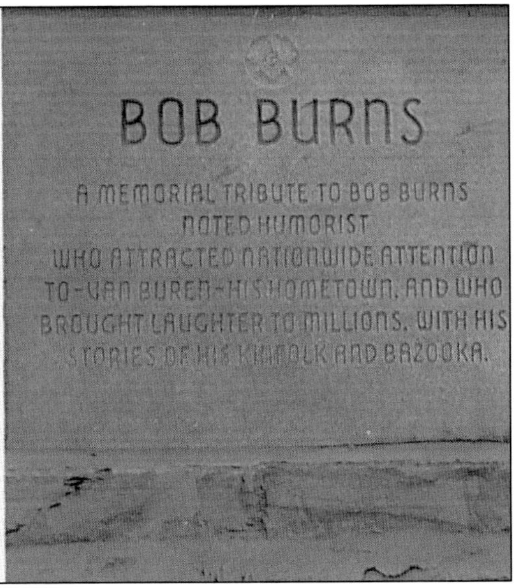

Bob Burns is likely the most well-known person ever to come out of Van Buren. A popular radio and movie comedian in the 1930s and 40s, Burns told jokes about his mythical relatives back home in Crawford County, where he was born in 1890. Burns, the son of a well-to-do but eccentric family, was forced to wear a dress until he was almost five. He taught himself to play the piano, mandolin, harmonica, trombone, violin, cornet, and guitar. He also played a homemade musical instrument that he dubbed a "bazooka" (from "bazoo" meaning a windy fellow). Fashioned from several pieces of gas pipe and a whiskey funnel, it was described by one listener as sounding "something like a wounded moose." During WW II, GIs nicknamed the army's new shoulder-held rocket launcher the "bazooka" because its appearance resembled that of Burns's unique horn. The memorial seen on the postcard above was erected in Van Buren after the native son's death in 1956. The postcard below was mailed to Indiana in 1936, with this message written on the back: "We saw Bob's town yesterday. It is plenty hot here."

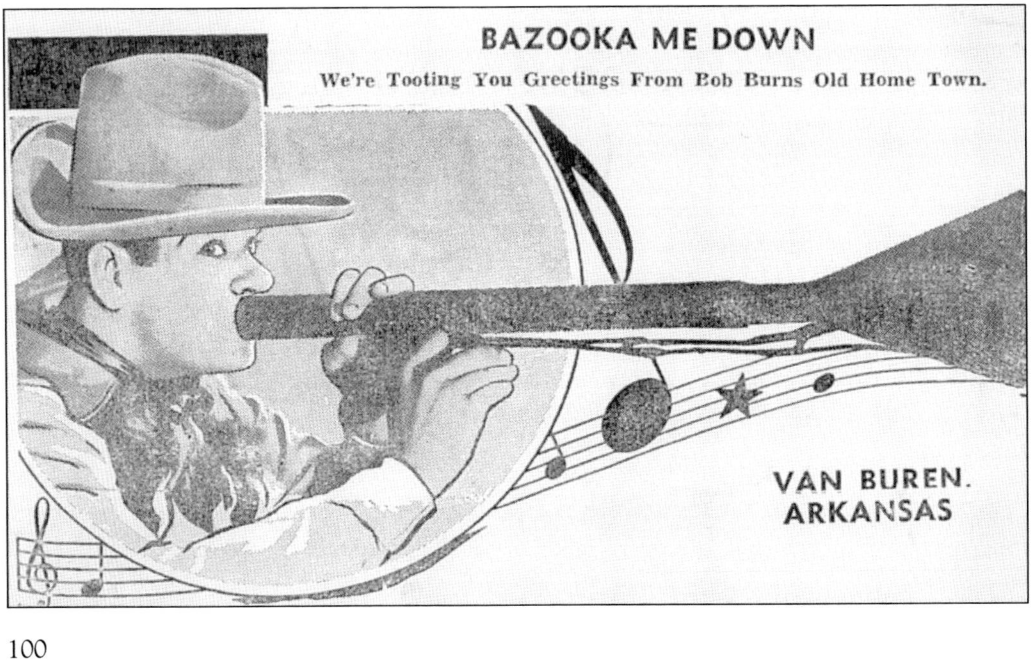

A PRIVATE FROM WILLIAMSVILLE* SAYS:

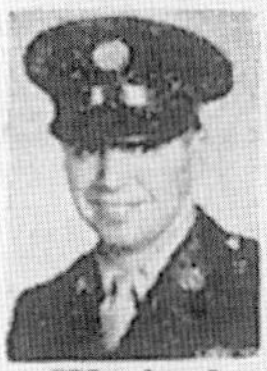

On Sunday afternoon, March 14, 1943, my pal and I went to Van Buren to visit Bob Burns' famous home. (See picture at right.)

We had a swell time there and saw many things of interest.

Van Buren, a nice little town of approximately 5000 people (which is about 2000 more people than we have back home in Williamsville), is only a few miles from Fort Smith. Our camp is near both places.

Pvt. Eugene B. Zielen
*N. Y.] *Camp Chaffee, Ark.*

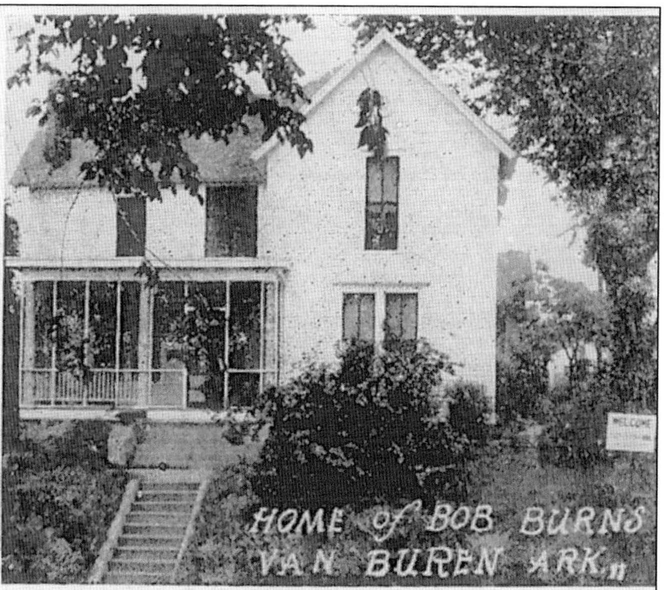

The pride and publicity value Van Buren found in its ties with Bob Burns were evident in the postcards his fame generated. Burns's boyhood home became a tourist attraction during the years of his radio and movie popularity, at the height of which his stepmother, Kate Burns, quit teaching school in order to give tours of the home. The sign on the tree in the yard shown above proclaims a welcome and touts the availability of Bob Burns souvenirs. The postcard was mailed in 1940 by Pvt. Eugene Zielen of New York, who visited the home while on a short leave from Camp Chaffee, across the Arkansas River. An enterprising photographer apparently printed postcards of the house with individual soldiers' pictures. Although still standing, the home is no longer open to the public.

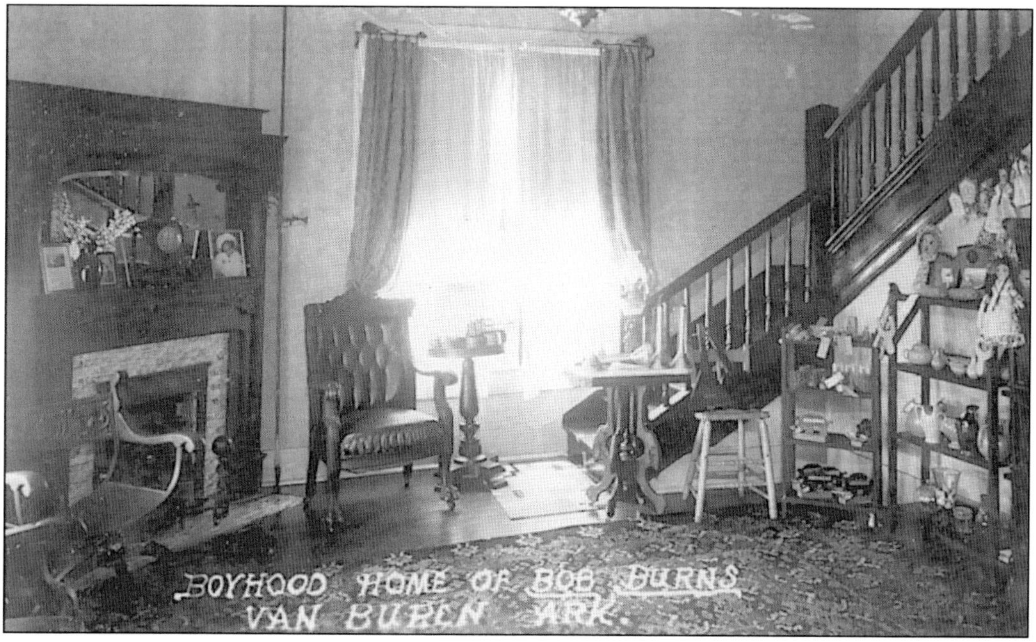

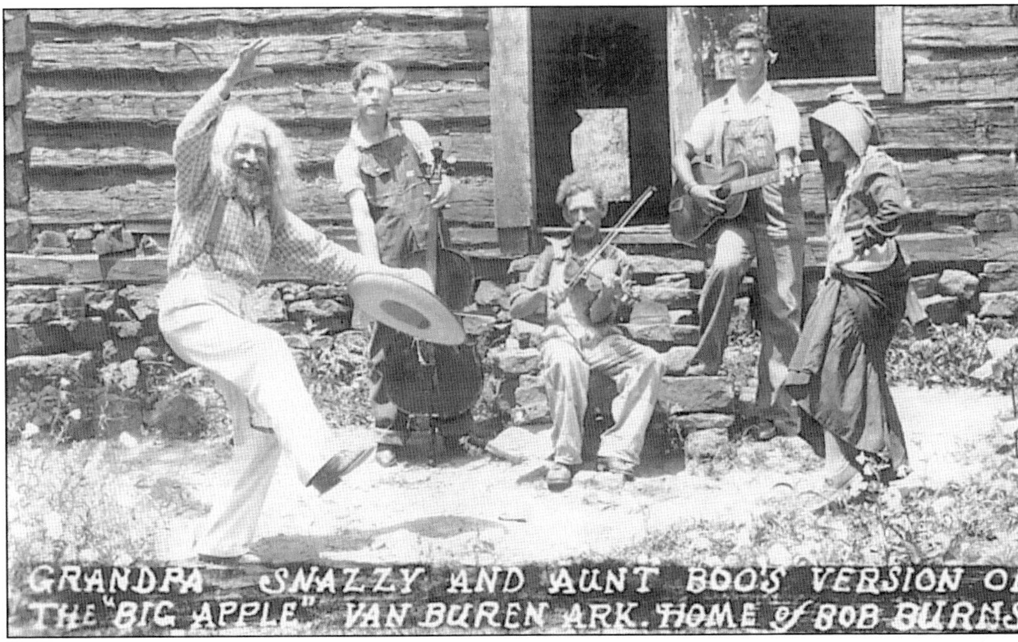

Bob Burns's mythical relatives, as described on his radio programs from New York and Los Angeles, were featured in a popular series of postcards. Responding to critics, Burns insisted that his humor did not offend rural Arkansans. "It is only the city slickers who complain," he asserted. "If the country folks I tell these stories about don't mind, I can't see why the city people want to kick. City folks are the same everywhere. They ain't different enough to be interesting." Images like the one seen above of Grandpa Snazzy and Aunt Boo's version of the "Big Apple" fueled much criticism and rebuttal. Below, two characters are posed in front of the theater renamed for Burns, re-enacting Burns's story in which "Uncle Hink" met "Uncle George" downtown and inquired about his recent doctor's appointment. "Well, you were limping pretty bad when you went to the doctor last week, George. What did the doctor say?" "The doctor said he would have me walking around in a week," replied George. "Was he able to?" asked Hink. "He sure did," responded George. "It's a good thing, too, 'cause I had to sell my car to pay his bill."

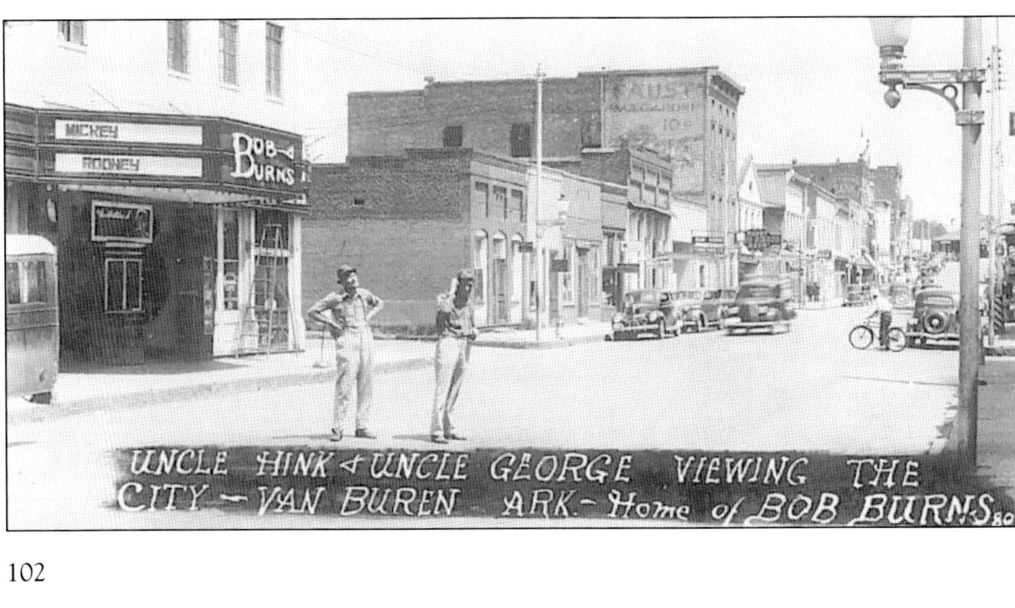

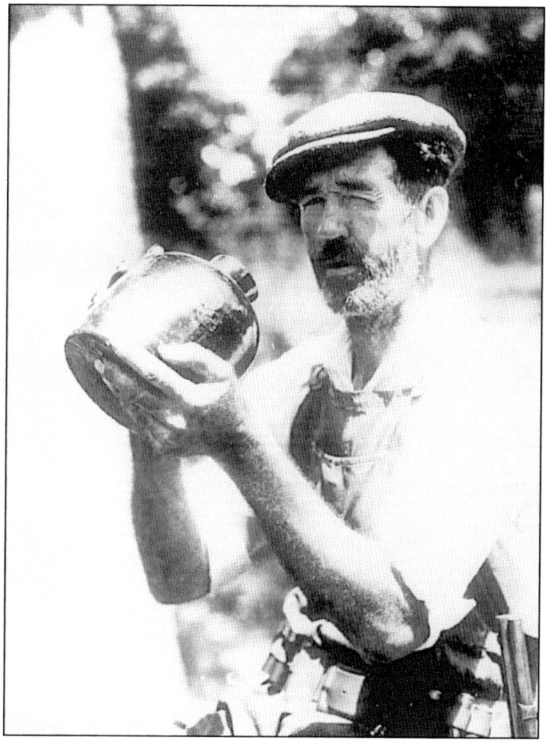

In one of Bob Burns's tales, "Uncle Slug" (so-named for an obvious reason) once went fishing and forgot his bait. Seeing a large snake with a frog in its mouth, Slug thought, "Well, I'll just take the frog and cut him up for bait," but the snake would not let go of the frog. Uncorking his jug, Uncle Slug poured a drink down the serpent's throat, causing it to turn loose of its prey. After catching several fish with the frog as bait, Uncle Slug felt a tap on his lower leg. He looked down, and there was the snake with another frog in its mouth, wanting to trade it for another slug of moonshine. Shown below, the blindfolded version of "Uncle Slug" was apparently related to a Burns tale of moonshine tasting at the Crawford County Fair. (Postcards *c.* 1940.)

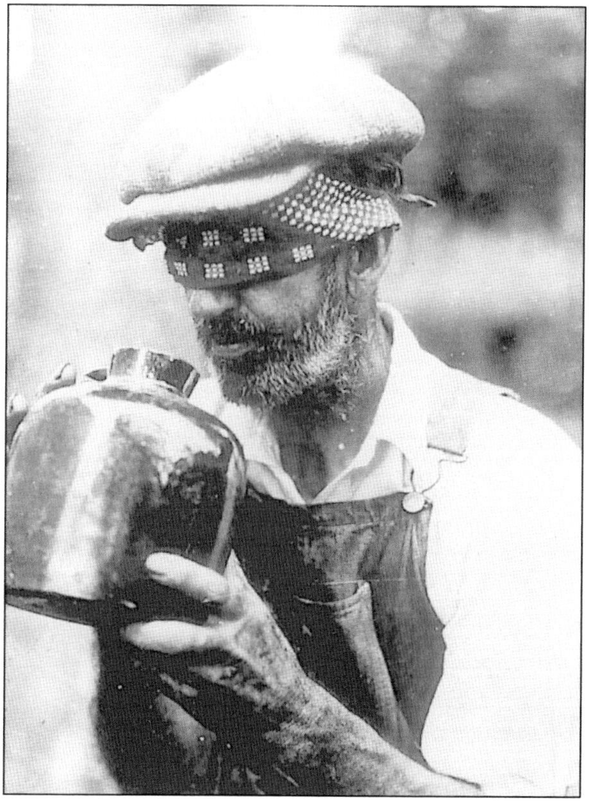

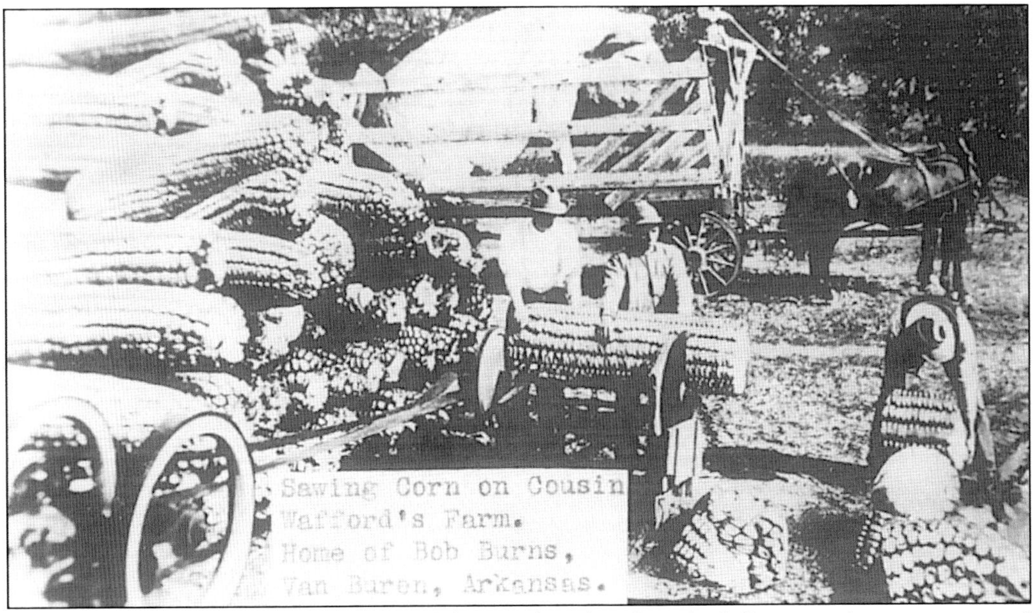

Bob Burns often joked about the size of the produce his Crawford County relatives grew, and this postcard capitalized on that exaggeration. Above, "Cousin Wafford" has produced some giant corn that required a crosscut saw to process. Behind them, an elephant-size hog waits in the wagon. The 1939 postcard's message reads as follows: "I had corn on the cob for lunch to-day." These exaggeration-theme postcards were part of a popular series used for postcards of different locations around the country, earlier in the century.

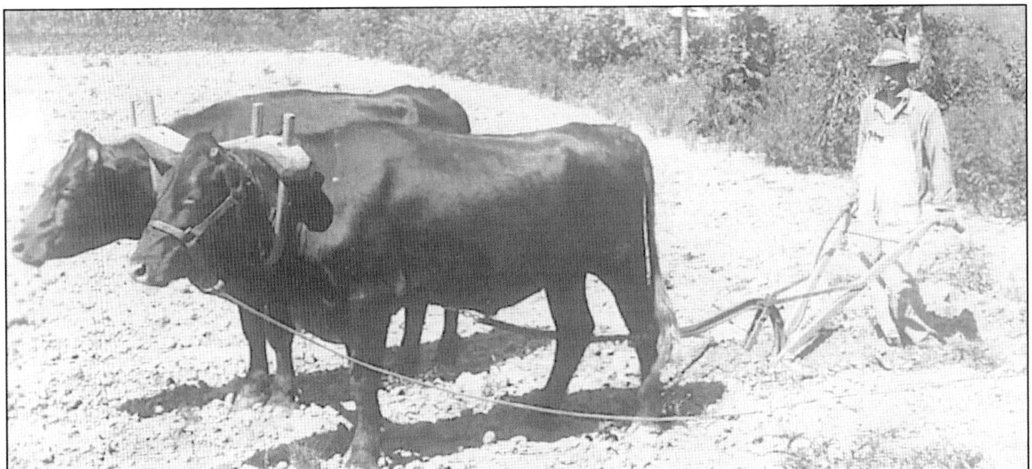

"Uncle Uni," seen here plowing a field for "Cousin Wafford," was the subject of another Bob Burns story in which a city slicker was driving down a country road and passed the home of Uncle Uni, who was sitting on his front porch. Thinking he could have a little fun with the hillbilly, the driver stopped the car and inquired, "Hey, Mister, can you change an $18 bill?" "Sure thing," responded Uncle Uni, who went inside to get his wallet. The city slicker took out a $10 bill, and using a pen, marked the zeros to look like eights. Returning, Uncle Uni took the bill without a glance. "Now," he asked, "how do you want your change? Two nines, or three sixes?"

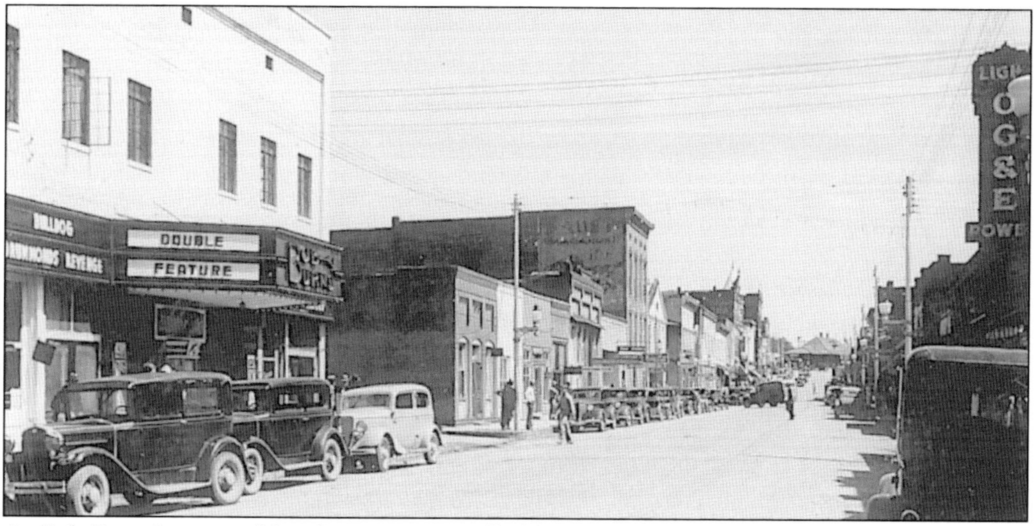

As Bob Burns's successful radio career propelled him into movies, the former Victory Theater was renamed for him. The film playing here was *Bulldog Drummond's Revenge*, a murder mystery about a former British army officer turned detective, starring John Barrymore. The theater, originally built in 1891, is today restored under its original name, the King Opera House. Among the entertainers and personalities who have appeared on its stage are William Jennings Bryant and Jenny Lind. In the rich lore of the opera house is a tale that the stage is haunted by the ghost of a young traveling actor who was shot by his girlfriend's father.

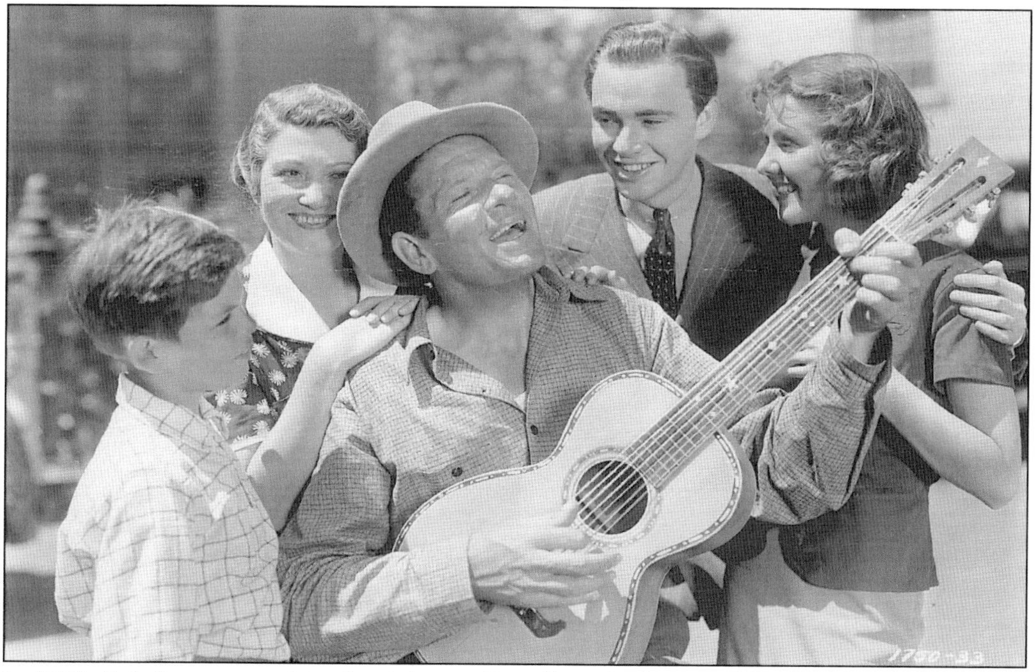

In 1938, Bob Burns starred in the *Arkansas Traveller*, which was publicized by the studio with this scene from the movie. The movie's plot centered on a guitar playing stranger (Burns) who comes to a small town and helps keep the local newspaper afloat, while at the same time playing cupid for the publisher's daughter and the mayor's son. The movie also featured Fay Bainter, Dickie Moore (seen to Burns's right), John Beal, and Joan Parker.

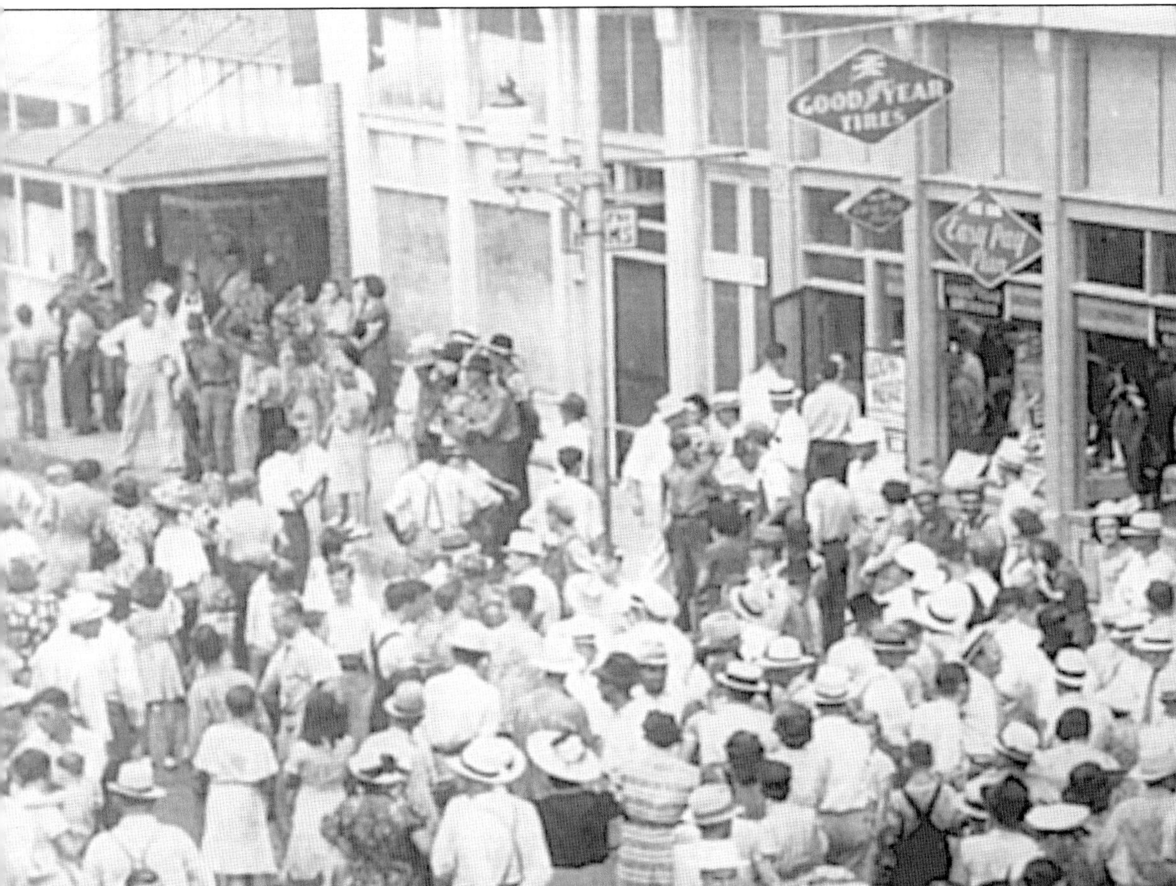

At the height of his Hollywood career, Bob Burns returned to be honored in his hometown of Van Buren in August of 1939. Burns came back home for the world premier of *Our Leading Citizen*, in which he starred as a small-town mayor. Among the guests of honor before the largest crowd ever assembled in Crawford County were Arkansas Governor Carl Bailey and the

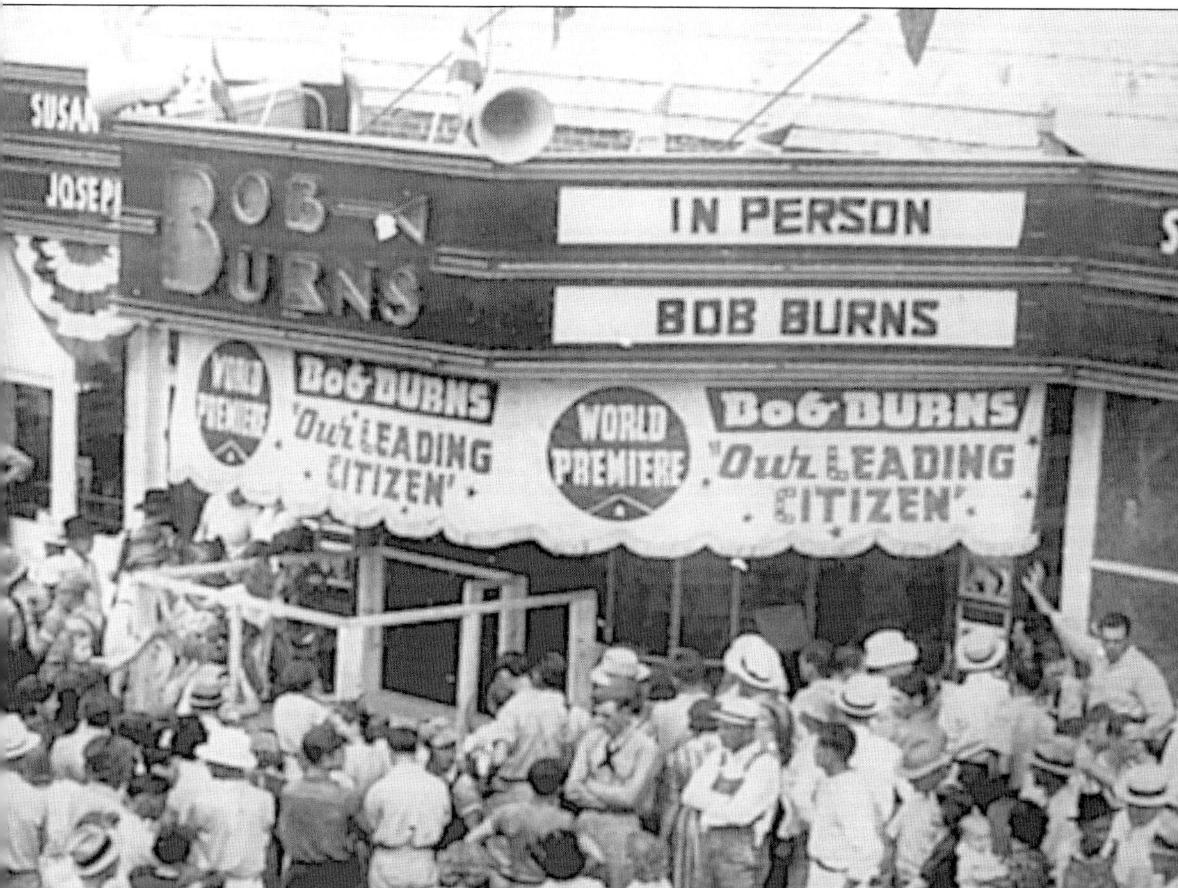

mayors of a dozen west Arkansas towns. During the festivities, Burns put on an apron outside Doc Meier's drug store, where he had once worked as a soda jerk, and served Susan Hayward, his co-star from the movie, at a sidewalk table. Bob Burns went back home to California after the event and never returned to Van Buren.

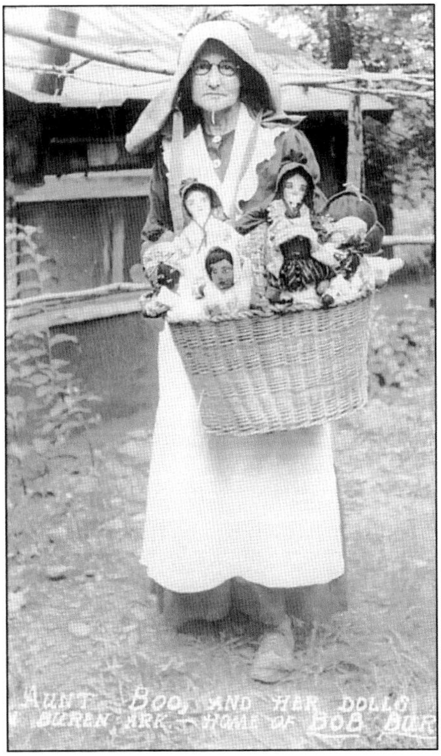

"Aunt Boo" was among the most popular of the characters lifted from the stories of Bob Burns to pose for postcard photographs. Often, she was photographed standing in the yard of her tarpaper-covered shack holding her handmade dolls or sometimes beside her husband, "Grandpa Snazzy." All these characters came from the childhood memories and fertile imagination of Bob Burns, who himself led a fascinating life. He was a gifted musician who could play almost any instrument, an army marksman during WW I, and a vaudeville comedian for most of the 1920s (sometimes appearing in blackface). It seemed he did a little of everything to earn a living before he found fame. He was a banana carrier in New Orleans, a waiter on an ocean liner, a streetcar operator, an Atlantic City carnival barker, a power company lineman in Utah, a boardinghouse operator in Nevada, and even a successful advertising man in Chicago. Yet the lure of show business and the joy of telling tales about characters back in Van Buren kept calling him, and it eventually brought him to wealth and fame. Burns died of cancer on his California ranch in 1956, ten years after retiring from show business to devote his time to real estate development.

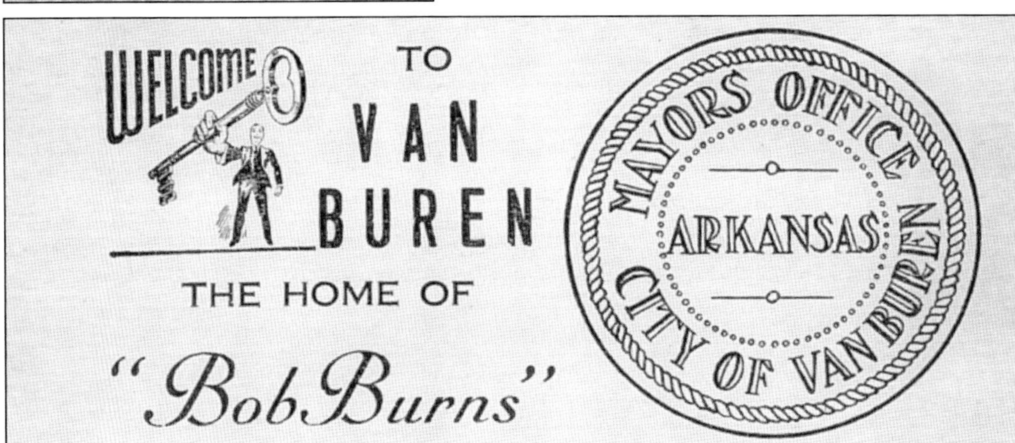

Despite his almost two decades of show business popularity, Bob Burns was not without his critics, especially in Arkansas. As recently as 1987, prominent Arkansas journalist Bob Lancaster received a letter of criticism, vowing that Lancaster's writing had "done more harm to the image of this state than anyone since Bob Burns and his bazooka"—this some 30 years after Burns's death. Yet as the late 1940s postcard above shows, Burns's hometown took pride in having produced the creator of "Aunt Boo," "Grandpa Snazzy," and so many others. The best summation of how the town felt might be found in what J.J. Izard, president of the Peoples Bank of Van Buren, told a reporter in 1956, "Bob Burns is the best thing that ever happened to us."

Four

CROSSROAD VILLAGES AND "TOURIST TRAPS"

While Van Buren was the seat of Crawford County government and business, the rest of the county remained rural in nature. A scattering of small communities grew up at railroad crossings, but with little more than a general store and occasionally a post office to mark a presence. However, by the 1920s, the push for a highway through the northern portion of the county toward Fayetteville, some 50 miles away, gave rise to a wide variety of enterprises. Some of the most interesting, captured on postcards, were the service businesses and tourist lures built to draw travelers off of what soon became State Highway 71.

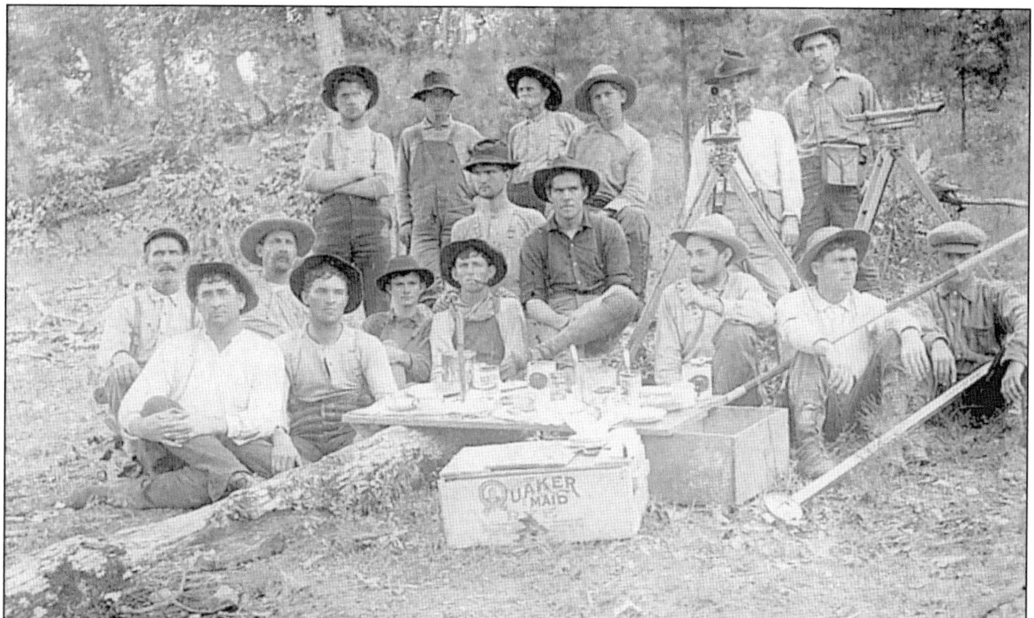

Surveying roads through the mountains and rocks of Van Buren County was hard work for man and beast. It is a safe assumption that these men were ready for lunch when the break came while doing survey work around 1906, near Uniontown, a tiny crossroads in northwestern Crawford County not far from the Oklahoma line. Lunch appeared to have consisted of canned fruit laid atop several wooden Quaker Maid rye crates. Today, the still small community of Uniontown may be reached via Highway 220.

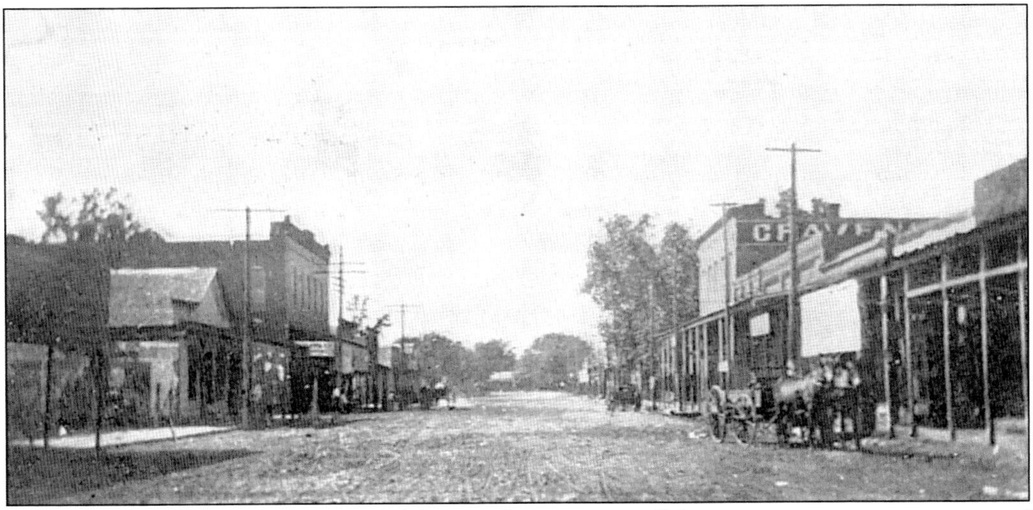

Alma, Van Buren's small-town neighbor to the east, is well known to recent generations of Arkansans as marking the I-40 exit to turn north to Fayetteville and the University of Arkansas. Alma, however, has a much older history that pre-dates the interstate. Settled in the 1800s, the residents first sought to name their new community Gum Town, but were denied this request by Postal Department authorities in Washington D.C. A postmaster in a neighboring town offered the name of his fiancee, Alma, and when submitted, the name was approved by the Washington bureaucrats. In this c. 1905 postcard, Fayetteville Avenue (the town's main street) was a sea of muddy ruts from wagon traffic.

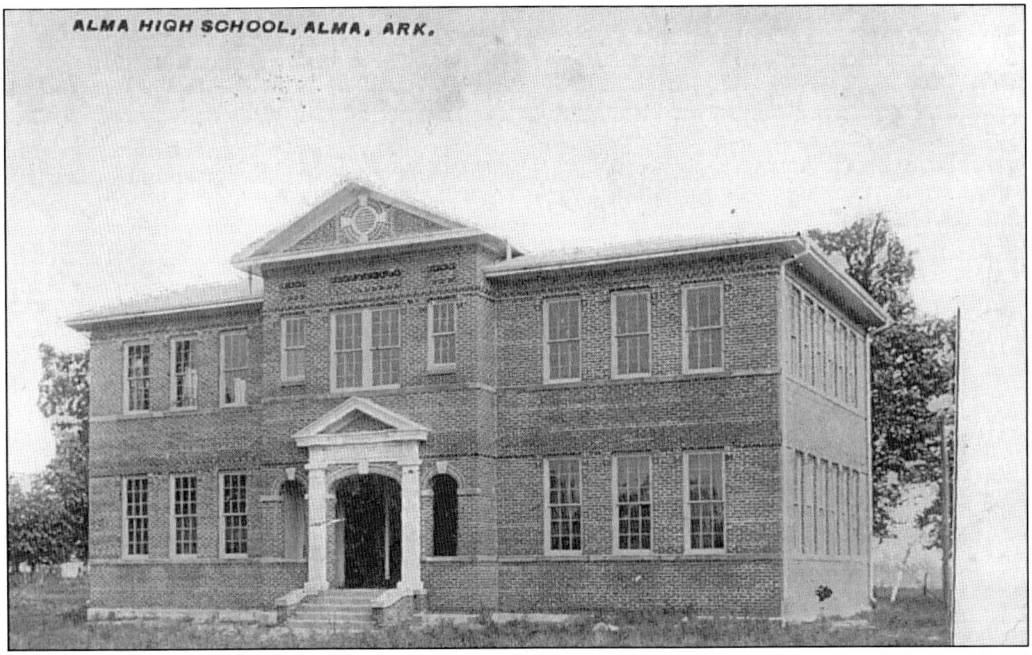

Although a very small town, Alma was able to erect a handsome, two-story brick high school shortly after the turn of the century. Such efforts were aided by passage of the state's first compulsory school attendance law in 1909. In 1910, about the time this postcard was made, annual state spending per student was $12. The school building no longer stands, but the small town of some 3,000 residents boasts a fine school system today.

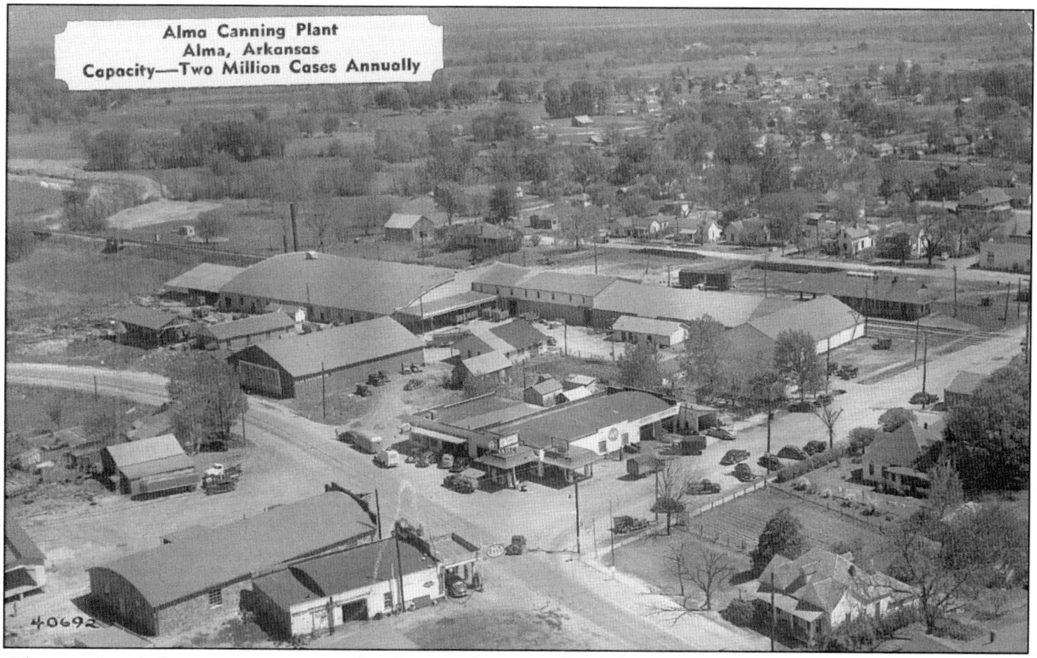

Alma gained the reputation as the "spinach capital of the world" and became home to what is supposedly the world's-largest spinach can. Each year, a parade festival features "Popeye" of cartoon fame. In the *c.* 1940 postcard above is an aerial view of the Alma Canning Plant, which at the time had a capacity of some 2 million cases of spinach a year. In the center and foreground are competing Conoco and Esso service stations and beyond is the sprawling cannery. In the postcard below is a view of the back-aching work of harvesting spinach at the Dean Brother's farm on Highway 71 outside of Alma. Note the two boys to the right (hands in pockets) and the trucks in the distance into which the pickers would have emptied their bushel baskets of freshly picked spinach. The trucks would have then hauled the crop to the cannery.

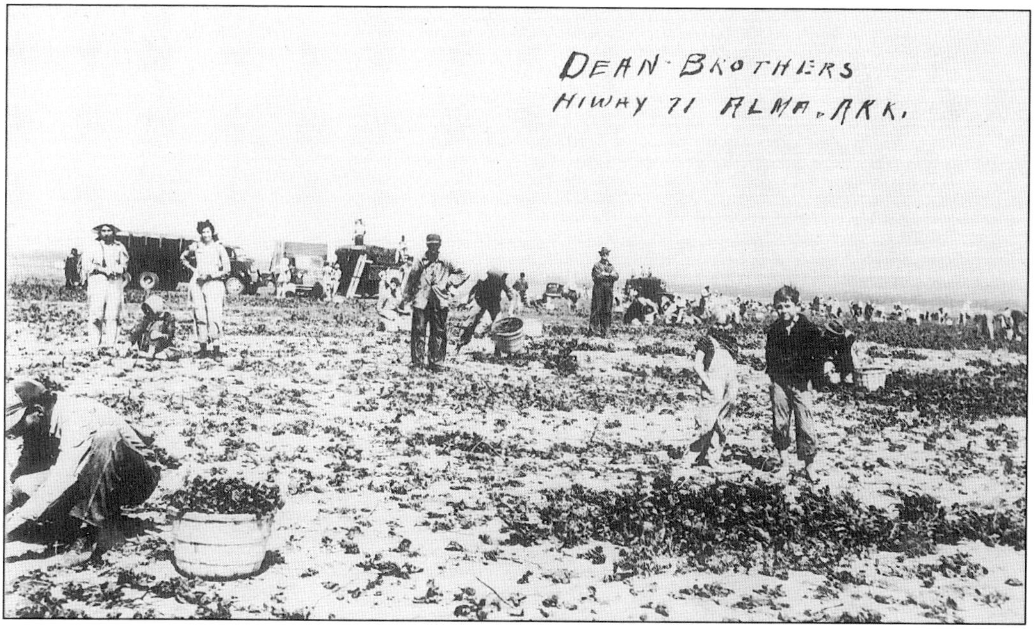

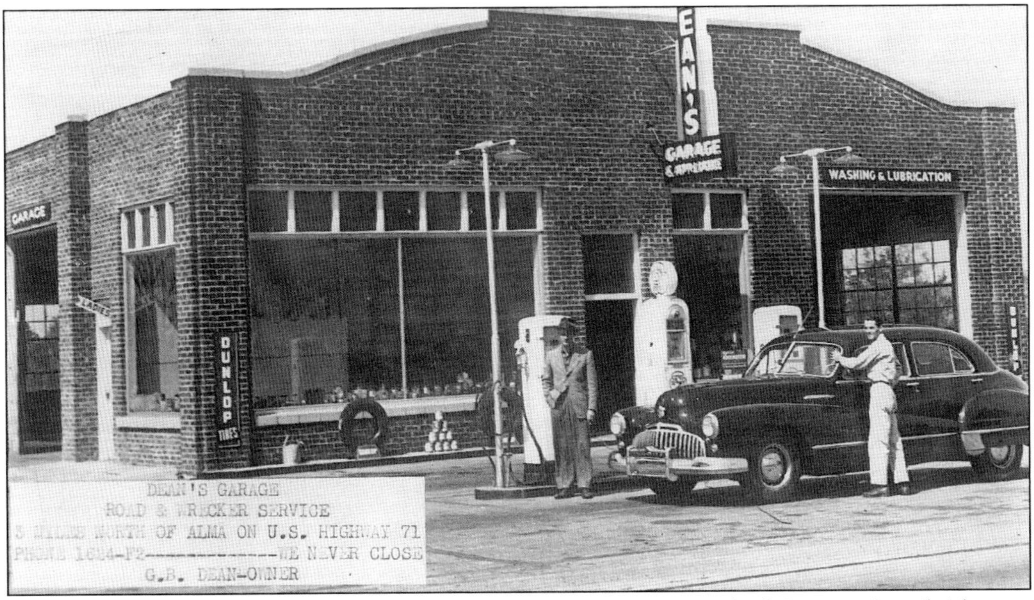

Motorists preparing to head into the Ozark Mountains from Crawford County found Alma to be a convenient stop along Highway 71 to buy gas, tend to car repairs, and perhaps enjoy a soft drink. Above is Dean's Garage, where a uniformed attendant cleans a windshield while the car's owner stands in front of the pump. Located 3 miles north of Alma, Dean's advertised a wrecker service and the fact that it never closed. Also on the outskirts of Alma, at the intersection of Highways 71 and 64, was T.J. Ballard's Texaco station and general merchandise store, a forerunner of today's gas and convenience stores. In the *c.* 1945 postcard below, Ballard placed a small round sign at the end of the gas pumps promoting "Ladies Restrooms," in a bid to lure motorists to pull off the road before heading toward Fayetteville. The business no longer operates today, but the building houses Chapter 42 of the Disabled American Veterans.

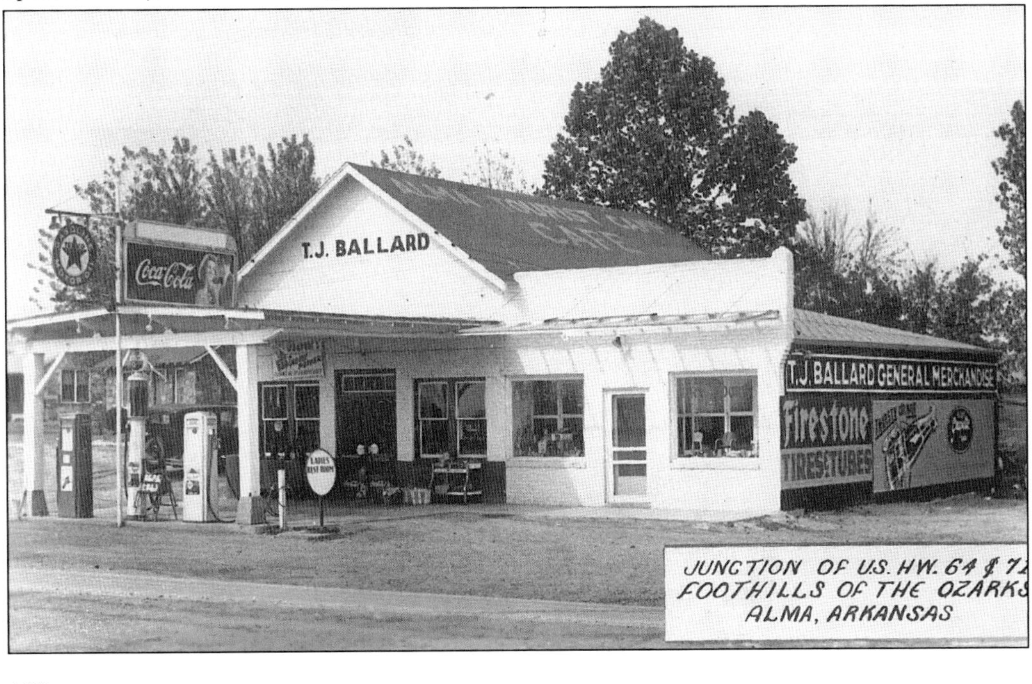

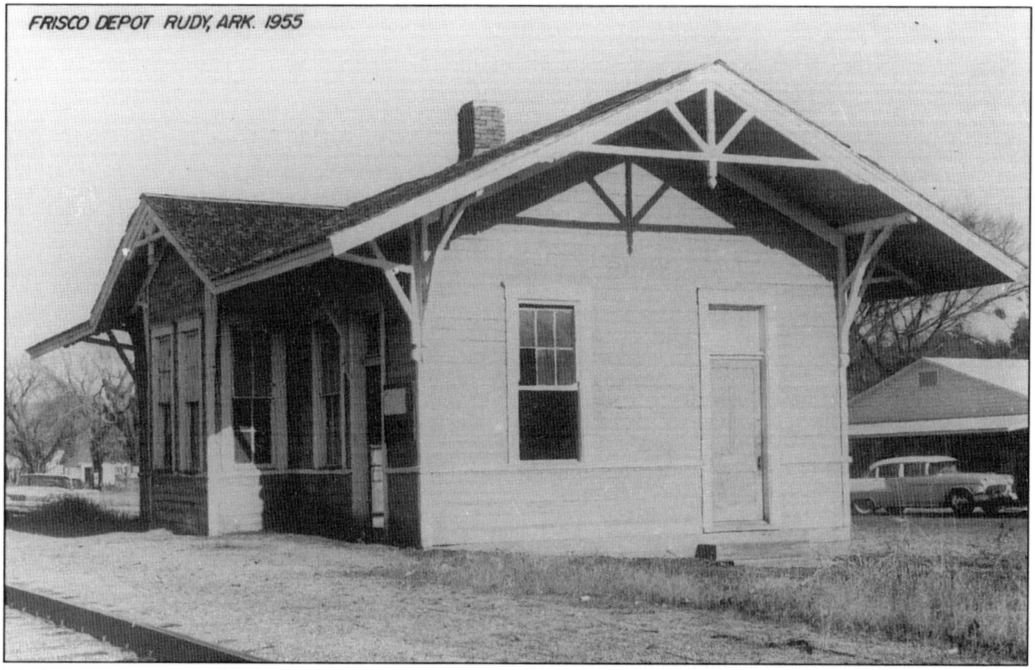

Today, moving north on Highway 71 from Alma, a short turn off on State Highway 348 brings a traveler to the small, bypassed community of Rudy. The land around Rudy was first settled in 1830 and was initially named Kenton, after a local farmer. In the late 1880s, an area resident, George Rudy, donated the land for the St. Louis & San Francisco Railroad to build a depot. Grateful for his gift and the prosperity that the railroad brought to the town, it apparently took his name. The Frisco Depot, shown above in 1955, is gone today. Seen below is the Rudy Post Office, typical for small towns in the 1930s and 40s. Crawford County's first paved road led from Alma to Rudy around 1930. Judging from the case of empty soft drink bottles at the right side of the building, it was most likely located next to the town's general store. The post office building is gone today, and the town is served by a more modern facility.

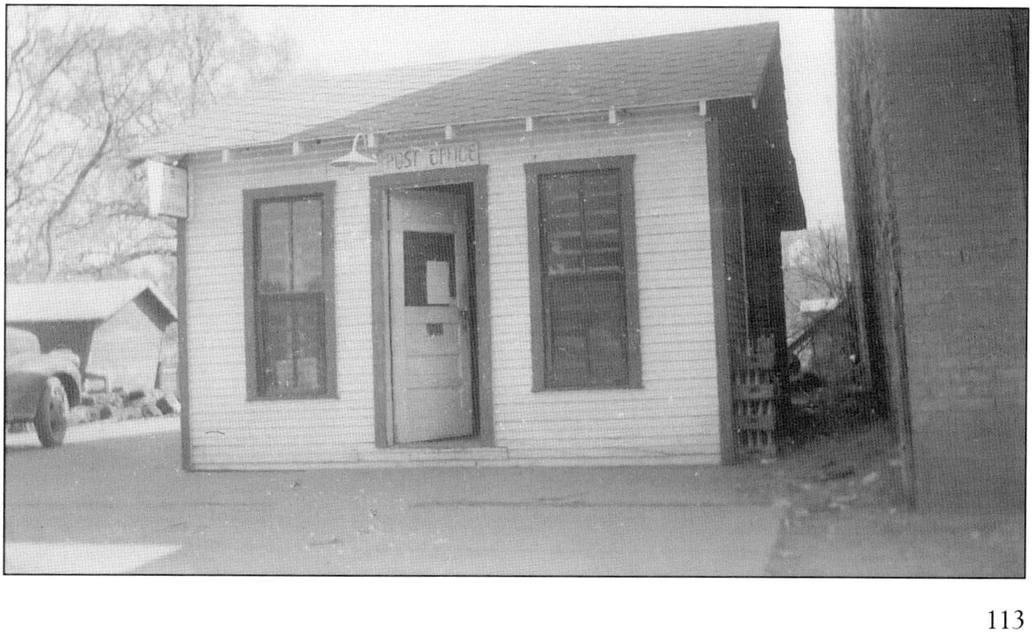

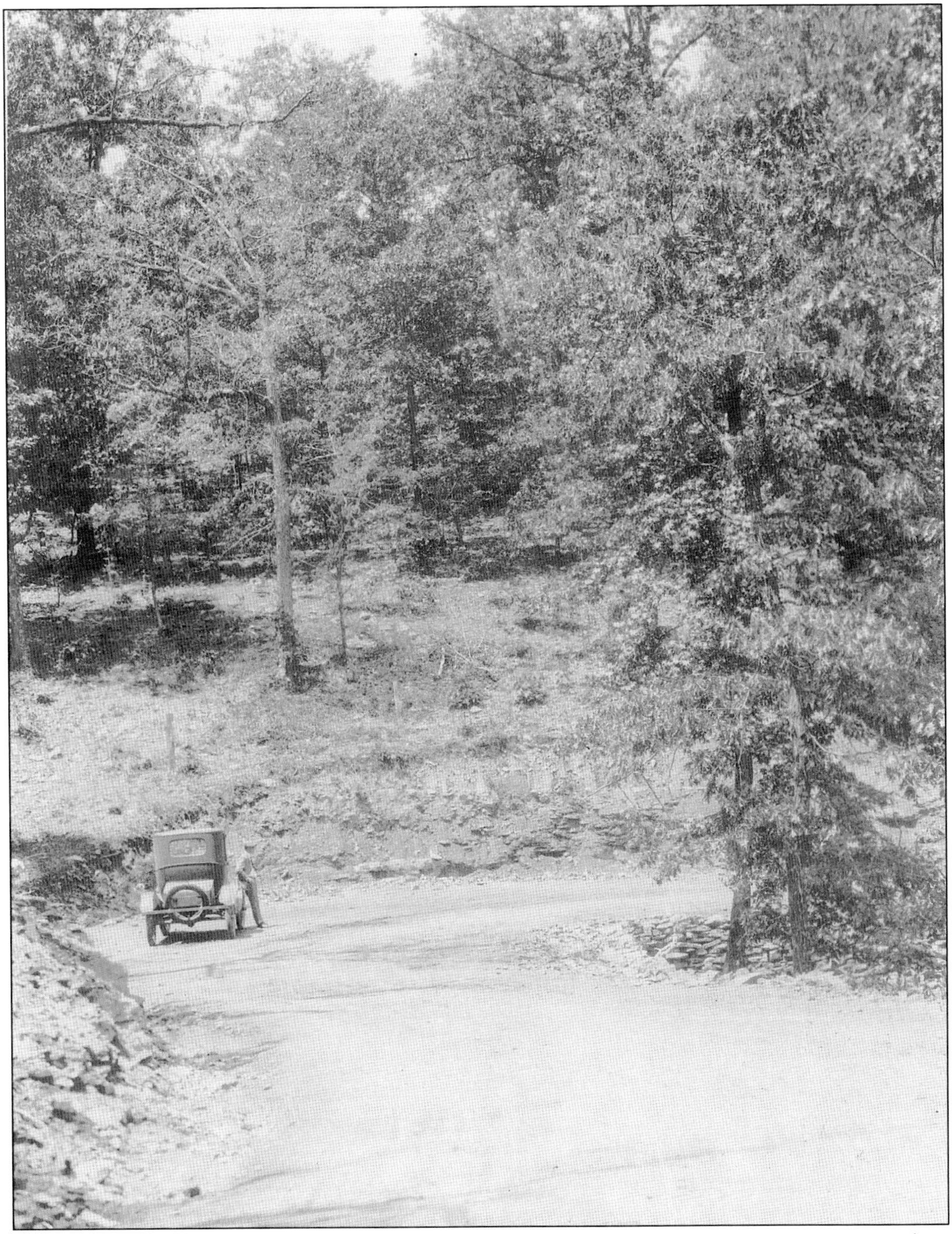

For decades, perhaps the best-known and most talked-about section of mountain road in Arkansas has been "Mountainburg Hill," an abruptly-rising, twisting, steep section of highway just beyond the small town of Mountainburg, on Highway 71. Only at the end of the 20th century was the dangerous road finally bypassed with a new interstate. This *c.* 1930 photograph shows the still rough, unpaved road and a driver beside his parked vehicle. He appears to be studying the steep climb before him, perhaps contemplating whether or not he can push the car up the mountain en route to Fayetteville.

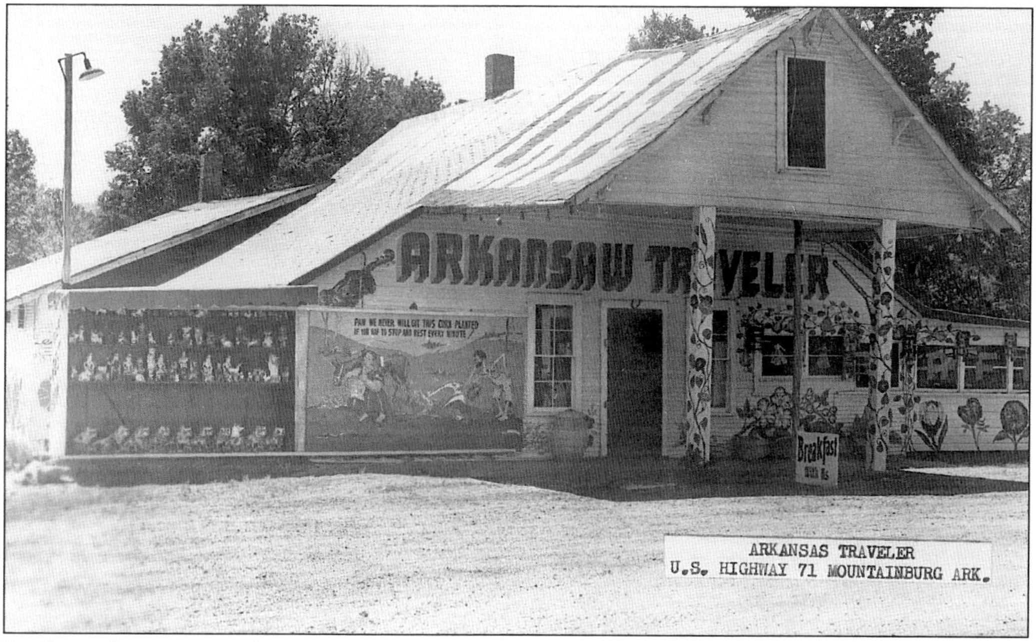

By the early 1930s, Highway 71 was paved between Fayetteville and Fort Smith. This led to the creation of more roadside businesses to support the ever-increasing number of motorists using the new road for business and pleasure. One such business was the Arkansas Traveler Gift Shop (as seen on this c. 1945 postcard), which offered breakfast and a variety of Ozark "Hillbilly" souvenirs. The remodeled building is presently an antique shop. Seen in the c. 1950 view below is Mr. and Mrs. Thomason's Basket Shop, for many years a fixture for tourists passing through Mountainburg. The couple sold dolls, novelties, and baskets fashioned from the white oaks found in the surrounding forest. The community of Mountainburg itself sprang up originally in 1859, so named because of its location at the foot of the Boston Mountains.

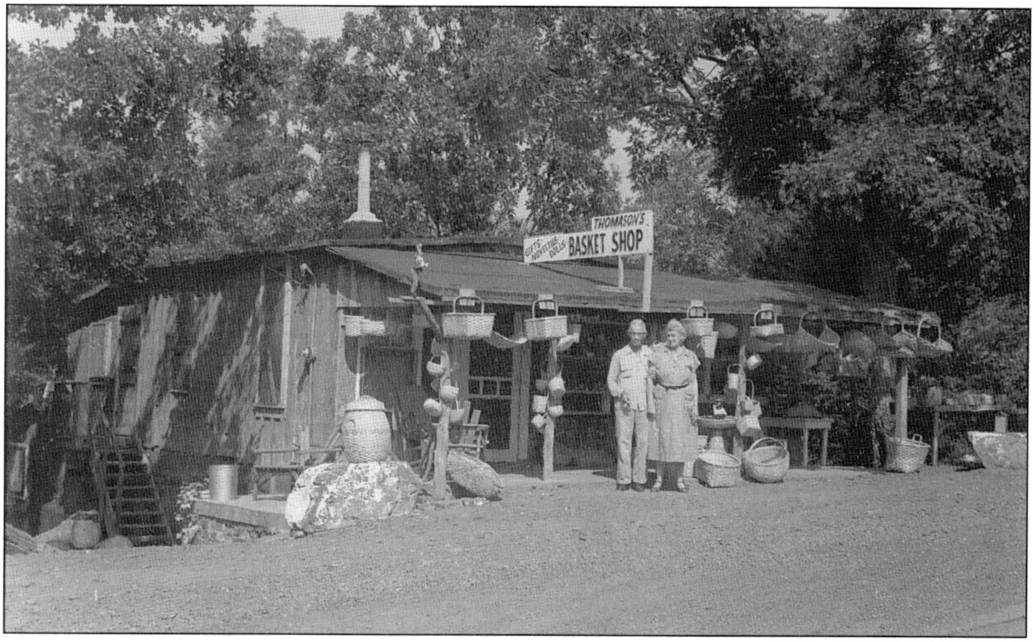

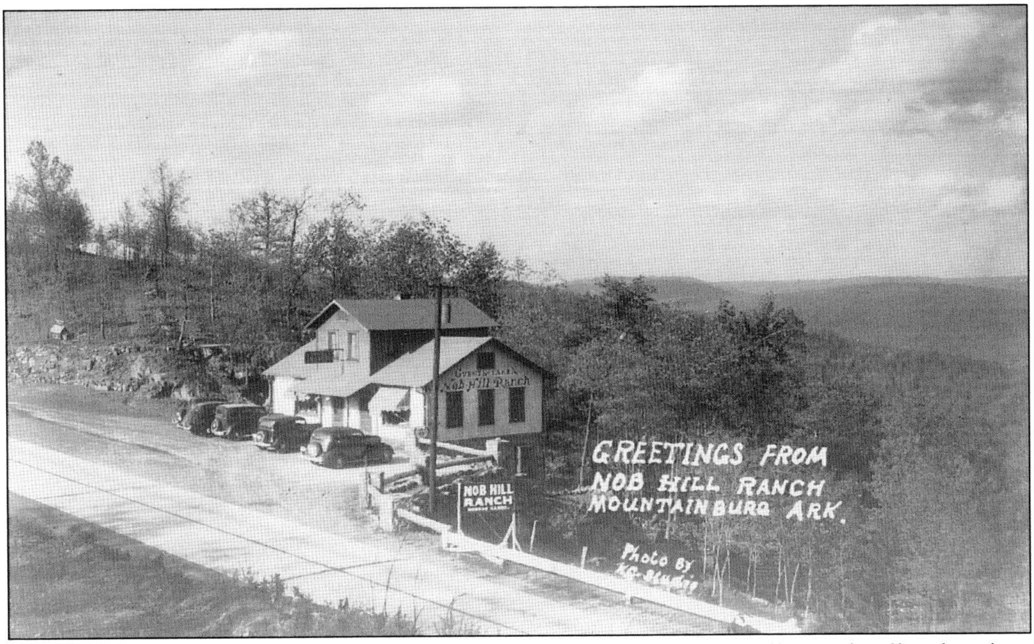

Seemingly hanging onto the edge of the steep mountain, the Nob Hill Ranch offered a place on the hill above Mountainburg to pull in for a meal or a night's stay in a "modern cabin" (according to the sign beside the road in this c. 1940 postcard). The building has at least one level of rooms, below the level of the parking lot. The building still stands, but it now serves as a residence.

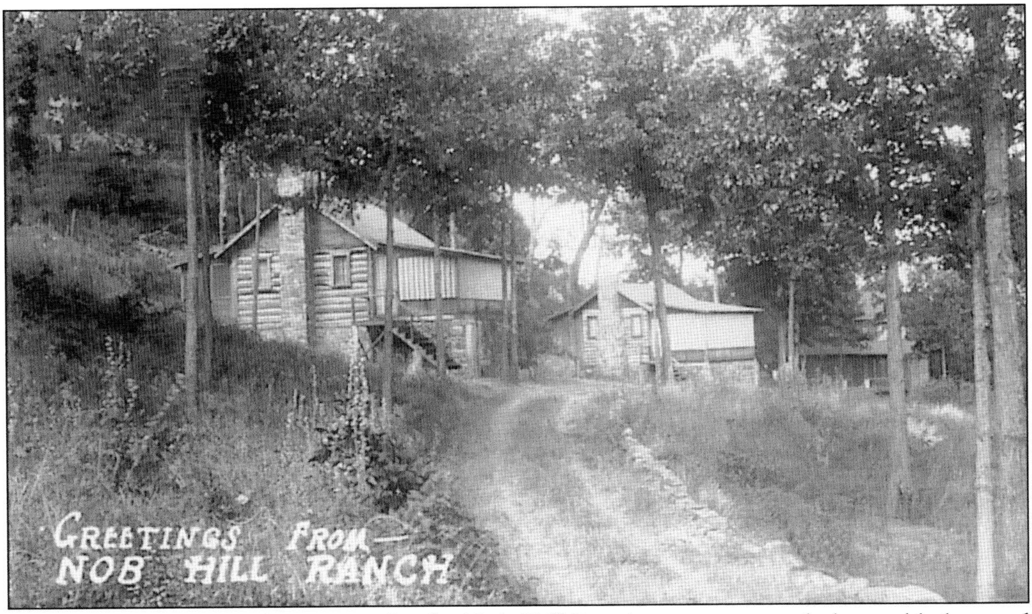

The rustic cabins rented to visitors by the Nob Hill Ranch were apparently located below and behind the office and cafe building seen above. The card's 1939 message reads as follows: "Am back again, it is delightfully cool up here after hot old Dallas. William and I stayed in a cabin like this, add these cards to Billy's postcard collection."

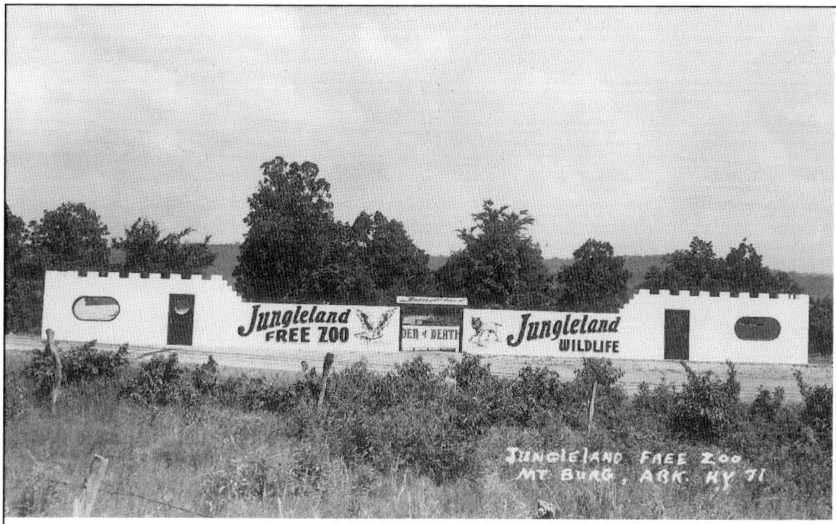

Among the most interesting "tourist traps" along the Crawford County section of Highway 71 outside of Mountainburg was the Jungleland Zoo, apparently an attraction with free admission. Seen here *c.* 1940, the intent may have been to lure travelers off the road to see the wildlife, while encouraging them to stock up on souvenirs. The attraction closed many years ago, but the sealed-up, whitewashed building still sits vacant beside the highway, its odd shape leaving no clue as to what it once was. Below is a view of the Dogpatch Cabin Camp, playing off the Al Capp cartoon strip and the ever-promoted Arkansas hillbilly image. The 1944 message from the business' owners reads as follows: "Lone Oak Court has been sold. Our court is for sale. It is located about two miles north of Lone Oak. If still interested in a court write for details." The owner, G.J. Peck, was attempting to sell out to O.B. Boyer of Oklahoma City. The building is gone today; it reportedly burned at some point in the past.

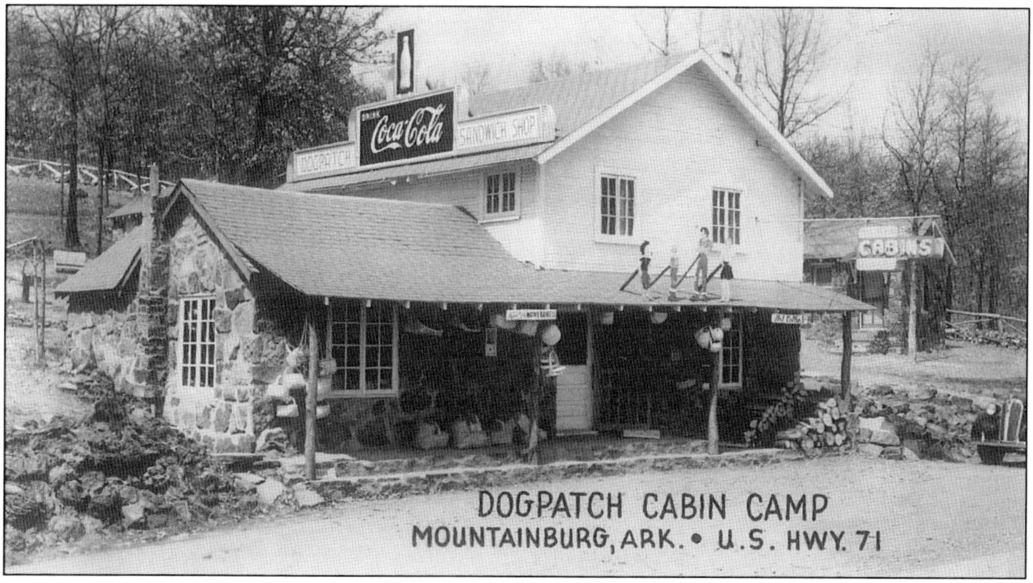

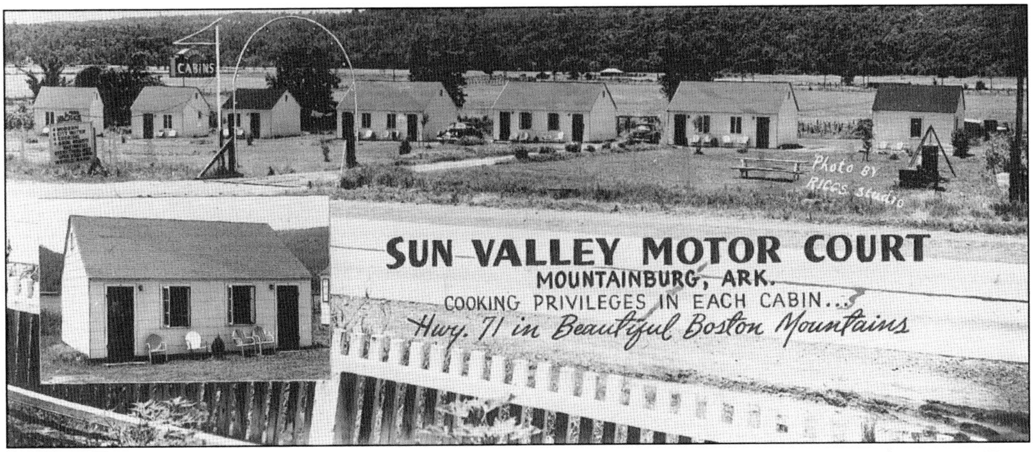

The most ambitious effort to lodge the rapidly expanding number of motorists between Fort Smith and Fayetteville almost surely was found in the Sun Valley Motor Court. The white frame cabins promised city water and in-room cooking facilities just off Highway 71 in Mountainburg, in the "Beautiful Boston Mountains." The site is the present home of Sun Valley Realty. The cabins are still there, but are apparently used as apartments rather than a tourist court.

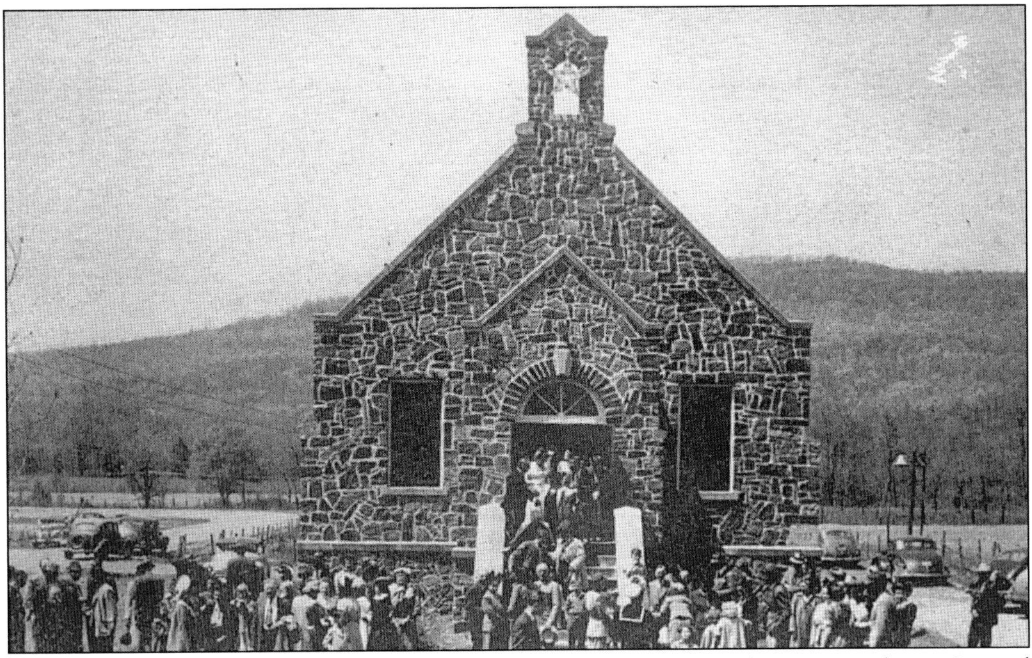

On a bright Arkansas Sunday around 1940, a photographer stood across Highway 71 and photographed many of the citizens of Mountainburg leaving worship services at the Presbyterian church. The tranquil scene belies a legendary event in the area, which is said to have occurred in 1857 on a day known as "Bloody Sunday." A missionary preacher held services while two feuding factions held their tempers, but after the final hymn was sung, total mayhem erupted—men used weapons against each other, while women and children reportedly did battle with kitchen utensils brought to serve Sunday dinner. For many years after the episode, no organized religious services were conducted in the area. Today, the church building is used as administration offices by the local school district.

Mountainburg was given its first post office in 1893, when the small village was still an isolated hamlet. This post office building dates from the early 1900s, and as the emblem embedded in the native stone at the top indicates, it shared space with the local Masonic Lodge. The building still stands, but the town of some 500 residents has a new post office today. The once-sleepy mountain village recently found itself with an interstate exit (with the opening of a new highway passing just to the west).

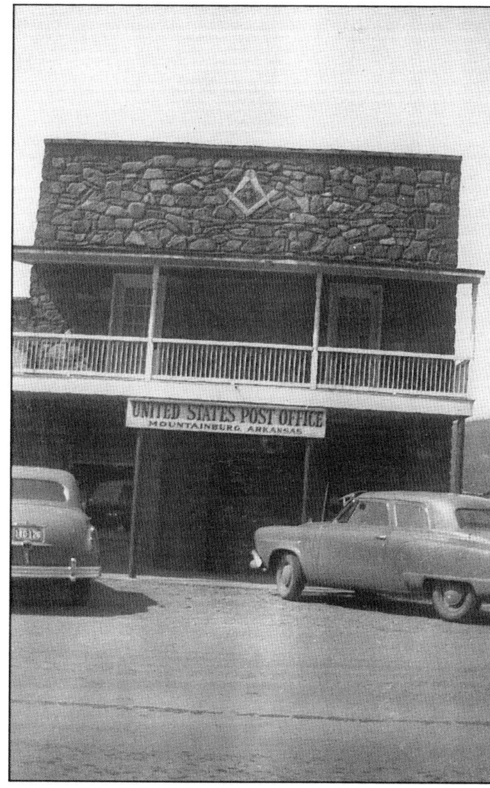

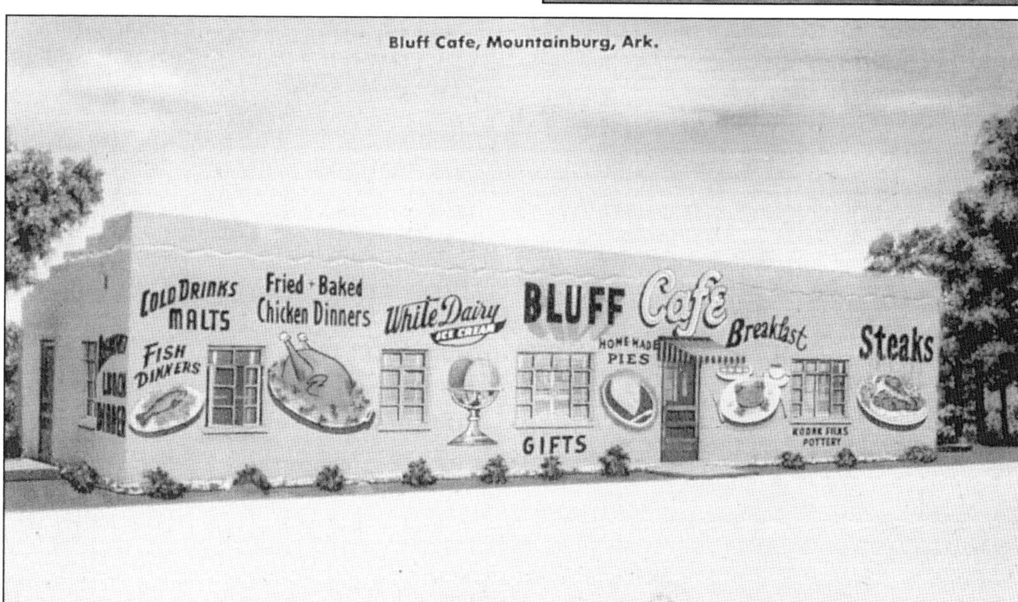

Around 1940, on the southern outskirts of Mountainburg, travelers dined at the Bluff Cafe, perhaps drawn in by its brightly painted exterior. The back of the postcard listed the phone number as 9F222 and described the business as being "on a mountain top overlooking peaceful valley and clear creek. Owned and operated by Mr. and Mrs. A.G. Houck & Sons." Today the building has markedly changed, as it has been converted into a residence.

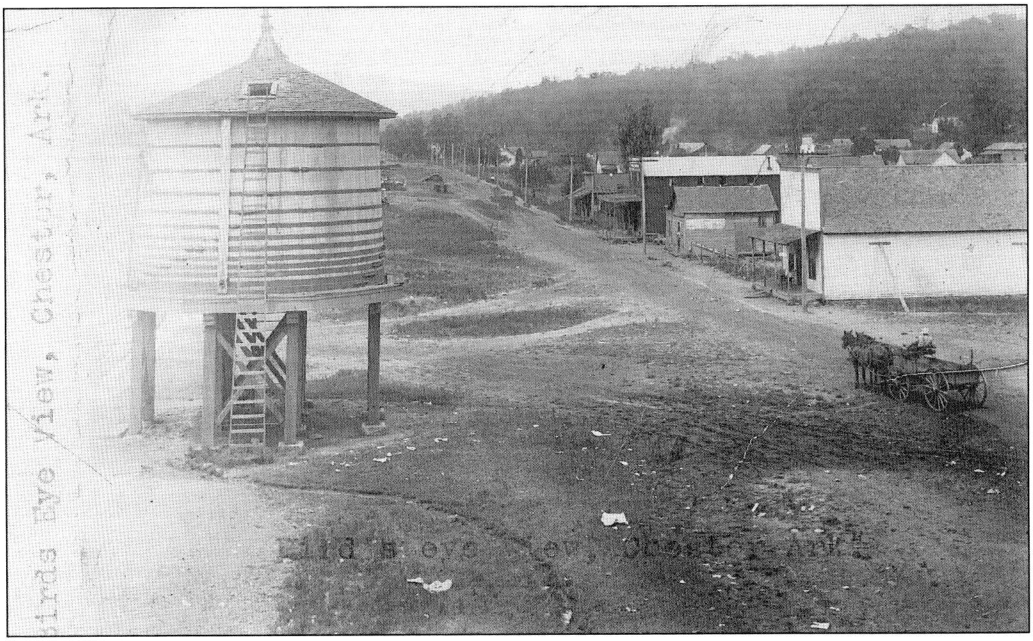

Chester, Arkansas, is located just north of Mountainburg, a few miles off of Highway 71. First settled in the 1850s, the tiny community found itself chosen as a stop on the Frisco Railroad in 1884. It was given the name "Chester" by a railroad engineer, reportedly after his hometown back east. In this 1912 view, a lone wagon makes its way down the dirt street. A water tower for the train engines is seen on the left and the general store is on the right.

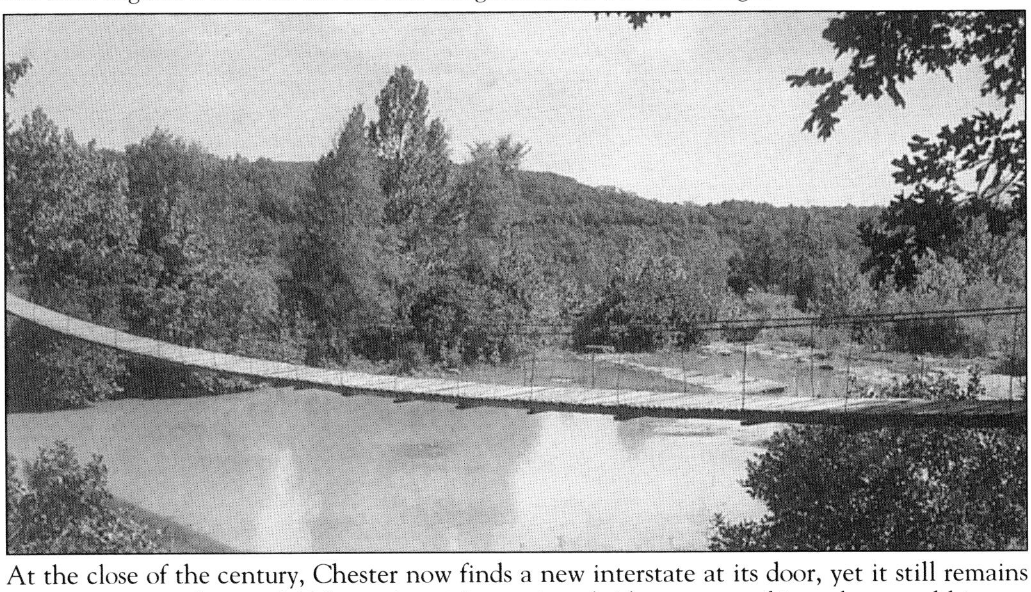

At the close of the century, Chester now finds a new interstate at its door, yet it still remains a country town of around 125 people, with a unique bridge as part of its culture and history. Since at least 1915, local school children have used a swinging bridge to cross Howard's Ford Creek, known locally as Chester Creek. The bridge provided a vital connection between the east and west sides of the village. When the first bridge washed out in a 1940 flood, it presented real logistical problems. Replaced at least twice since then, the bridge still remains an important feature of the mountain community.

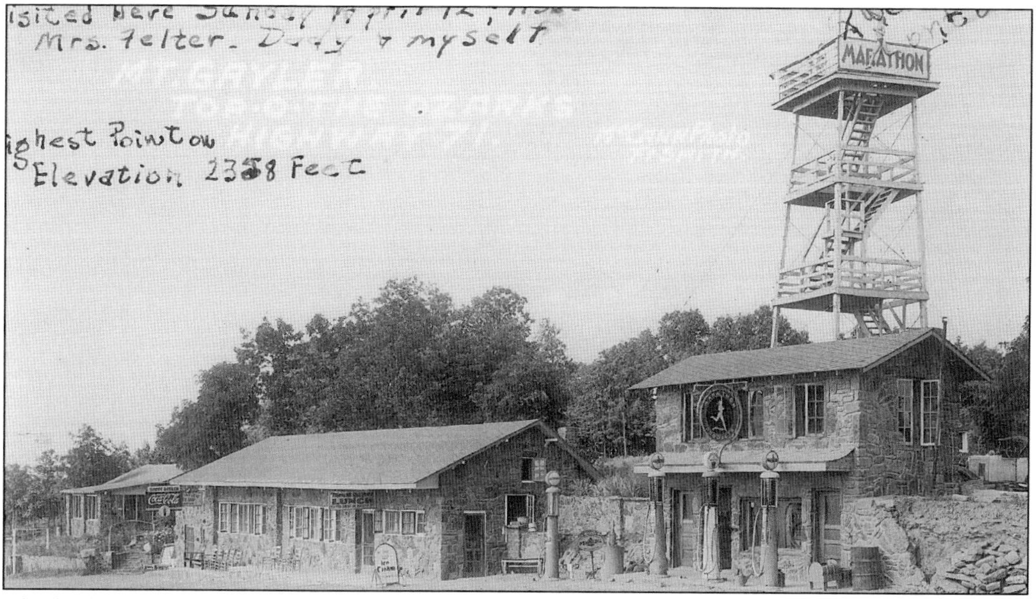

The highpoint, both in altitude and in memory, for many travelers on Highway 71 in northern Crawford County was atop Mt. Gaylor, so named for an early settler, Reuben Gayler. The road connecting Fayetteville and Fort Smith was finally paved in the early 1930s, and roadside commerce soon followed, providing some of the most photographed scenes atop what was billed as "the highest paved roadway between Canada and Mexico." On the west side of the crest stood a Marathon Oil station, several cabins, and a wooden observation tower built by Ed Bellis, all of which represented the first enterprise on the mountain. For a dime a visitor could go up on the tower and take a 360-degree look from atop its 2,358-foot summit. Across the highway was built the most popular stop on the road for hungry travelers. Burns Gables, with its dining room and novelty shop, was the motorist's reward for making it up the mountain. John Burns, a pharmacist who moved from Fort Smith, built the establishment in 1936, at a time when no commercial deliveries of food were yet made to the area. He and his large family set about growing a large garden and curing hams, and soon Burns Gables was *the* place to stop.

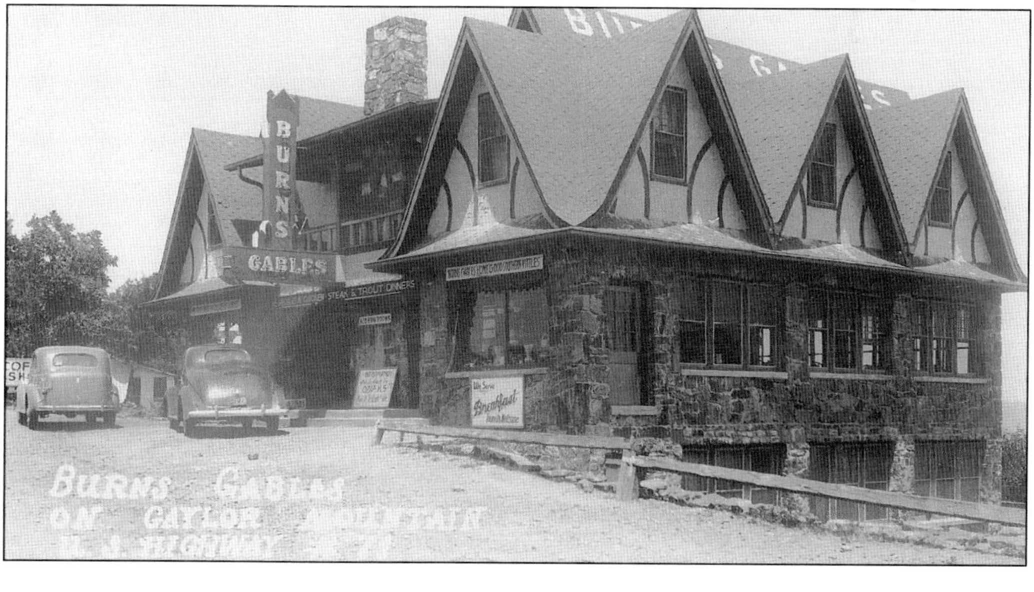

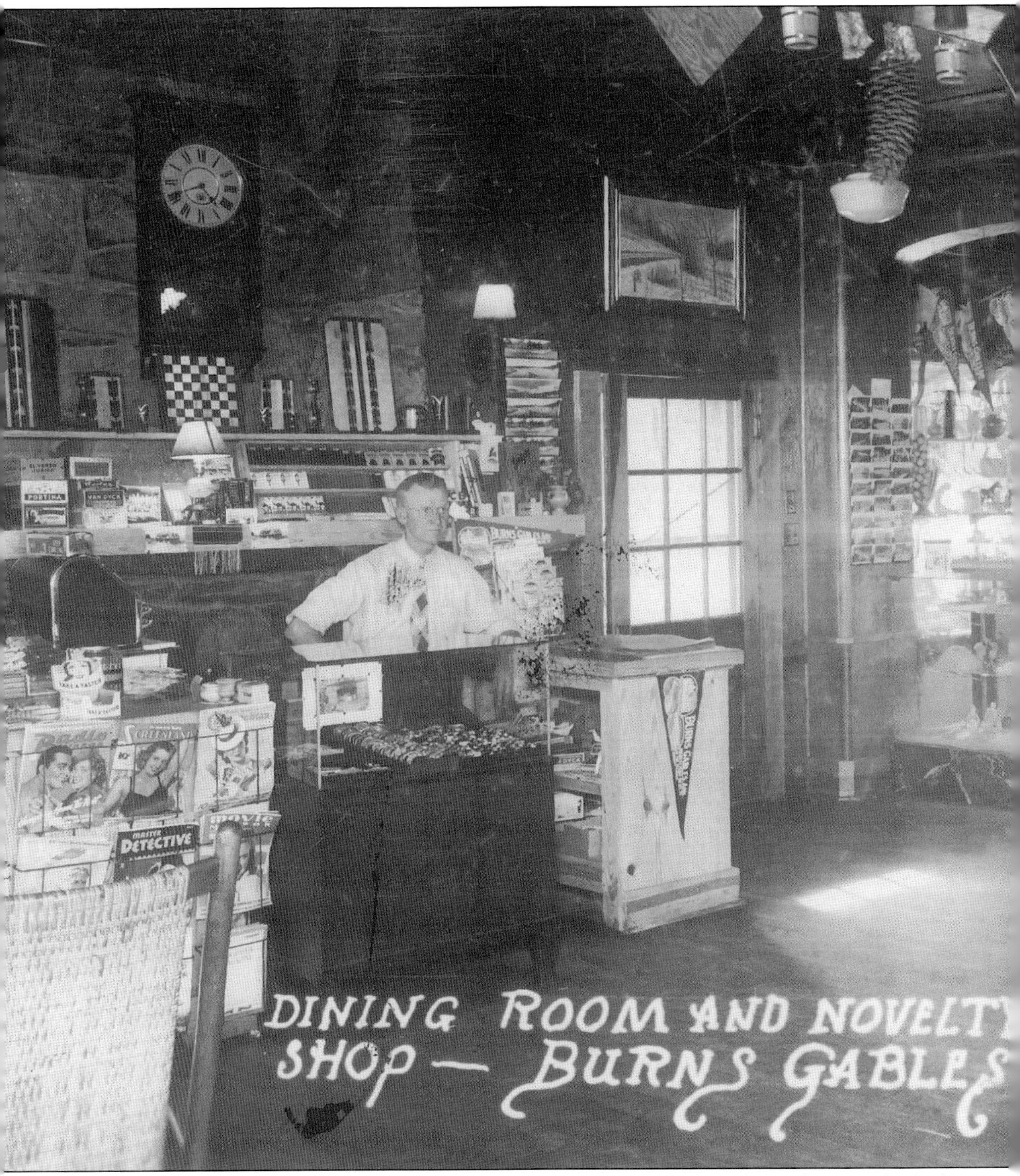

A tourist stepping through the door at Burns Gables would likely have been drawn to both the decor and to the pretty girl named Polly, shown on the right, behind the counter. After Polly Caveness finished high school in El Paso, Arkansas, (where John Burns originally lived) she came to Mt. Gaylor, began working at Burns Gables the day it opened in 1936 and continued to work there until the day it closed in 1979. A look around this enlarged, 1940 postcard gives us a good sense of

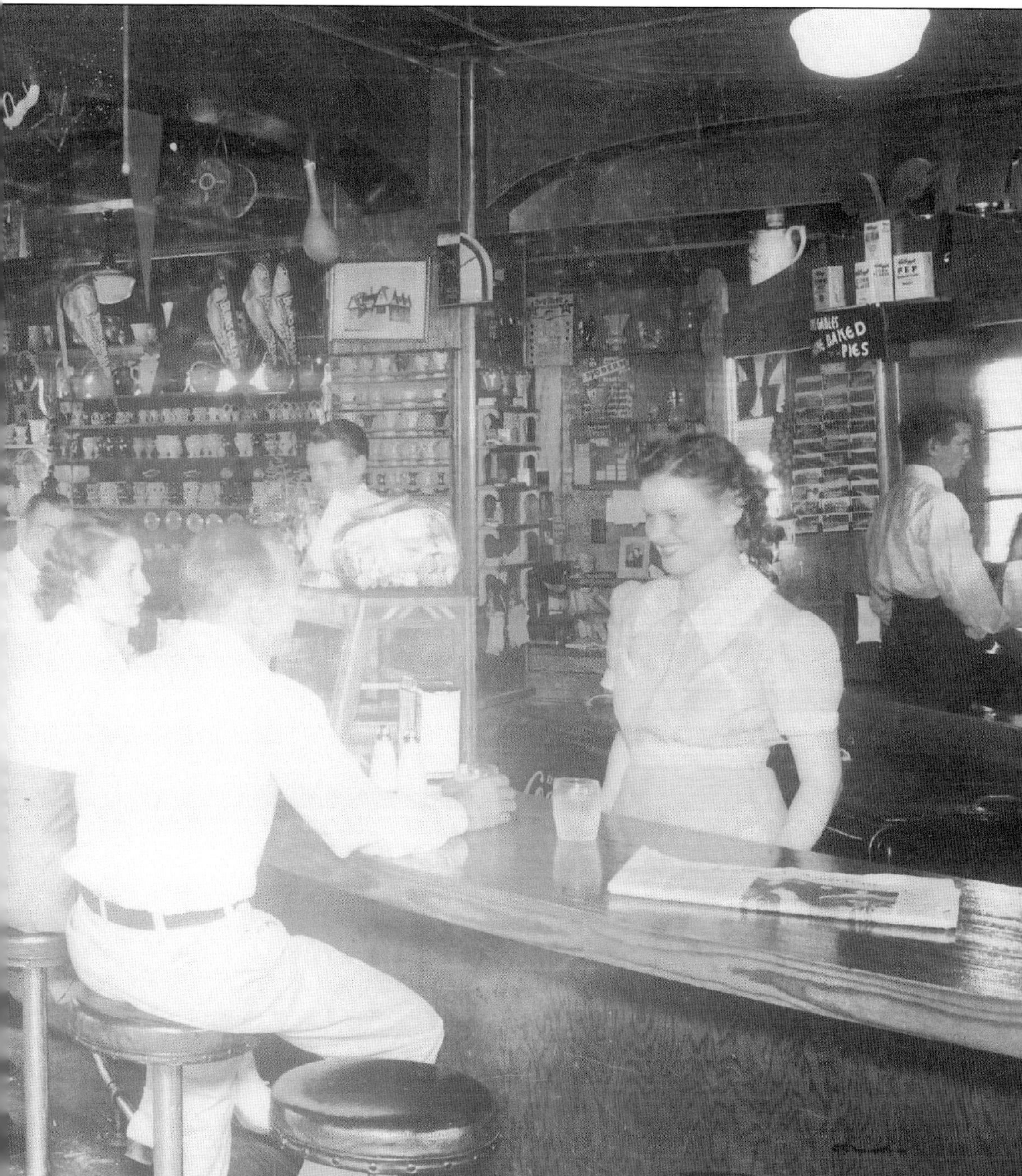

what it might have been like to shop and dine at Burns Gables. Not visible is a "sit down" dining room where Polly and other young ladies waited tables. In the dining room or at the counter they served wild huckleberry pie and fresh bread, baked daily in large ovens on the premises. Note the popular magazines of the day to the left, the novelties for sale against the wall, and the rather stern look on the face of the gentleman (perhaps Mr. Burns himself) behind the cash register.

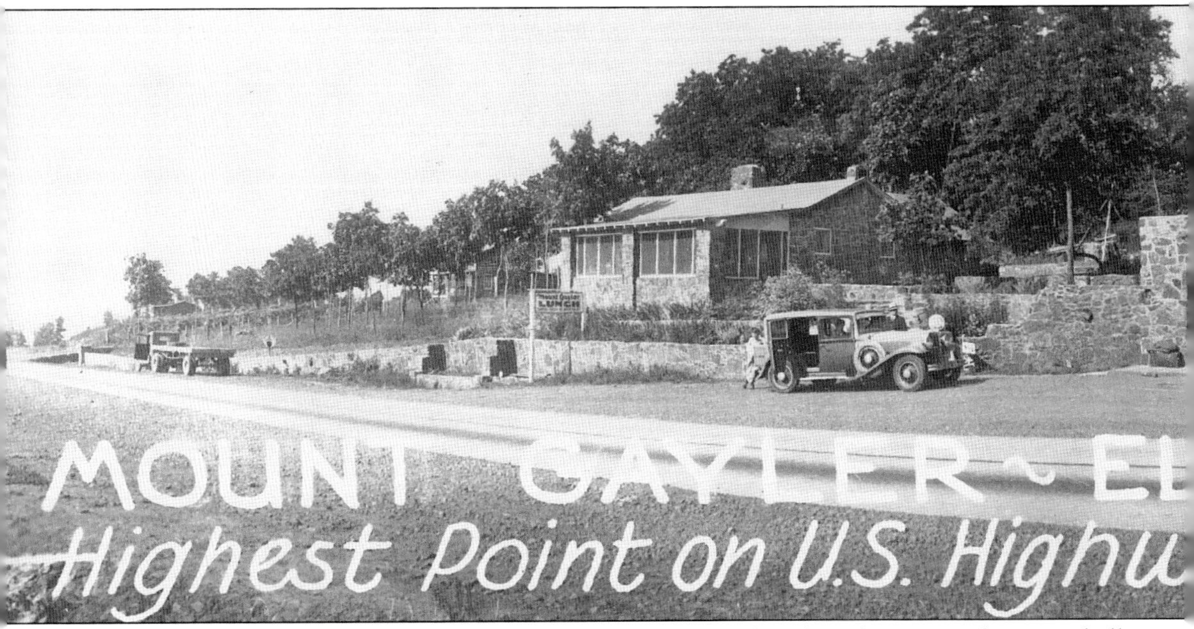

Ed Bellis and his wife, Stella, along with their young son, Ed Jr., lost their Texas home and all their worldly possessions as a result of the stock market crash of 1929. After unsuccessful efforts at such jobs as selling washing machines, Mr. Bellis scraped together enough money to buy five acres of what was almost wilderness atop Mt. Gaylor in 1931. At the time, the highway ended at the summit, but the Bellises gambled on the future when the road would be completed between Fort Smith and Fayetteville. Mr. Bellis, formerly trained as a bookkeeper, poured his sweat equity into the new business, himself laying each of the stones seen in the gas station, cabins,

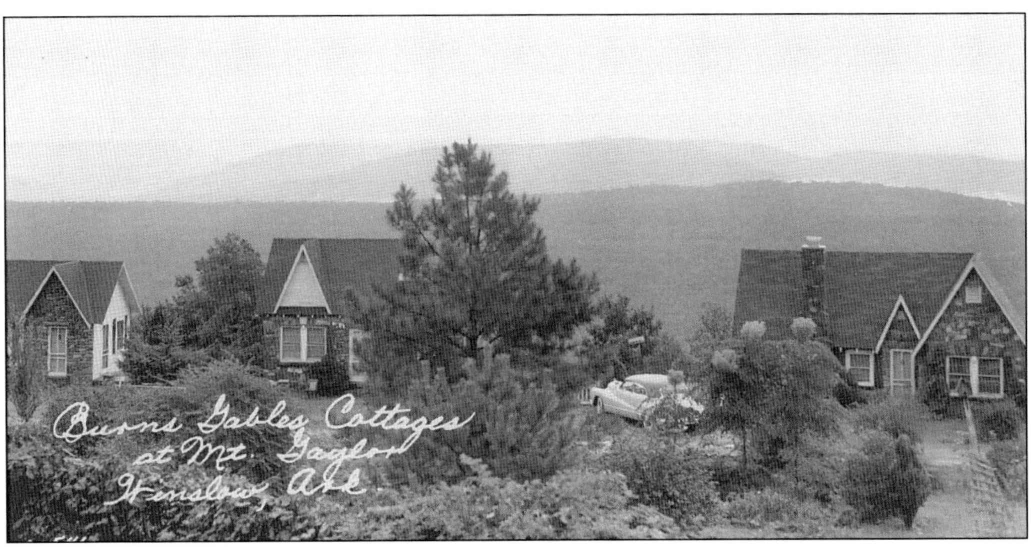

After John Burns came to Mt. Gaylor in 1936 and built Burns Gables across the road from the Bellis's business, a seemingly friendly competition ensued to see which man could pull the most tourists off to his respective side of the increasingly popular highway. Burns built the cabins seen in this c. 1945 postcard behind his restaurant, adding a gabled effect suggestive of the style of the rest of the business.

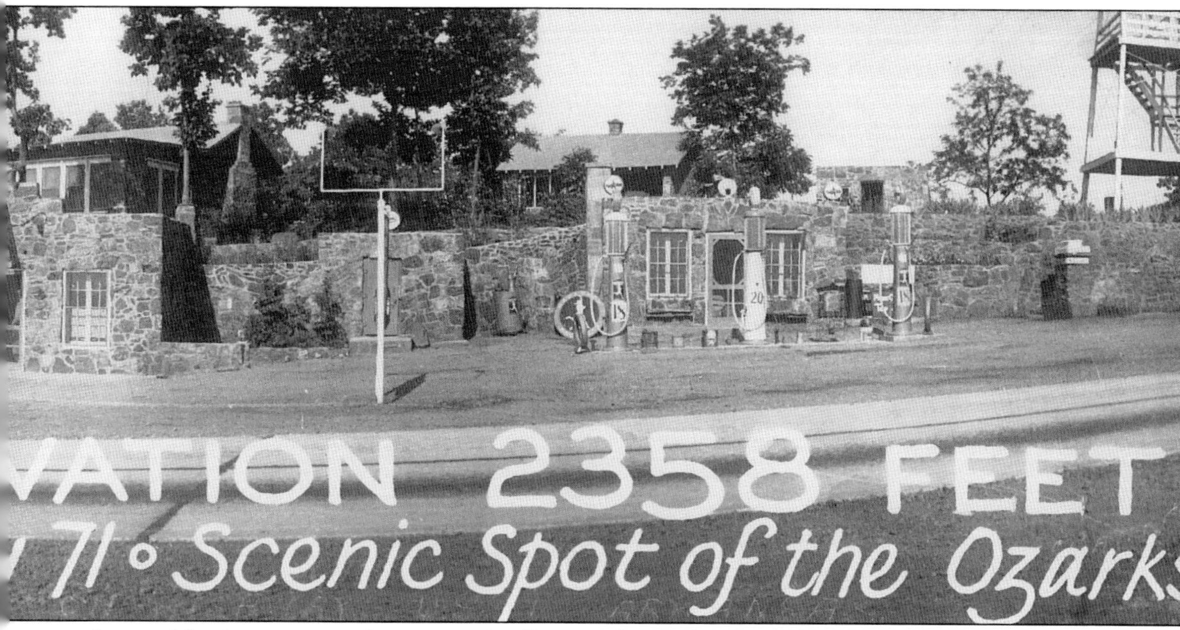

and store. Until a two-room house was finally completed, the family lived in a tent in the bed of their truck. Mrs. Bellis pumped gas while her husband did the mechanic's work, which was often needed after cars struggled up the steep mountain. The Bellises soon opened a restaurant and found themselves sharing their tiny house with the eight young women whom they had brought to the mountain to work in the business. It is said that one day in 1937, a long sedan driven by cowboy star Tom Mix pulled up to the gas pumps, creating an understandable stir among the employees. The wooden observation tower, with its four platforms, is seen to the right.

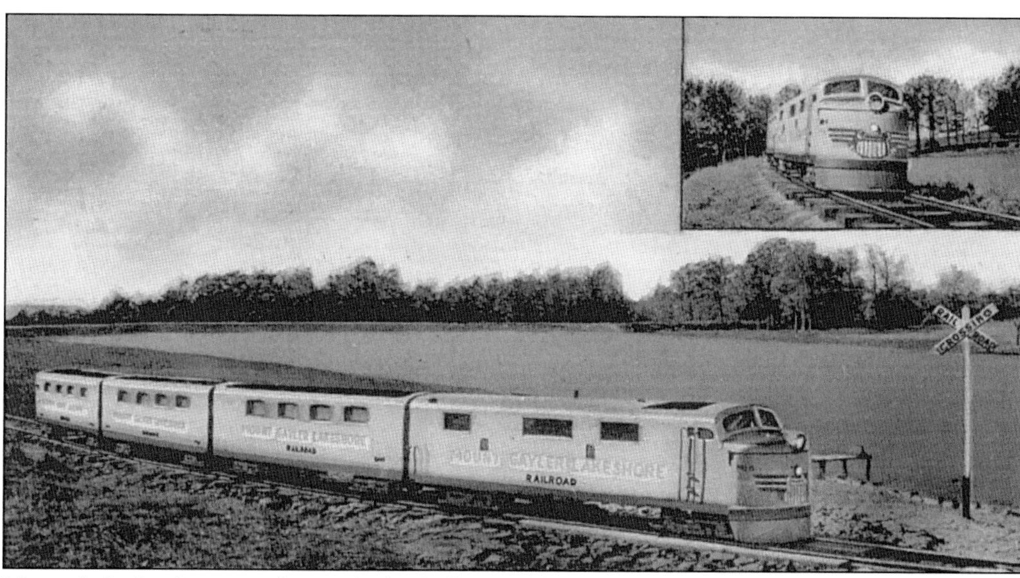

Meanwhile, back across the road, the Bellises added a miniature railroad (seen in this c. 1950 postcard) that gave visitors a ride around a small lake behind their gift shop and observation tower. Some of the cabins remain today but have been out of use in recent years. The train has long since been dismantled.

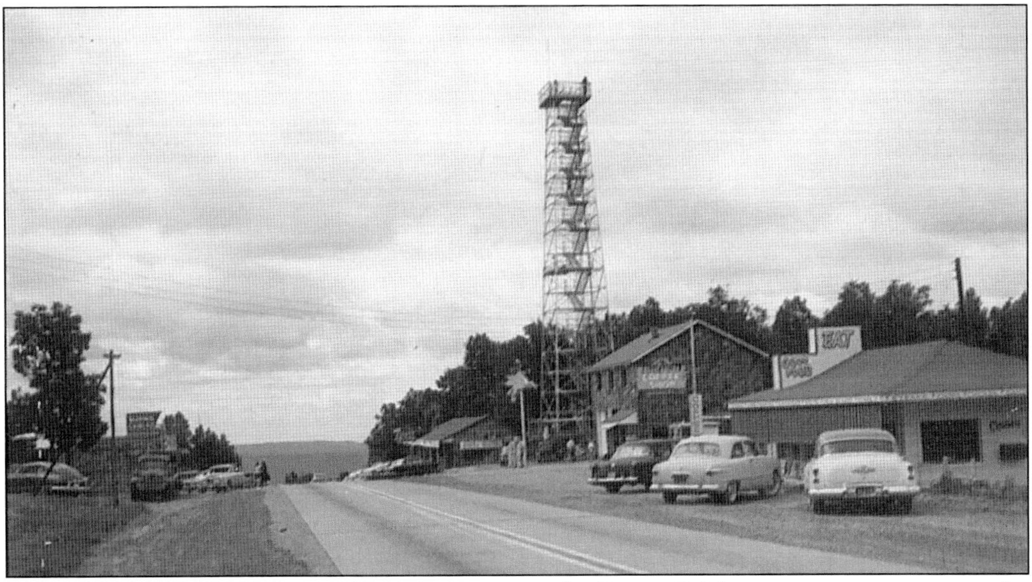

In 1939, Ed Bellis, perhaps watching the ever-popular Burns Gables upstart prosper across the road, enhanced his side of the tourist artery by replacing his wooden observation tower with a 100-foot steel tower (seen in this c. 1955 postcard) erected by the Fort Smith Structural Steel Company. There was no elevator, but for a dime visitors could walk up some 20 flights of steps to the observation deck at the top. The tower is still open today, costing about a dollar to take in the view.

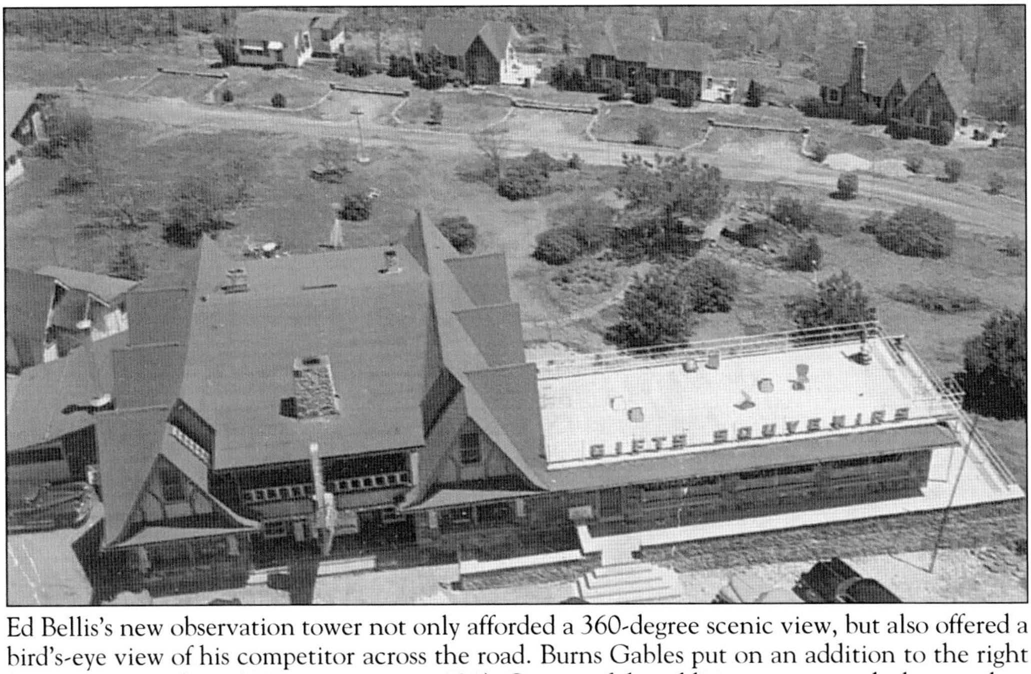

Ed Bellis's new observation tower not only afforded a 360-degree scenic view, but also offered a bird's-eye view of his competitor across the road. Burns Gables put on an addition to the right (not present in the c. 1940 view on page 121). On top of the addition was a sun deck, complete with a variety of lounge furniture, where guests or employees on break could lay back and look up at the people looking down on them from atop Bellis's tower. In this c. 1950 view can be seen some of the cabins operated by the Burns business, to the rear of the restaurant.

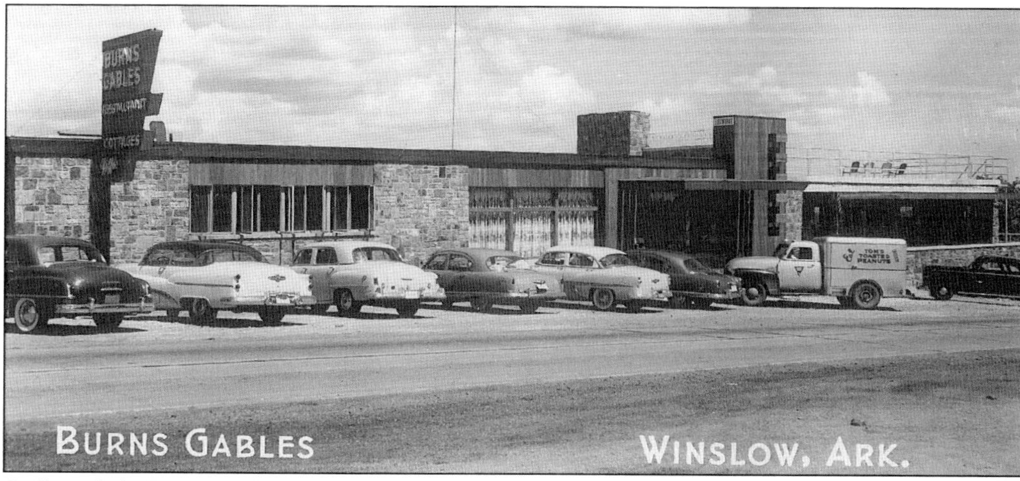

Sadly, while Burns Gables is still open as a souvenir and snack shop today, it is without its trademark gables, already absent in this 1955 view. Late one night in 1952, flames erupted in the building and with the nearest fire trucks almost 50 miles away in Fort Smith, little could be done. Heroically, Ed Bellis raced from across the road and formed a bucket brigade that saved the addition to the right of the main building. The business was rebuilt, with materials salvaged where possible, but it would never be the same as in its heyday. John Burns is now deceased, though his family continues to operate the business. Some years ago, the mountain suffered another great loss when Ed Bellis was killed in a traffic accident on the twisting, dangerous Highway 71. His was one of dozens of fatalities over the years that sparked a movement for a new interstate, which finally opened in 1999, a few miles to the west.

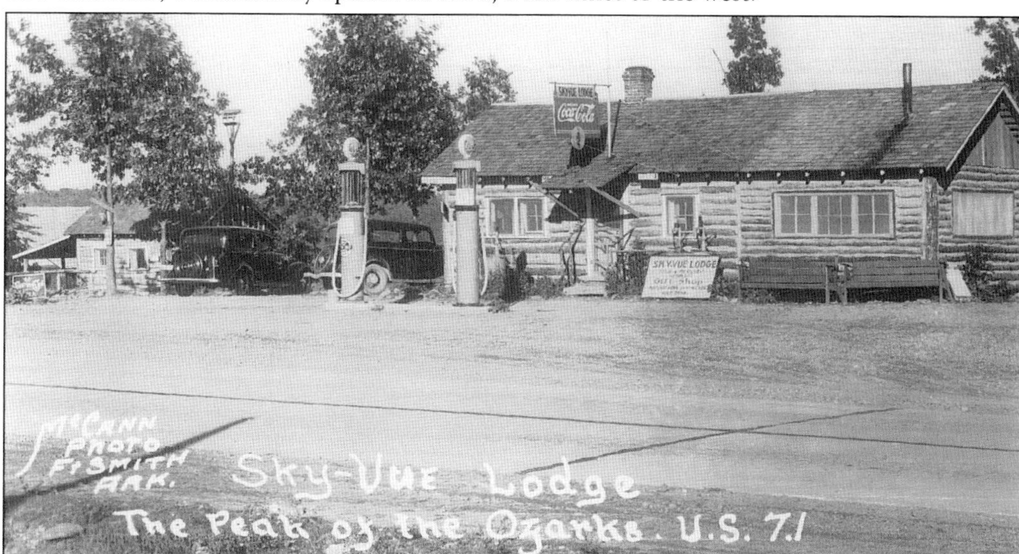

If Fayetteville-bound motorists failed to stop at Burns Gables or the Mt. Gaylor Gift Shop, they had one last chance before leaving Crawford County. Just up the road was the Sky-Vue Lodge, seen here c. 1940, which sold gas, food, postcards, and even rented out cabins. Providing a link from past to future, the Sky-Vue Lodge is still in business today, advertising itself as "Your back porch view of the Ozarks, at the longest continuously operating lodge & cabins [sic] in the Boston Mountains." As in years past, many travelers each year book a cabin that provides a unique combination of the history and scenery of western Arkansas.

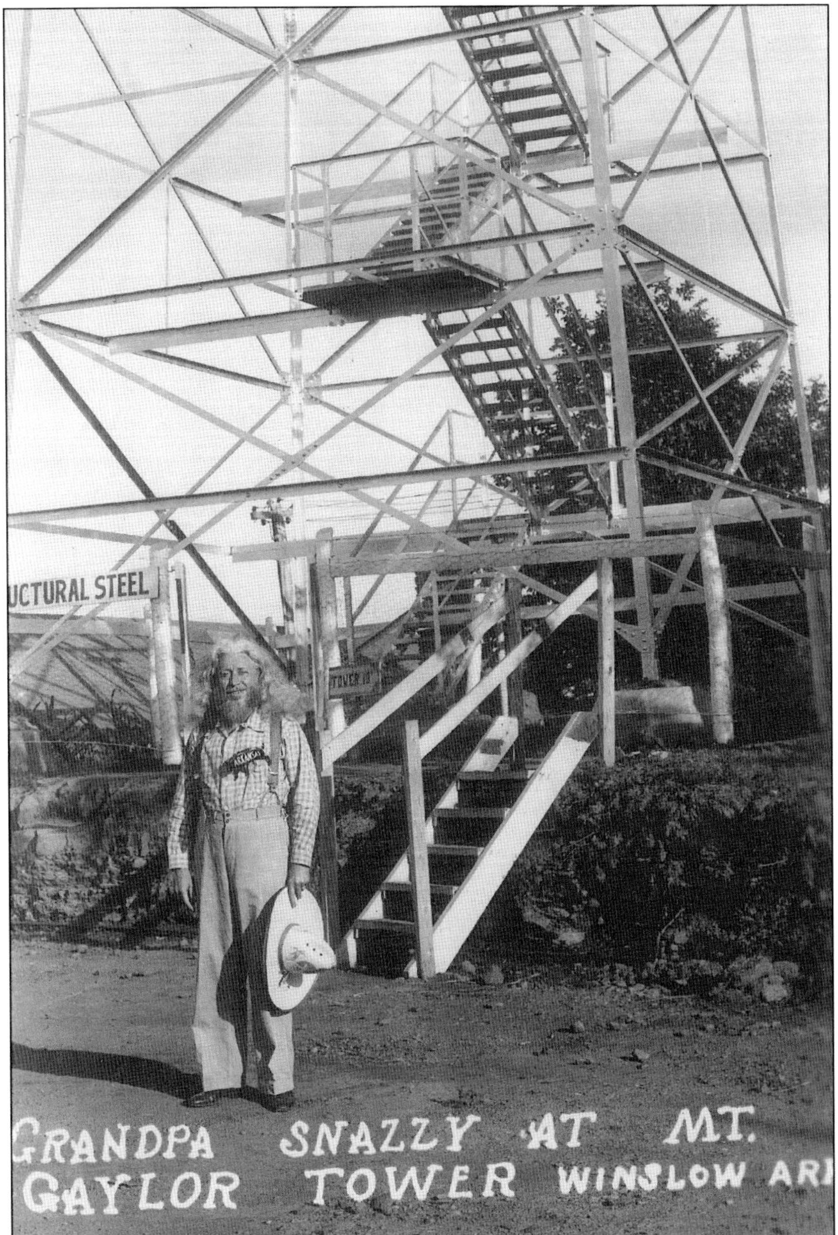

The 216 steps of the Mt. Gaylor tower have been tested by the feet of thousands of visitors over the past six decades. Those who climbed to the top have marveled at all that lay within their view. Around 1940, one of these visitors was Bob Burns's "Grandpa Snazzy," who was perhaps pondering whether or not his old legs were up to the climb. Although it is hoped that this book will help rekindle memories for older Arkansans and inform later generations, we also hope it prompts people to spend a little time sampling what Sebastian and Crawford Counties still offer to visitors. Much of the history and scenery of the area are still available, including the Mt. Gaylor tower. In the age of interstate highways, it will at times be necessary to slow down and search for the simple delights that, once found, are worth the effort. As Grandpa Snazzy and Aunt Boo might have said, "Y'all come see us."